ALSO BY NOAH FELDMAN

After Jihad: America and the Struggle for Islamic Democracy

What We Owe Iraq: War and the Ethics of Nation Building

DIVIDED BY GOD

DIVIDED BY GOD

AMERICA'S CHURCH-STATE PROBLEM—
AND WHAT WE SHOULD DO ABOUT IT

NOAH FELDMAN

FARRAR, STRAUS AND GIROUX

NEW YORK

Farrar, Straus and Giroux
19 Union Square West, New York 10003

Copyright © 2005 by Noah Feldman
All rights reserved
Distributed in Canada by Douglas & McIntyre Ltd.
Printed in the United States of America
First edition, 2005

Library of Congress Cataloging-in-Publication Data
Feldman, Noah, 1970–
    Divided by God : America's church-state problem—and what we
should do about it / Noah Feldman.— 1st ed.
        p.   cm.
    Includes bibliographical references and index.
    ISBN-13: 978-0-374-28131-1 (hardcover : alk. paper)
    ISBN-10: 0-374-28131-9 (hardcover : alk. paper)
    1. Church and state—United States—History.   I. Title.

BR516.F43 2005
322'.1'0973—dc22

                                                        2005007064

Designed by Debbie Glasserman

www.fsgbooks.com

1   3   5   7   9   10   8   6   4   2

In memoriam
Alan Heimert
1928–1999

CONTENTS

DIVIDED BY GOD

For ten days in August 2003, with an insurgency brewing and soldiers dying in newly conquered Iraq, the nation's attention suddenly became riveted on sleepy Montgomery, Alabama. Late one night the previous winter, Judge Roy Moore, the elected chief justice of the Alabama Supreme Court, had arranged for a two-and-a-half-ton block of granite to be erected in the rotunda of his courthouse. The enormous rock, which took a team of men and machinery to move, was inscribed with the Ten Commandments. A federal district court found the monument to be an unconstitutional infringement on the separation of church and state, and ordered its removal; in late summer, a federal court of appeals agreed.[1]

What happened next grabbed the public eye: Moore refused. This extraordinary act of civil disobedience by a judge sworn to uphold the law brought out spokespeople and activists for both of the two most prominent schools of thought about church and state in the contemporary United States. On the front steps of the courthouse and on live television, their arguments began with the framers of the Constitution. The evangelicals declared that our entire system was built on Judeo-Christian values, and that the founding fathers, whose moral sense was based on the Bible, would have been astonished and horrified to see the Ten Commandments proscribed by court order. The secularists invoked Thomas Jefferson and James Madison to support their view that the symbols of religion ought to be kept out of the governmental sphere altogether. Both sides shared the assumption that they could win the argument if they could prove that history was on their side.

The Montgomery controversy mattered for reasons greater than the specter of a politically ambitious Alabama judge refusing to follow a federal court's order, or the constitutional question of whether the Ten Commandments may lawfully be displayed in public places, which the Supreme Court had yet to resolve. With a presidential election looming, the evangelicals and the secularists were enacting in microcosm the national debate about the right relationship between religion and government in the United States. The stakes of that debate extend beyond statues to billions of dollars in government funding, basic moral questions of life, death, and family, and the recurrent challenge of what it means for Americans to belong to a nation. The Ten Commandments were just a symbolic stand-in. Judge Moore had struck a vein of division that runs deep in America's history and its psyche.

INTRODUCTION

In the darkest days of the Civil War, the absolute low point of division in American history, Abraham Lincoln could still imagine religion as a potentially unifying force. North and South, he observed in his second inaugural address, prayed to the same God and read the same Bible, even if they interpreted it differently. Through a shared faith, the American people could someday bind up the nation's wounds, inflicted by a just God as punishment for the original sin of slavery.

Today, the overwhelming majority of Americans still say they believe in God, but a common understanding of how faith should inform nationhood can no longer bring Americans together. To the contrary, no question divides Americans more fundamentally than that of the relation between religion and government. For many, moral values derived from religion are the lodestar of political judgment. Almost a quarter of the electorate in the 2004 presidential election described values as the most important issue to them, and of these, some four-fifths voted for President George W. Bush.[1] Yet many Americans believe with equal commitment that religion is a private matter that should not figure in the sphere of politics—a view expressly adopted by Senator John Kerry in the presidential debates, where he explained his pro-choice stance by asserting that his personal beliefs as a Catholic must not be imposed on women who held different beliefs about abortion.[2] Although church membership did not predict which candidate a voter would choose, one statistic stood out sharply: the more often you attended church, the more likely you were to vote for President Bush.

A HOUSE DIVIDED

The deep divide in American life, then, is not primarily over religious belief or affiliation—it is over the role that belief should play in the business of politics and government.[3] Consider same-sex marriage, which appeared on ballots in eleven states in 2004 and shows no sign of disappearing from public debate. Many Americans insist that marriage is "between one man and one woman" but say they have no objection to civil unions that give gay couples the same rights as married people. If there is no legal difference between civil union and marriage, why object to the word "marriage"? What's in a name? The obvious answer is that even though marriage is a state institution, it has a traditional religious definition, which opponents of same-sex marriage do not want to change. The reason so many people oppose same-sex "marriage" is that they believe the state's sanction of marriage should take account of a moral value derived from religion.

Religious values also figure prominently in the debates about stem-cell research, abortion, euthanasia, and the death penalty. On each of these life-and-death issues, one school of thought insists that citizens' private religious values should not decide government policy, while an equally vociferous alternative view maintains that the right answers to such ultimate questions must come from the wisdom of religious tradition. In each case, the debate is as much about whether faith should inform political debate as about the rights or wrongs of the issue. "We are a religious people," the Supreme Court said in 1952, "whose institutions presuppose a Supreme Being."[4] Clearly, not everyone agrees. Is the Court's dictum true today? Was it ever true in our history?

The essential question of how religion and government should interact becomes most salient when we confront the controversial constitutional problems that arise under the heading of church and state: Should the government be able to fund religious schools or social programs through the model of charitable choice? May courthouses display the Ten Commandments? Do the words "under God" in the Pledge of Allegiance amount to an establishment of religion? No one lives or dies as the result of our resolution of these hard questions on which the Supreme Court inevitably opines, but they are nevertheless lightning rods for debate, because they go to the very heart of who we are as a nation. They raise the central challenges of citizenship and peoplehood: who belongs here? To what kind of nation do we belong?

This book sets out to address these crucial questions, turning to our history to understand the origins of today's controversies and exploring how we might chart a course for the future. Two sides dominate the church-state debate in contemporary American life, corresponding to what today are the two most prominent approaches to the proper relation of religion and government. In this book, I call those who insist on the direct relevance of religious values to political life "values evangelicals." Not every values evangelical is, technically speaking, an evangelical or born-again Christian, although many are. Values evangelicals can include Jews, Catholics, Muslims, and even people who do not focus on a particular religious tradition but care primarily about identifying traditional moral values that can in theory be shared by everyone. What all values evangelicals have in common is the goal of evangelizing *for* values: promoting a strong set of ideas about the best way to live one's life and urging the government to adopt those values and encourage them wherever possible. To them, the best way to hold the

United States together as a nation, not just a country, is for us to
know what values we really hold and to stand up for them. Convergence on true, traditional values is the key to unity and strength.

On the other side of the debate are those who see religion as a
matter of personal belief and choice largely irrelevant to government, and who are concerned that values derived from religion will
divide us, not unite us. I call those who hold this view "legal secularists," not because they are necessarily strongly secular in their
personal worldviews—though many are—but because they believe
that government should be secular and that the laws should make it
so. To the legal secularists, full citizenship means fully sharing in
the core legal and political commitments of the nation. If the nation defines itself in terms of values drawn from religion, they
worry, then it will inevitably tend to adopt the religious values of
the majority, excluding religious minorities and nonreligious people
from full citizenship.

Despite their differences, both approaches, values evangelicalism
and legal secularism, are trying to come to terms with the same
fundamental tension in American life. The United States has always
been home to striking religious diversity—diversity that has by fits
and starts expanded over the last 230 years. At the same time, we
strive to be a nation with a common identity and a common project. Religious division threatens that unity, as we can see today
more clearly than at any time in a century, yet almost all Americans
want to make sure that we do not let our religious diversity pull us
apart.[5] Values evangelicals think that the solution lies in finding
and embracing traditional values we can all share and without
which we will never hold together. Legal secularists think that we
can maintain our national unity only if we treat religion as a personal, private matter, separate from concerns of citizenship. The
goal of reconciling national unity with religious diversity is the
same, but the methods for doing it are deeply opposed.

CHURCH, STATE—AND PEOPLE

The conflict between the two groups itself now threatens to destroy a common national vision. What can be done about it? Is there a third way that could produce reconciliation between Republican and Democrat, red and blue, evangelicals and secularists? In the pages that follow, I propose a different approach to the question of religion and government, one that eschews the extremes of both the values evangelicals and the legal secularists. In place of their mutually exclusive visions, I suggest that we should permit and tolerate symbolic invocation of religious values and inclusive displays of religion while rigorously protecting the financial and organizational separation of religious institutions from institutions of government.

I develop my argument through the lens of history. Both evangelicals and secularists like to claim that our constitutional past and tradition support their approach. Both are wrong. By reconsidering and reinterpreting the way Americans in different eras have tackled the church-state question, broadly understood, I want to point us forward to a solution that draws on the best of what we have done in the past, while rejecting our not-insignificant mistakes.

The reason to look to history is not that we must always do just what our forefathers did. We have to be prepared to acknowledge that our extraordinary, even heroic founding fathers built a Constitution that not only heralded religious liberty and free speech, but protected slavery, excluded women, and failed to anticipate developments as important as public schools and political parties. The reason to look backward in order to move ahead is that our constitutional, democratic, and republican form of government is at its core an experiment in nation building—now glorious, now ignominious; now brilliant, now misled. In our history, and only there, can we see the results of the experiment, in order to understand them, judge them, and make the next adjustment or change. Nor is it up to the courts alone to make these changes. We can make them ourselves, in myriad ways, at every level of government and in the way we think and act as citizens.

In fact, it is the popular nature of our constitutional experiment that has made the relation of religion and government so central to our national experience, especially compared to the relatively secular and secularized nations of Europe. During the roughly thirteen hundred years from the time the Roman Empire became Christian to the American Revolution, the current constitutional church-state question in the West always began with the assumption that the official state religion was the religion of the sovereign. Sometimes the sovereign king fought the church for control of religious institutions; other times, the church claimed authority over the state by claiming religious authority over the sovereign himself.[6] The wars of religion that followed the Reformation were halted at Westphalia by a treaty specifying that each region would have its own religion, namely, that of its ruler.[7] The rulers, meanwhile, used religion to serve their own ends. Writing just before the American Revolution, Edward Gibbon explained that the people believed, the philosophers were atheists, and the rulers found religion a convenient tool to encourage obedience.[8] Gibbon's nominal subject was ancient Rome, but his readers understood that he was talking about their world, too.

The revolutionary American idea that the people were sovereign profoundly disturbed the old model: How could the state establish the religion of the sovereign if the sovereign people belonged to many faiths? Suddenly the sovereign who would make the laws would believe in religion, instead of cynically manipulating it, and the elite skeptics who enabled the ruler's game would no longer be in the same position of influence. This new model of popular sovereignty called for a new church-state arrangement.

The framers rose to the occasion. For the first time in recorded history, they designed a government with no established religion at all. The Articles of Confederation that preceded the Constitution remained silent on religion. The Constitution in its original form went further by prohibiting any religious test for holding office. And the first words of the First Amendment to the new Constitution, enacted by the first Congress as an understood condition of ratification, stated that "Congress shall make no law respecting an establishment of religion, or prohibiting the free exercise thereof." If the people were to be sovereign, and belonged to different religions, the state religion would be no religion at all. Too many religious denominations would have been in competition to make theirs the official choice, and none could have prevailed without excluding the others. Establishment at the national level was prohibited. Religious diversity had done its work. The experiment had begun.

PAST AS PROLOGUE

New circumstances brought new developments. In successive eras, repeated infusions of religious diversity brought original ideas about church and state—new answers to the challenge of preserving unity in the face of expanding diversity. By charting the emergence of new solutions to the church-state problem in response to fresh pulsations of diversity, we can trace the birth of the full range of contemporary positions on how government and religion should interact. This book, then, tells a story of growth, development, and conflict—but it does so by revealing complex people inventing ideas that remain alive and relevant today, and that readers may find themselves embracing or rejecting, sometimes forcefully. Those ideas mattered profoundly to the people who first had them, and, right or wrong, they should matter just as much to us today, since we are building our own country and Constitution on the foundations they laid.

The early republic was religiously diverse in that it was inhabited by several different Protestant denominations. This "multiplicity of sects," as James Madison brilliantly realized, ensured that no one denomination had the capacity to establish its own state religion at the national level. Yet Madison was almost alone in recognizing this demographic reality, and even he did not rely on it when drafting what became the First Amendment. The dominant idea organizing church-state relations in the framers' era was the liberty of conscience, understood to protect religious dissenters—representing the religious diversity of the time—against compelled taxation to support teachings with which they disagreed. Aided by the reality of religious difference within and among the states, the ideal of liberty of conscience drove the argument for institutional separation in precursor states like Virginia, in the federal Constitution, and eventually in the hold-out New England states when their relative religious homogeneity gave way to schism. In the presence of religious diversity, protecting religious liberty by prohibiting coercive taxation was a mechanism for preserving unity.

The Second Great Awakening of the early nineteenth century split old sects and created new ones, and the response was the identification of "nonsectarian Christianity" as the basis for common morality that would be taught in the new public schools and produce the republican virtue needed to hold the country together. Yet no sooner had the nonsectarian idea been put into practice than it ran headlong into a wave of Catholic immigration from famine-stricken Ireland. For many Catholics, nonsectarianism was nothing more than Protestant sectarianism, forcibly imposed—and instead of fostering unity, it generated half a century of intense and sometimes violent fighting over state funding of parochial education and the role of the Bible in the public schools, culminating in a proposed constitutional amendment barring states from funding Catholic education. Although the amendment failed at the federal level, by and large Catholics lost the fight and accommodated themselves to nonsectarianism even as nonsectarianism sought to assimilate them to itself.

Next, in the last quarter of the nineteenth century, Darwin-inspired agnosticism and atheism entered the picture, further adding to religious diversity by fueling a strong secularism that denied religion's truth and proceeded to the conclusion that religion should be banished from all of aspects of life—government affairs included. As mainstream Protestantism liberalized itself in response to evolution, fundamentalism was born in reaction to the liberals. Reacting against the elitism associated with strong secularism, and goaded by the idiosyncratic political genius of the aging William Jennings Bryan, the new fundamentalism sought to combine political populism with exemplary legislative enactments that would keep secularism at bay, enshrine the faith, and keep ordinary, believing people united in their faith, not divided by modern heresy. From the ideal of religious populism were born dozens of anti-evolution statutes and the extraordinary spectacle of the Scopes monkey trial. Eventually, strong secularism faded from the American political scene.

Jewish immigration then created diversity of a new sort, and with it a movement for a new kind of secularism that was not anti-religious but rather legal, nominally neutral toward religion, and devoted only to keeping religion away from the governmental sphere. Legal secularists believed that unity could never be achieved in an America that felt like a Christian country, so long as some Americans were not Christians. Looking to the courts to instantiate its ideal of secular government, this movement had great success in the thirty years after World War II, until the tide began to turn again.

Fundamentalism, it turned out, was not out of the picture. Impelled by what some sociologists would call America's Third Great Awakening and angry with the successes of legal secularism, it returned to the political scene carrying the banner of the Moral Majority and, later, the Christian Coalition. Once again, an infusion of new religious viewpoints encouraged a new view on church and state—this time, the ideal of disseminating moral values grounded in religion. Unlike earlier fundamentalists, the new evangelicals claimed to advocate not their own particular creed but values that could be shared by all persons of faith and so produce national unity; in this sense they were drawing on the rhetoric that had made nonsectarianism such a success. Not content with popular politics, the evangelicals pushed for judicial appointments and, when they got them, developed their own innovative legal strategy, depicting religious people as a persecuted minority in need of the courts' protection.

TENSIONS AND RESOLUTIONS

All this brings us to our present predicament, and the failings of both values evangelicalism and legal secularism. In short, both are self-contradictory: they fail precisely where they want to succeed, because neither successfully reconciles religious diversity with national unity. The values evangelicals want to find shared values, but that leads them to rely on the unexamined assumption that, deep down, Americans agree on what matters. The trouble is that "we"—which includes today not only Jews and Christians but also Muslims, Hindus, Buddhists, and more—often do *not* agree; to reach consensus, the values evangelicals would have to water down the "values" they embrace to the point where they would mean nothing at all. They are left either acknowledging disagreement about values, or else falling into a kind of relativism that is inconsistent with the very goal of standing for something rather than nothing.

Meanwhile, the legal secularists have the opposite problem. They claim that separating religion from the public, governmental sphere is necessary to ensure full inclusion of all citizens. The problem is that many citizens—values evangelicals among them—feel excluded by precisely this principle of keeping religion private. Keeping religion out of the public sphere might protect the feelings of religious minorities, but it also sends a message of exclusion to those who believe that public acknowledgment of religion would signal commitment to shared values. Increasingly, the symbolism of removing religion from the schools, courthouses, or the public square is experienced by values evangelicals as excluding them, no matter how much the legal secularists tell them that is not the intent.

It emerges that neither contemporary approach works—and in the book's final chapter I propose an alternative. The core separation of church and state in the American experiment, I argue, has historically been *institutional*: keeping government and religious entities apart, in sharp contrast to the arrangements of established churches in the framers' Christian Europe or today's Islamic world. Our legacy of institutional separation is not untainted by anti-Catholic sentiment, but it is nonetheless deep-rooted, and indeed it predated the peak of Catholics' arrival in the United States. The reason for such separation is straightforward: to prevent churches and other religious organizations from entering into the fight for public resources, where taxes would go to support religion. With billions of dollars going to support religious programs and schools, we have gone too far in breaking down this separation, and we need to draw back. Values evangelicals may not like it, but they must recognize that government funding of religion will, in the long run, generate disunity, not unity.

By contrast, the goal of ensuring that religion remains in the private sphere, that religious symbols or acts be kept out of politics and out of schools, is the product of a further step taken by legal secularism in the years since World War II. Though motivated by the sincere desire to facilitate inclusion of minorities, this experimental step has outlived its usefulness, as it has become a symbol of exclusion, not inclusion. The constitutional decisions marginalizing or banning religion from public places have managed to alienate millions of people who are also sincerely committed to an inclusive American project.

The answer is to allow public religion where it is inclusive, not exclusive, and to allow religious displays and prayers so long as they accommodate and honor religious diversity. No one should ever be coerced into a religious exercise, but so long as no one's rights are violated, it makes no sense to ban public religion on the theory that someone might be offended or feel excluded. This shift would symbolize a broader acceptance that religious faith does indeed inform the political choices of many Americans. Legal secularists may resist, but they need to acknowledge that, in a democracy, their concerns over exclusion cannot effectively trump the sense of exclusion shared by the many Americans who want to express their religious values through politics. Once a shift to symbolic inclusion occurs, the fevered pitch of debate should tone down. Instead of arguing about who is offended by whose religious faith (or disbelief), we should be able to focus more on how we as a people ought to resolve hard moral and policy questions. Values evangelicalism as a militant movement should begin to lose some of its ardor as legal secularism ceases to be its equally implacable enemy. Basic disagreements about issues will persist, as well they should when the issues are tough. But the conflict will be less threatening to our national unity and more easily subject to being managed.

HISTORY AND DESTINY

I undertook this book in the spirit of seeking reconciliation between the warring factions that define the church-state debate and, increasingly, much else in American politics. Perhaps the reason for my perspective (and my aspiration) inheres in my background. Raised and educated in a Modern Orthodox Jewish milieu, I saw that religion could offer a powerful grounding in a set of practices and beliefs both identifiably American and distinctively Jewish. I felt I had a foot in the camp of legal secularism with its concern for minorities, and values evangelicalism with its search for common values. Confident in what I knew and believed, I did not find Christianity to be a threat to me or my religious community. I welcomed and recognized my status as a religious minority, which I saw as basic to a two-thousand-year-old tradition of diaspora Judaism.

Yet I also think it would be too simple to consider upbringing as destiny, for me or for the people I discuss in this book. I myself have not always remained squarely within the normative bounds of traditional Judaism. New experiences and challenges have led me to recognize the tensions among religious, personal, and citizen selves more fully than I otherwise might have done. I have also studied and written about Islam and constitutional democracy—topics in mosque and state, as it were—and concluded that different arrangements of religion and government might work for different societies with different demographics and social norms. This comparative study has powerfully informed my thinking about church and state in the United States. Had I read differently, lived differently, or not experienced the ups and downs of constitutional promise and disappointment in Iraq, where I have had the chance to advise various constitutional actors, I might have reached different conclusions—but these are the ones I reach today.

We as a nation are no more the inevitable product of our historical past than are we as individuals. What we do and who we are can be shaped and molded, not with complete freedom but at any rate with reflection and forethought. The tools we need to make it happen, though, are honesty about the past and a vision of what we seek to achieve in the future. The United States and its people continue through time, even as culture, faith, and Constitution change. In what follows, I am asking you to join me in relearning a past less familiar than it may at first seem and in rethinking a future that is not unavoidably fixed. Throwing over received ideas is never easy—but unless we can manage it, we are going nowhere.

1

THE ORIGINS

On June 12, 1788, James Madison, the father of religious liberty in America, stood before the Virginia convention debating the ratification of the Constitution and opposed the First Amendment. There was no need for the Constitution to prohibit an established religion or to protect religious liberty, Madison argued. Religious diversity would guarantee religious freedom by itself: "For where there is such a variety of sects, there cannot be a majority of any one sect to oppress and persecute the rest."[1] There were so many different religious denominations in the United States that no one group would ever be able to impose its will over the others. It was pointless to prohibit what no one group could ever hope to accomplish.

The assembled Virginians knew Madison as the man who had led the fight to disestablish the Anglican church in Virginia, guarantee religious liberty, and block the state even from collecting an assessment that could be earmarked for distribution to the religious teacher of one's choice. No American, not even Jefferson, had better credentials on the separation of church and state. Virginia's religious dissenters, Presbyterians and Baptists who had been Madison's close allies in the five-year struggle in the state legislature, wanted a guarantee in the federal Constitution that would parallel what they had won at the state level. Notwithstanding Madison's predictive judgment about the likely effects of diversity, they still feared the possibility that someday one denomination really might be able to establish a national religion that would make them pay taxes in support of a church to which they did not belong. The solution they demanded was an amendment to the Constitution to guarantee religious liberty. Why was Madison suddenly on the wrong side?

PRINCIPLE AND POLITICS

In the solution to this puzzle lies the key to the most basic question about the relationship between church and state in the United States: Why *do* we have a First Amendment prohibiting the establishment of religion and protecting the free exercise thereof? The answer combines principle and politics. The principled reason behind the religion clauses of the First Amendment was to protect the liberty of conscience of religious dissenters—and everybody involved in the process understood that fact. The political reason for the clauses was that no one in the new United States opposed the idea of religious liberty, and given the religious diversity among Americans, no one denomination seriously believed it could establish a national religion of its own. Although 95 percent were Protestants of some sort (as of 1780 there were just fifty-six Catholic churches and five Jewish congregations in the whole country), American Protestants ranged from Anglican (soon to be renamed Episcopalian) and Congregationalist to Presbyterian, Baptist, Quaker, and beyond.[2] Practically speaking, the fact of religious diversity made a nationally established religion impossible. The sovereign people belonged not to one faith, but several. The solution, adopted by the first Congress, which wrote the Bill of Rights, passed it, and sent it to the states for ratification, was to prohibit a national establishment and guarantee free exercise.

Madison was profoundly committed to religious liberty and opposed to religious establishment of any kind; in fact, he believed that no government had the right to take any action in the religious sphere—certainly not the proposed new federal government, whose powers were limited to those granted in the draft Constitution he had done so much to produce. In addition to principle, Madison had another reason for judging an amendment unnecessary. In thinking about the creation of a new federal republic that would perfect the union of thirteen still-disparate states, he had developed the world-changing idea that America's diverse factions could counterbalance each other, instead of tearing the country apart. Applying this notion to religion convinced Madison that only national politics, not a parchment promise, could guarantee religious liberty and nonestablishment.

But Madison was also a politician, and his constituency of religious dissenters was having none of his argument. So Madison did what any politician would do, only better: he abandoned the stance he took at the Virginia ratifying convention, got himself elected to the first House of Representatives, and took the lead in drafting the religion clauses of the First Amendment. Because he combined principle and politics when it came to the religion clauses, Madison's story is central if we want to understand the early history of the church-state relationship in the United States.

That history is under dispute today as never before. In the media, in scholarly writing, and in judicial opinions, one can hear both that the framers gave us a "Godless Constitution" with strong separation between church and state,[3] and, to the contrary, that the Constitution assumed a Christian nation and prohibited the federal government only from officially preferring one denomination to others. The story we tell about our founding is our creation myth, so it is not surprising that the framers' decisions and beliefs regarding religion and government loom very large in the current debate about the subject. Both legal secularists and values evangelicals have a huge stake in claiming the framers' original authority for their views.

But the truth is that both of these perspectives are wrong, both developed over the last fifty years in order to justify positions in a contemporary legal and cultural fight under circumstances very different from the framers'. In what follows, I briefly sketch the most prominent views on the subject—then go back to the beginning and set the record straight.

THE BATTLE LINES

The framers undertook an extraordinary experiment when they broke from past practice and prohibited the establishment of religion by the federal government while guaranteeing free exercise —on that much, everyone can agree. In England and on the European continent, in Catholic and Protestant countries alike, it had long been assumed that a close relationship between established religion and government was necessary to maintain social order and national cohesion.[4] The framers were experimenting across the board, trying to create a federal union out of self-governing states despite the certainty of mainstream theorists like the influential Montesquieu that a geographically large republic could not survive.[5] That innovation came out of necessity. The Articles of Confederation, loosely tying the original thirteen states to one another, had failed politically and economically, and the framers had little choice but to try something new. But why experiment in the realm of church and state?

One traditional answer begins with Thomas Jefferson, the most controversial founding father in his lifetime and beyond, and the author of the Virginia Statute for Religious Freedom, which ended state financial support for organized religion in Virginia.[6] Determined to be remembered for the statute, Jefferson ordered it mentioned on his tombstone as one of his three greatest accomplishments, alongside the authorship of the Declaration of Independence and the foundation of the University of Virginia.[7] As president, Jefferson also coined what would become the single most influential metaphor in American constitutional law when he wrote, in an official letter to the Baptists of Danbury, Connecticut, that the Constitution had "erected a wall of separation between church and state."[8]

According to the dominant historical interpretation, Jefferson's personal religious skepticism and his faith in unfettered reason combined to create a deep desire to separate church and state in order to protect each from the other. Individual thought must be protected from government-enforced orthodoxy, and government must in turn be saved from the baleful effects of organized religion. Denounced in his lifetime as a nonbeliever, and in all likelihood a deist at most, Jefferson left evidence in his personal letters of a powerful streak of anticlericalism and disdain for organized religion.[9] For secularists this has long made Jefferson an attractive hero, precursor to their view that the reasons for separation lie as much in keeping religion from meddling in state affairs as in protecting religious liberty.

The problem with this emphasis on Jefferson's role in the shaping of religious liberty in America is that although he did write the Virginia statute, he was in Paris as the American ambassador in 1786 when it was actually passed, and he was still there in 1789, when the Bill of Rights—including the First Amendment—was added to the Constitution. Indeed, Jefferson missed the entire Constitutional Convention. Those who put Jefferson at the center of the story therefore have to treat Madison, his trusted lieutenant, as the instrument whereby Jefferson's views were executed. According to this view, Madison's activities on behalf of religious liberty, conducted during Jefferson's long absence, directly connect the Jeffersonian triumph of strong separation in Virginia and the adoption of the same policy in the federal Constitution. At least since

the 1870s, when the Supreme Court dusted off Jefferson's metaphor of the "wall of separation," there have been voices arguing that
strict separation was the American plan of government from the
beginning.[10]

Yet an alternative, revisionist view of the history, first articulated
by Mark DeWolfe Howe in the 1960s,[11] adopted by several Justices
of the Supreme Court, and recently redeveloped and deepened in
an important book by Philip Hamburger,[12] emphasizes not Jefferson's concern for the protection of the state from religion but rather
eighteenth-century religious dissenters' concern to protect the
church from the state. This school points out that the phrase "wall
of separation" appears nowhere in the Constitution, nor indeed in
the state ratification debates leading up to the enactment of the
First Amendment. The troublesome metaphor surfaced first almost
150 years before Jefferson, in the writings of the great dissenter
Roger Williams, who broke from Massachusetts Bay Puritanism,
embraced Baptist views—among other unorthodoxies—and
founded the colony of Rhode Island, in which religious liberty was
assured from the beginning. For Williams, the wall of separation
came between the "garden" of religion and the "wilderness" of temporal government—and it protected the garden from the wilderness, not the other way around.[13] Williams's metaphor was
rediscovered by Isaac Backus, a New England Baptist of Jefferson's
generation, who believed, like Williams, that an established
church—which he considered to exist in the Massachusetts of his
day—would never protect religious dissenters like himself and must
be opposed in order to keep religion pure.[14]

According to this revisionist view, Jefferson may have distrusted
religion and wanted to protect the state from it, but that was his
personal view, not that of the Constitution or indeed of the Baptists and other eighteenth-century religious dissenters who demanded an amendment to the Constitution protecting religious
liberty. Alongside a Jeffersonian line emphasizing the protection of
the state from the organized church was a distinct line of thought

associated with Baptists like Backus and the itinerant preacher and ideologue John Leland, which sought to protect religious dissenters from government coercion. Together, early protosecularists (Jefferson and Madison) and proto-evangelicals (Backus, Leland, and others) made common cause in the fight for nonestablishment—but for starkly different reasons.[15]

So in prohibiting "an establishment of religion," according to this alternative view, the framers did not follow what they characterize as the antireligious motivations of Jefferson, who was not even in the country. Rather, they must have meant to prohibit only the kind of arrangement they knew from the Church of England as established in the colonies. An established church existed when the government officially recognized, supported, and by law favored one organized denomination in particular, to the exclusion and detriment of all others.[16] As long as the government does not prefer one religion or denomination, this view concludes, the constitutional ban on establishment has not been violated. It follows that, today, the government may support religion at will, so long as the support is "nonpreferential," available to all religions on equal terms.[17]

What is more, say the revisionists as well as some other scholars, the First Amendment operated only at the federal level when it was enacted. It stated simply that "*Congress* shall make no law respecting an establishment of religion," leaving the states free to legislate as they wished and essentially placing religious questions within their jurisdiction rather than that of the federal government. Both before and after the Bill of Rights became law, some states collected taxes and distributed them to congregations and ministers, as they had in the colonial period. This interpretation understands the First Amendment as enacting a type of federalism, found elsewhere in the Constitution, guaranteeing the states autonomy in certain domains. A handful of constitutional historians—and one Supreme Court Justice—go even further, maintaining that the words "no law *respecting* an establishment of religion" not only left the state arrangements untouched but were actually intended to protect those state establishments of religion from congressional interference by barring Congress from legislating with respect to existing religious arrangements in the states. According to one version of this more extreme view, whatever the federal government may or may not do, states should not be barred from establishing religion, even after most of the other freedoms in the Bill of Rights were extended by the Fourteenth Amendment so that they apply not just to the federal government, as originally intended, but to the states as well.[18]

One can find large measures of historical truth in both the traditional and the revisionist approaches. Jefferson and Madison did play major roles in formulating the canonical ideal of religious liberty that made its way into the Constitution. They did, in fact, form an alliance in Virginia with evangelical Presbyterian and Baptist dissenters from Anglicanism whose religious beliefs were very different from their own. When Congress wrote the First Amendment, it did intend that it apply only to Congress, not the states.

But the historical story needs to be told anew. Both existing versions slight the clearly articulated principled rationale for free exercise *and* nonestablishment that was common to deists, Baptists, as well as everyone in between: the liberty of conscience. Both, too, miss the motivating political reality that pushed the liberty of conscience onto state and then federal agendas: the sudden increase in religious diversity that resulted from bringing the states together into a federal union. Within the individual states, some, especially in the mid-Atlantic, already had a great deal of religious diversity. But in New England, Congregationalism dominated, and in the South, the Church of England remained the denominational choice of the majority. Where religious diversity within individual states was small, religious establishments, acknowledged or unacknowledged, were possible. Now that these states were to be joined in a single national government, though, the religious diversity *between* states made a national establishment impossible. So when

Congress wrote what became the religion clauses of the First Amendment, it meant to do much more than leave religion to the states. It intended to enshrine in the federal Constitution the protections against religious coercion that Americans had learned to think of as natural rights.

LIBERTY OF CONSCIENCE: THE ORIGINS OF AN IDEA

The idea of liberty of conscience is so commonsensical today that we hardly imagine that it has a history at all. Americans in the decades leading up to the First Amendment broadly agreed that government—whether state or federal—had no authority to coerce individuals in matters of religious conscience. They shared this view regardless of educational background or religious stance.[19] The remarkable convergence of views about liberty of conscience had an origin: it reflected the diffusion of arguments for religious toleration made a century earlier by John Locke, the seventeenth-century British philosopher who had greater influence on the thought world of the framers than any other one writer.

The idea that reached fruition in Locke's thought had grown gradually out of the Christian notion of conscience, understood as a spark of inner moral guidance that exists in every soul.[20] St. Jerome was the first to mention conscience of this kind, a distinctively human faculty for telling us what is right and what is wrong. Subsequent church fathers, most importantly Thomas Aquinas, developed the idea that such an individual faculty enables people to make internal moral judgments and that it is sinful to act against the inward directives that conscience provides.[21]

Thomas thought that it was possible for the individual conscience to make a mistake and to require correction by the legitimate religious authorities of the church who carried the weight of tradition and divine sanction. It followed that, for Thomas, one should ordinarily defer to authority in deciding controversial moral questions.[22] Martin Luther diverged from this view when he insisted that he alone was responsible for making up his own mind about what God required of him. In his pivotal appearance at the Diet of Worms, in the presence of Emperor Charles V, Luther refused to "give up" his conscience and retract beliefs about grace and free will that differed from official church doctrine. He could retract his views in good conscience, he explained, only if he were convinced to do so by Scriptures or reason. It was not enough that the pope or the church councils (who formulated doctrine) thought something was true, because they were fallible. "I cannot and I will not retract anything," Luther concluded in a formulation that lay at the heart of early Protestantism, "since it is neither safe nor right to go against conscience."[23]

The idea that no one else can make up my mind for me proved to be central to the development of the idea that conscience should be free. In the writings of John Calvin, "Christian liberty" meant that even the church, whether Catholic or Reformed, could not bind the conscience of the believer with respect to any belief or practice not absolutely necessary for salvation. It followed that government, too, lacked the authority to make binding laws "concerning religion and the worship of God."[24] This was still far from separation of church and state. In Calvin's Geneva, the magistrate was expected to pay attention to God's laws, and Calvin insisted that good government would prevent idolatry, blasphemy, and "other public offenses against religion." But in the hands of Calvin's followers, especially the English Puritan writer William Perkins, Calvin's views were expanded to include the proposition that only God, not human government, could make laws that were entitled to bind the individual conscience on pain of damnation. If human law and divine law conflicted, the human law would have no binding effect at all.[25]

The step from the belief that God's law trumps man's law to the conclusion that government should not enforce religious worship took more than a hundred years to become accepted as an American commonplace. In the years after Perkins's death, religious minorities such as Baptist dissenters in early seventeeth-century England were arguing that they should not be compelled by the government to attend Church of England services, which their consciences told them were not what God desired. Offering religious worship without faith and against one's conscience, they argued, was sinful, and government had no right to force anyone to commit sin.[26] This amounted to a claim for exemption from the rites of the established Church of England. Roger Williams, himself a sometime Baptist, similarly insisted that government had no right to coerce anybody in the realm of religion, and in the colony of Rhode Island that he founded, he refrained from creating a state-established church. But many, both in England and in America, continued to insist that false beliefs and opinions—that is, those that contradicted Christianity—must be regulated by the state to avoid the spread of sinful error.[27] It would be wrong for the government to coerce someone whose conscience was right about his religious faith, argued New England Puritan John Cotton.[28] But an erroneous conscience needed to be corrected, by force if necessary, and it would be truly dangerous to allow people who suffered from an erroneous conscience to propagate their sinful views among the innocent and unsuspecting public.

It took John Locke to translate the demand for liberty of conscience into a systematic argument for distinguishing the realm of government from the realm of religion. A participant in the internecine politics that accompanied the aftermath of the English civil war, Locke eventually fled to Holland, where he saw firsthand the consequences that wars of religion had had on the Continent and the advantages of the Dutch preference for tolerating religious dissent. In his *Letter Concerning Toleration*, first published in Holland because it would have been banned in England as subversive, Locke began by arguing that the commonwealth came into being by the consent of its individual members solely to promote their interests in life, liberty, and property. This argument for a government of limited, delegated powers, expanded in his *Two Treatises of Government*, implied that the state had no authority to do anything that its citizens lacked the authority to give it.[29]

Locke went on to maintain that God had not given any one person the authority to compel another in matters of religion. From this premise, it followed that government, deriving its power from the individual's consent, lacked the power of religious compulsion. Furthermore, he argued, even if an individual wanted to delegate his own personal religious choices to government, he could not logically do so. It would be impossible for me to grant someone else the power to make me believe anything, and if I were to delegate to another the power to tell me how to worship outwardly, I would be guilty of the sin of hypocrisy if I followed the prescribed forms without believing in them. Religious faith without sincere belief cannot bring about salvation: "No way whatsoever that I shall walk in against the dictates of my conscience, will ever bring me to the mansions of the blest."[30] Even if I wanted to give somebody else the right to use the law to influence me in religious affairs, it would be counterproductive for that person or state to coerce me to practice my religion in any way other than my conscience required, because such worship would be hypocritical: "Whatsoever is not done with that assurance of faith, is neither well in itself, nor can it be acceptable to God. To impose such things, therefore, upon any people, contrary to their own judgment, is, in effect, to command them to offend God."[31]

From the argument that it would be impossible and spiritually illogical for the individual to delegate religious choices to government, Locke concluded that government lacked the legitimate authority to coerce anyone in matters of conscience. Religious choice, Locke reasoned, was a matter of inward conscience, and true faith must flow from free choice; liberty of conscience and religious liberty were therefore indistinguishable. Religion, he concluded, belonged in a sphere of its own, protected from the coercive authority of the state. Parallel to the unalienable rights to life, liberty, and property that Locke made famous, there existed a natural, unalienable right to liberty of conscience, derived from the autonomy of the conscience and the impossibility of allocating religious authority to government. It followed that government must tolerate religious practices of all kinds, so long as they did not infringe on the government's responsibilities to keep the peace and protect the basic natural rights of others. In embryo, this formulation captured the idea of liberty of conscience as it is still widely held today.

Of course, Locke's views were not fully modern and not perfectly consistent. He maintained that atheists should not be tolerated, because they threatened the state by being untrustworthy in the taking of oaths, and because, by definition, they denied the existence of religious conscience.[32] (It was assumed that most people would tell the truth under oath because they would be afraid of being damned if they lied, but atheists would have no such fear and would therefore have no incentive not to lie.) Catholics and Muslims, who according to Locke owed temporal allegiance to the pope and caliph respectively, were also denied protection on the ground that the state could not tolerate political loyalties to a foreign power. But Christians of sincere religious faith should be tolerated in their beliefs and practices, so long as those practices did not interfere with the maintenance of civil order. Jews, too, were to be tolerated. Short of child sacrifice or other lawbreaking, the government should let religious idiosyncrasies alone.

Over the course of the eighteenth century, Locke's views on liberty of conscience and toleration of religious minorities spread through colonial America, alongside his views about government derived from the consent of the governed, who reserved to themselves certain inalienable rights. Religious establishment existed alongside official toleration. All the Southern colonies, including the Carolinas, whose original colonial charter Locke himself had helped draft, treated the Church of England as an established church, just as it was in the motherland.[33] Locke's views did not necessarily rule out state support for religion, so long as the governed did not understand payment of taxes to support the established church as a violation of their liberty of conscience. Although it was possible to interpret Locke to mean that government's lack of authority in the realm of religion barred even noncoercive government action to promote religion, Locke never said so outright, and never called for the disestablishment of the Church of England, so this reading generally remained outside of mainstream public debate.

Influenced by their collective obsession with coercive government taxation, the generation of the American Revolution took the next step of coming to believe, beyond anything Locke had said himself, that the government could not forcibly collect taxes for religious purposes in violation of individuals' conscience. There, paths parted. Some Americans, particularly those who belonged to denominational majorities, felt that the individual's liberty of conscience would not be violated if he were required to pay taxes in support of religion but allowed to direct his taxes to the religious denomination of his choice. They therefore supported, with success in New England if not elsewhere, compulsory taxes to support religious institutions, with a legal right to choose which body would receive one's funds. Indeed, so concerned were they to avoid the appearance of coercing conscience that they were prepared to exempt Quakers and Mennonites, who believed that coerced taxation even to their own denominations violated God's law.

Meanwhile, other Americans, especially dissenting religious minorities, argued that even a scheme in which the individual could decide which religious body would get his tax dollars inevitably compromised liberty of conscience. While politically important, this disagreement took place against the backdrop of a common Lockean commitment to the liberty of conscience, which had come to be seen as an inalienable right in the pantheon that featured life, liberty, and property.[34] Liberty of conscience provided the principle motivating the American experiment in the nonestablishment of religion. But this was liberty of conscience with a distinctly American twist. Its stakes were felt as much in the pocketbook as in the pew. The ideals were lofty—but the fight was about money.

LIBERTY AND TAXES: AN AMERICAN COCKTAIL

The national experiment with institutional separation of church and state began to gestate in 1776, when the thirteen colonies, reborn as states, replaced their colonial charters granted by the king with written constitutions deriving their authority from the consent of the governed. In New England, the Puritan legacy of state laws mandating the collection of local taxes to support local religious ministers chosen by their congregations was maintained over objections by religious dissenters. Roger Williams's Rhode Island and William Penn's Quaker-founded Pennsylvania never had established churches. But where, as in all the Southern colonies, charters had established the Church of England, with the king as defender of the faith and head of the church, it was generally recognized that something had to change.[35]

Almost from the moment of independence from England in 1776, Baptists, Presbyterians, and others began to lodge formal protests with state legislatures around the country, demanding to be freed of the responsibility to pay taxes to support churches from whose doctrines they dissented. Within individual states, these dissenters were the voices of such religious diversity as there was. Some, like Scotch-Irish Presbyterians in Virginia, were the descendants of immigrants; others, like Isaac Backus and many of his New England Baptist colleagues, were the progeny of splinter churches that had sprung up during the First Great Awakening of the 1740s and were eking out a difficult existence now that the wave of religious enthusiasm had crested.[36] The antitax rhetoric of the American Revolution emboldened these dissenters to demand exemption from coercive religious taxation, and the fact that their states were now loosely united with other states where other dissenters were making similar claims further emboldened them.

In New England, the dissenters made few inroads. The Congregationalist majority in the state legislatures simply denied that it was violating their rights, insisting instead that it had satisfied its obligations by permitting dissenters to formally apply for tax exemptions. In practice, these exemptions angered Baptists who considered requiring them a form of subordination. Dissenters who wanted to remain within the Congregationalist doctrinal fold complained bitterly that they could get them only if they formally declared themselves to be Baptists or Quakers, not if they told the truth.[37] Some, like Backus, asserted that even acquiring the certificates of exemption would mean admitting that the state had the right to collect religious taxes and coerce conscience if it chose, thereby "implicitly acknowledging that power in man which I believe belongs only to God."[38] But the response of even such a liberal as John Adams was that the Congregationalists were as likely to give up their mode of collecting funds for churches as was the sun to revolve around the earth.

In Virginia, by contrast, the colonial legislature, transformed into a revolutionary constitutional convention in June 1776, enacted a Declaration of Rights that included the statement that "religion, or the duty which we owe to our Creator, and the manner of discharging it, can be directed only by reason and conviction, not by force or violence; and therefore all men are equally entitled to the free exercise of religion, according to the dictates of conscience."[39] This bold declaration expressing the basic theory of the liberty of conscience was followed in October by a law stating that no one would be compelled to attend or to support "any religious worship, place, or ministry whatsoever."[40] The same law also guaranteed freedom of belief and opinion, but the crucial institutional change was the exemption from compulsory taxes to support religious institutions. Although the Anglican church—soon to be renamed the Episcopal church to avoid the embarrassing reference to England[41]—technically remained the official church, the majority, and perhaps as many as two-thirds of Virginians, were Presbyterians, Baptists, or members of other denominations.[42] Discontinuing the taxes that these citizens had previously paid to the Church of England fundamentally altered the nature of the relationship between church and state in Virginia. It left the Episcopal church without an obvious means of support, even after the state legislature in 1784 officially granted it title to the property that had belonged to its predecessor church.

Virginia supporters of the old established church, concerned with the precarious situation of ministers, responded by proposing a new law that would tax citizens to support the denomination of their choice. They bent over backward to explain that they "would have no Sect or Denomination of Christians privileged to encroach upon the rights of another," and that they wished to see "a General and equal contribution of the whole State upon the most equitable footing that is possible to place it."[43] In their view, this approach was consistent with the liberty of conscience, and it was necessary to avoid the rapid decline of religion that would in turn be "fatal to the Strength and Stability of civil government." It was a conventional view, imported from England and repeated in the colonies since the beginning, to believe that obedience to the law depended on men's belief in divine punishment. Weakening religion would threaten the stability of the state. Taxes, administered consistently with the liberty of conscience, were the solution.

The great revolutionary patriot Patrick Henry, now a staunchly Episcopalian Virginia politician, took up this cause, and indeed a bill creating a general assessment was near passage when Henry was elected governor in November 1784. At the same time, Madison assumed leadership of the anti-assessment movement, building a coalition of Baptists and Presbyterian laypeople—the Presbyterian clergy were prepared to accept the assessment[44]—who believed that the tax was too close to the traditional practice of collecting funds

for the established church. Madison is often described as sharing
Jefferson's supposed concern to protect government from religion,
but in fact this concern never figured in the fight over the assessment bill. Madison left very little evidence of his personal religious
faith and may possibly have shared Jefferson's deism. But unlike Jefferson, Madison was never hostile to organized religion per se. At
Princeton, then a Presbyterian school known as the College of New
Jersey, Madison had studied under college president John Wither-
spoon, a conservative Calvinist Presbyterian, who had made his
name in Edinburgh by criticizing the antireligious sentiments of
enlightened contemporaries such as David Hume.[45] While Madison did not follow his teacher in all things, he seems in any case to
have developed a respect for sincere faith, alongside a healthy dis-
taste for religious persecution.[46]

The evidence of Madison's views during the Virginia debates
may be seen from his famous 1785 polemic against state funding of
religion, written to consolidate support for the anti-assessment
coalition. In this petition-pamphlet, called *Memorial and Remonstrance*, Madison did not set out to make an argument about the
dangerous effects of organized religion on government. Such an approach would have been unpopular and probably unconvincing to
the great majority of Virginians, who took the conventional view
that religion was good for government, not bad for it. The overwhelming thrust of Madison's argument, derived directly from
Locke, was that coercing individuals in matters of conscience is
fundamentally wrong because religious faith can be meaningful
only when it follows from the individual's own belief and judgment, not from force. The right to make one's own choices about
religion is therefore "in its nature an unalienable right." Government has no authority to make decisions for the individual in matters of belief, because the individual cannot logically delegate to
government the ability to make up his mind for him. For this reason, Madison intimated, government and religion must be considered two distinct spheres.[47]

Madison also felt the need to refute his opponents' argument that government could not survive without established religion to back it up. "In some instances," he suggested, established religions "have been seen to erect a spiritual tyranny on the ruins of the civil authority." (Madison's readers would have taken this to refer to the Catholic church succeeding the fallen Roman Empire.) Religious establishments had also "been seen upholding the thrones of political tyranny"—apparently a reference to the Church of England's conduct during the late Revolution.[48] These two sideswipes at easy targets pass almost unnoticed in a document that otherwise frames its arguments against assessment by means of a thoroughgoing defense of religious liberty.

Yet as its supporters insisted, the proposed assessment bill that Madison was opposing required people only to pay taxes that would be directed to the ministers that they themselves designated. It provided an exemption for Quakers and Mennonites, denominations without clergy, allowing them to direct their taxes to general funds administered by their communities, and it provided for undesignated funds to go to the state for use promoting "seminaries of learning," which in context did not need to be religious.[49] George Washington, for one, wrote a friend in a personal letter that he was "not amongst the number of those who are so much alarmed" by the proposed bill.[50] (Ever the careful politician, and not yet president, Washington avoided taking a public position in the debate.) How, then, did the bill violate the individual's liberty of conscience? The answer was tricky, even for Madison. It lay with the compelled payment of taxes, which was, after all, the only coercion that the bill would have created. Compelled taxes to support religion, Madison suggested, *always* violate religious liberty, even when the taxpayer does not directly object.

The substance of this remarkable argument was made most explicit in the text of the law that Jefferson had earlier drafted and that Madison managed to get passed after he had defeated the assessment bill. The preamble to the Virginia statute put it this way:

"[T]o compel a man to furnish contributions of money for the propagation of opinions which he disbelieves and abhors, is sinful and tyrannical . . . even the forcing him to support this or that teacher of his own religious persuasion, is depriving him of the comfortable liberty of giving his contributions to the particular pastor whose morals he would make his pattern, and whose powers he feels most persuasive to righteousness."[51] The suggestion was apparently that the individual, freed from mandatory taxation, might not direct his taxes to the local minister of his own denomination but would choose some other spiritual guide whose morals he preferred. This alone would constitute free choice, and by extension, compulsory taxes were always against conscience. With this rather doubtful claim in place, the statute went on to enact the exact words that had already been made law in 1776: "that no man shall be compelled to frequent or support any religious worship, place, or ministry whatsoever, nor shall be enforced, restrained, molested, or burthened in his body or goods, nor shall otherwise suffer, on account of his religious opinions or belief." The only difference between 1786 and 1776 was Jefferson's extraordinary preamble, with its famous declaration that "truth is great and will prevail if left to herself," and its highly quotable dictum that "our civil rights have no dependence on our religious opinions, any more than our opinions in physics or geometry."

Despite the fact that Jefferson's statute said not a word about protecting the state from the effects of religion, and a great deal about protecting religious belief from the state, secularists have long emphasized what they characterize as Jefferson's secular orientation as the key to his position on religious liberty. Jefferson certainly provides excellent material for the claim that he was the very model of an early secularist. In private writings, he extended Locke's views to the conclusion that government had no authority—not even noncoercive authority—over matters of religion, and one can also find private outbursts against organized religion. But close analysis of his approach to matters of church and state reveals a more nuanced picture than is usually depicted.

Jefferson's time in France coincided with the most anticlerical, antireligious period in Western history to that date. Not coincidentally, Jefferson's thoughts and writings from the years before he went to France and became immersed in the distinctive intellectual style of the French Enlightenment differ from those that came after. During this early phase of his career, in which he drafted the Virginia statute, Jefferson rarely, if ever, took an anticlerical tone in private, and certainly never in public. His private writings on religion do not focus at all on protecting government from the church. To the contrary, Jefferson's own handwritten notes on religion center on the protection of religion from coercion by government. In his notebooks, he copied extensively from John Locke's *Letter Concerning Toleration*, far and away the most influential text on church and state in late colonial America, and one that was in no sense antireligious.[52]

After his sojourn in France, though, Jefferson became more radical about religious matters. The anticlerical views to which he was exposed in revolutionary France seem to have stuck, and they must have seemed particularly apt to him when he ran for president in 1800 and was subjected to a systematic campaign of vilification by the clergy in the New England states. The Federalists' attacks on Jefferson famously featured the (apparently accurate[53]) allegation that he had fathered children with his slave Sally Hemings. But the attacks also regularly included the charge that Jefferson was an atheist, and that anyone who voted for him would be an infidel by association.[54] The Congregationalist clergy who leveled these attacks no longer dominated New England life as they had until the 1760s, but they still received salaries from the public coffers and used their pulpits to bully equally on matters of faith and politics. Jefferson faced a formidable enemy in these ministers, and his private excoriations of them, as well as his sense of triumph when the

New England states eventually stopped funding the clergy,[55] must be understood as intimately connected to his experience of their condemnation. In fact, even Jefferson's letter to the Danbury Baptists, in which he invoked the "wall of separation," must be read in the context of Jefferson's electoral battles with New England Federalists. The Baptists, dissenters from the New England Way in church and state, hated the Congregationalist clergy as much as Jefferson did, though for their own reasons. Jefferson's letter to the Connecticut congregation memorialized their political allegiance and common opposition to the New England power structure as much as or more than it embodied a self-conscious statement of deep principle.[56]

The crucial point for the background of the religion clauses of the Constitution, though, is that it was the early Jefferson, not the late Jefferson, whose written formulations were enacted into law in Virginia—and it was Madison whose advocacy and political activism did the real work. The Jefferson who drafted the Virginia statute in 1779, seven years before it passed, had not yet encountered the full weight of French Enlightenment anticlericalism, nor had he yet been vilified by the state-supported clergy of New England. His focus was on the liberty of conscience and the necessity of individual judgment in finding truth, which he feared that the state might infringe. This was no antireligious secularism of the late-nineteenth- or early-twentieth-century variety, nor was it legal secularism of the kind that was to emerge after the Second World War and that still exists today. The focus was still on protecting religion from government, not the other way around.

At the same time, Madison and his supporters in opposing assessment and urging religious freedom also had the goal of protecting religion, and not the state. The dissenters who stood with Madison were the opposite of secularists: they thought that religion was essential to the shaping of important decisions in their personal and political lives alike. They sought an absolute liberty of conscience in making such decisions, in the form of freedom from government coercion in the payment of taxes for religious purposes. The Virginia debates thus provide little support to the anachronistic view that secularism was afoot in the years before the enactment of the First Amendment.

But neither do the Virginia debates provide evidence for the revisionist view that the Constitution did not mean to prohibit non-preferential support of religion when it banned "establishment." To the contrary, the "establishment" (in Madison's words) that was proposed and defeated in Virginia in the form of the assessment bill was precisely a system that purported to treat religious sects non-preferentially. Similarly in New England, where the states continued to collect taxes to support ministers right into the 1820s, the laws were written so that, in theory, the taxpayer could choose the recipient of his compelled contribution. Dissenters attacked the New England arrangement by calling it an establishment. They protested that laws requiring both dissenting taxpayers and congregations to be certified by local authorities made it difficult in practice to avoid supporting what was in effect the "established" Congregationalist system. But for some fifty years, the dominant majority answered that the so-called New England Way could not be considered an established church, because it made provision for opting out of the system by exemption. An established church, the Congregationalists conveniently maintained, was one that did not allow for liberty of conscience by permitting taxpayers to avoid compulsory support for the church.[57]

In the debates that led up to the drafting and ratification of the First Amendment to the Constitution, then, the participants were well aware of the possibility of nonpreferential government support for religion. In principle, all condemned use of coercive taxes to support religious institutions with which the taxpayer might disagree. The framers' generation could not agree, though, on whether systems that allowed for government support of religion with the possibility of exemptions or choice of recipient qualified as establishments of religion. The critics of those systems, whether in Virginia or New England, invariably depicted them as unjust instances of establishment. Defenders denied that nonpreferential support counted as establishment at all. For everyone, "establishment" was a dirty word.[58]

CHURCH AND STATE AT THE FRAMING: THE DEBATE IN THE STATE RATIFYING CONVENTIONS

What, then, was the decision that the framers reached about the relationship between religion and government in the federal Constitution? The answer, as we shall now see, is that the politics of religious diversity led them to agree on enacting the principle of the liberty of conscience by prohibiting a national establishment and guaranteeing free exercise of religion.[59]

By the time of the American Revolution, it would have been difficult to find any American who disagreed with the proposition that every person was entitled to liberty of conscience and that no government could legitimately coerce people in matters of religion. The debate was almost entirely over the application of that principle to institutional reality. Supporters of the old way of doing things feared that religion would shrivel and die if it were required to depend on voluntary contributions for support. Dissenters took the opportunity to redouble their claims that forcing them to pay taxes would violate their liberty of conscience. They rejected even the nonpreferential arrangements according to which everyone could designate a church of his own choosing. In practice, they insisted, such arrangements denied them their liberties. The revolution gave dissenters an even better basis for the argument that they should not be obligated to pay taxes with which they disagreed, because, after all, so much of the American resentment against England had to do with the imposition of unjust taxation.

As a result of this situation, every single state guaranteed the liberty of conscience to its citizens in its new, postrevolutionary constitution. The process of drafting state constitutions brought the importance of protecting the liberty of conscience into the national consciousness. When the draft federal Constitution was proposed in 1787, without any general guarantee of religious rights or prohibition on the establishment of a national religion, the state ratifying conventions objected. The objections came from those who feared that they might be minorities with respect to the rest of the population of the United States.

In Pennsylvania, where Quakers still held considerable political power, and there was no state support of religion, delegates protested that in the new Constitution the "rights of conscience are not secured" and that "Congress may establish any religion."[60] Ordinary citizens submitted petitions to the ratifying convention asking for an amendment that would guarantee the rights of conscience and specify "that none should be compelled contrary to their principles and inclination to hear or support the clergy of any one religion."[61] The Virginia Baptists worried that the freedom from compulsory taxes for religious purposes that they had won in Virginia could be lost at the federal level: "if a majority of Congress with the President favor one system more than another, they may oblige all others to pay to the support of their system as much as they please."[62] Under their influence, and over Madison's objection, the Virginia ratifying convention proposed a constitutional amendment derived from its own state constitution, protecting the "unalienable right to the free exercise of religion, according to the dictates of conscience," and specifying "that no particular religious sect or society ought to be favored or established, by law, in preference to others."[63] North Carolina, Rhode Island, and New York adopted similar or identical proposed amendments.[64]

Religious diversity drove this push for a constitutional amendment on religious liberty. The new form of government under consideration was intended to bind together the states into a union that was more complete—"more perfect"—than under the Articles of Confederation. The resulting bound-together union would contain a degree of religious diversity much greater than existed in any of the several states. Under these conditions, various religious groups worried about the possibility—unlikely, to be sure—of the federal government coming under the control of some other particular denomination. This made them especially eager to prohibit this eventuality in constitutional terms.

Moreover, the religious dissenters within particular states who previously had sought to avoid compulsory taxation at the state level now had a national stage on which to express comparable concerns. Religious diversity within states combined with religious diversity among the various states. Majorities that, confident in their dominance, had supported traditional modes of state support for religious institutions at the state level had no realistic hope of such dominance nationally. New England Congregationalists dominated Massachusetts, Connecticut, and New Hampshire, but they were not close to being a majority vis-à-vis the rest of the country.

We can return, then, to the Virginia ratifying convention and the puzzle of why James Madison rose to argue that the federal Constitution did not need an amendment protecting religion or prohibiting establishment. Madison, it must be recalled, was the primary architect of the federal constitutional draft that was being proposed for ratification. He had supported the decision not to include a Bill of Rights in the Constitution, fearing that specifying some rights might lead to the exclusion of others. At the Virginia convention, he still hoped to see that draft ratified without alteration and initially pressed the argument that, since the federal government had only limited, delegated powers, it already lacked the authority to do the things that a Bill of Rights would repetitively block it from doing. "There is not a shadow of a right in the general government to intermeddle with religion," he explained.[65]

This argument, like Madison's overarching view that a Bill of Rights was unnecessary in a scheme of limited government, proved unsatisfactory to his audience. Patrick Henry, Madison's old adversary and now the leading opponent of ratification at the Virginia convention, denounced the absence of a guarantee of religious liberty from the new document. Henry saw no contradiction between his support of a general assessment in Virginia and his support of the principle of religious liberty more generally. More important, he knew a good political opportunity when he saw one: the criticism stood to win over Madison's erstwhile allies, the religious dissenters, against the cause of ratification. Even Jefferson, in a private letter to Madison, insisted on the necessity of an amendment to protect religious liberty.[66]

Madison was second to none in his support for nonestablishment and religious liberty. But Madison had a deeper political and practical reason why a religion amendment was unnecessary, which he pressed in the convention and on Jefferson in private: he believed that without religious diversity to ensure nonestablishment from the practical standpoint, a constitutional amendment would do no good, since it would be ignored by the majority. "If there were a majority of one sect, a bill of rights would be a poor protection for liberty."[67] His proof was Virginia, where, he wrote to Jefferson, "I have seen the bill of rights violated in every instance where it has been opposed to the popular current."[68] Indeed, Madison believed that the Virginia assessment bill, had it passed, would have violated the state's Declaration of Rights, and that he had won the fight against it only because of the state's religious diversity. Should that change—"if a majority of people were now of one sect"—the assessment would be back, "and on narrower [i.e., less inclusive] ground than was then proposed."[69]

For Madison, then, the danger was the tyranny of the majority, and the solution lay in diluting that majority by introducing diversity, not in "parchment barriers"[70] like a Bill of Rights. This view of religious diversity as the guarantor of nonestablishment ran exactly parallel to Madison's famous and extraordinary argument in the tenth Federalist Paper[71] that the diversity of political interests in the United States would combat the dangers of faction that inhered in small republics; indeed in Federalist 51, another contribution to the series that was penned to advocate ratification, Madison made explicit the comparison between religious diversity and political diversity. In politics as in religion, he explained, diversity was the best security to avoid one faction capturing the reins of government and turning it to its own interests.[72]

This argument, brilliant though it was (or perhaps *because* of its brilliance), went nowhere. Dissenters in Virginia and defenders of religious liberty elsewhere were experiencing the entrance into a meaningful union as a threat to religious liberty, not a guarantor. Madison had the political sense to realize that ratification of the Constitution could not ultimately succeed without a Bill of Rights attached. He then took up the cause of a constitutional amendment guaranteeing religious liberty, pursuing it with characteristic vigor in the first Congress. But Madison was still right in an important sense. Religious diversity was indeed the best guarantor of nonestablishment and religious liberty because it became the engine for the passage of the religion clauses in the First Amendment. The dissenters got the guarantees of religious liberty that they wanted— but they got them for a political reason that only Madison fully understood.

THE FIRST AMENDMENT IN THE FIRST CONGRESS

The draft language that Madison proposed in the House of Representatives once he had joined the cause of seeking a constitutional amendment guaranteed that no one's civil rights would be "abridged on account of religious belief or worship"; it said that no national religion could be established; and it protected "the full and equal rights of conscience" from being infringed "in any manner, or on any pretext."[73] This language grew from the proposals of the state ratifying conventions, all of which mentioned conscience or religious liberty. A House committee changed the draft language to "no religion shall be established by law, nor shall the equal rights of conscience be infringed."[74]

Congressman Benjamin Huntington of Connecticut immediately objected, expressing his concern that if this ban on established religion were understood to apply to the states, his own New England practice of requiring taxpayers to support their own churches "might be construed into a religious establishment" and therefore prohibited or at least not be enforced in the federal courts.[75] Madison did not assuage Huntington's concern by saying that the New England arrangement was not an establishment—Madison no doubt believed that the Connecticut system was indeed an establishment, unjust to New England dissenters. Instead, Madison told Huntington that the Constitution was talking only about the federal government, not the states. He proposed inserting the word "national" into the amendment, so that it would specify that no "*national* religion" could be established by law.[76] This, Madison suggested, should satisfy Huntington by making it clear that the proposed constitutional amendment was intended to regulate only at the national level.

To make the federal emphasis even more explicit, the draft language was then changed to say that "*Congress* shall make no laws touching religion, or infringing the rights of conscience," clarifying that the issue on the table was national, rather than local.[77] After several more iterations, and proposed language from the Senate, a conference committee of House and Senate settled on the final language, subsequently ratified by the states and unchanged for the last 213 years: "Congress shall make no law respecting an establishment of religion, or prohibiting the free exercise thereof."

It is uncertain why the proposed Senate version and the final language adopted by the conference committee omitted reference to the liberty of conscience. The phrase "exercise of religion" was borrowed from the English Act of Toleration of 1688. No debate was recorded on the change, and no one, so far as we know, objected to the inclusion of the idea of the liberty of conscience in the First Amendment. To the contrary, it is certain that everyone understood that the liberty of conscience was the principled reason to prohibit establishment and guarantee free exercise. An established religion would, by definition, compel citizens to contribute to its support. No one in 1791 was especially afraid that an established religion would force people to attend church; even the Church of England no longer did that. The advocates of a constitutional ban on establishment were concerned about paying taxes to support religious purposes that their consciences told them not to support.

These same dissenters, whether in Virginia or New England, further believed that even nonpreferential government support would, in practice, place them in this untenable position. That is probably the reason why Madison ignored the language, proposed by several state ratifying conventions, according to which "no particular religious sect or society" would be favored "in preference to others." Madison knew from his Virginia experience that this language could still potentially have been construed to allow nonpreferential government support of religion in the form of compulsory taxes that could be designated for the church of the taxpayer's choosing. By selecting broader language that encompassed a ban on any establishment at all, Madison swept in a prohibition on nonpreferential establishment as well. As Madison's exchange with Huntington shows, this broader sweep was acknowledged. With the exception of Huntington's concern to clarify the federal scope of the amendment, no opposition to a prohibition on establishment and the guarantee of free exercise is recorded.

This exchange between Madison and the New Englander Huntington shows definitively that, despite what is sometimes claimed, the framers understood perfectly well that nonpreferential support for religion could and probably would be understood as an establishment of religion. At the same time, it is absolutely correct to say that the First Amendment to the federal Constitution was drafted so that it would not apply to the states when it was enacted. The

Bill of Rights, as initially ratified, did not stop the states from abridging the freedom of speech or from inflicting cruel and unusual punishments. It was not until the post–Civil War passage of the Fourteenth Amendment, and its subsequent interpretation in the twentieth century by the Supreme Court, that the Bill of Rights came to apply to the states as well.

But that does not mean that the Establishment Clause (as it is now called) of the Constitution was actually intended to protect state establishments of religion from congressional interference by specifying that Congress could make no law "respecting an establishment of religion." The framers would never have imagined that *Congress* would possess the power to change state arrangements with respect to religion. Moreover, in 1791, no state was prepared to acknowledge that its church-state arrangements counted as an establishment, because "establishment" was a term of condemnation. Even Congressman Huntington did not admit that his home state of Connecticut actually had an establishment of religion; he just acknowledged that the New England Way could be "construed into an establishment" by its opponents. At the time that the First Amendment came into being, Americans were almost universally prepared to say that establishment of religion was a bad thing. They understood perfectly well that the federal Constitution prohibited Congress from creating arrangements like those in New England. It is therefore historically incorrect to claim that the Constitution, by banning an establishment of religion, allowed the government to support religion generally or nonpreferentially.

The new constitutional amendment, then, guaranteed two things. The Establishment Clause guaranteed that the government would not compel anybody to support any religious teaching or worship with which he conscientiously disagreed. The Free Exercise Clause guaranteed that the government would not stop anybody from worshipping or practicing his religion as he chose. Both clauses were necessary because the framers understood that there was a difference between making somebody do something against his will

and stopping him from doing something he wanted to do. Prohibiting establishment protected citizens from being placed in the
position where they must act against conscience in the realm of religion. Guaranteed free exercise protected their right to worship in
the way their consciences told them they must.[78] These guarantees
still apply to us today—but their interpretation has been much
contested, and some of their contemporary applications would
seem very strange indeed to those who framed them.

THE FRAMERS AND THE SYMBOLS OF RELIGION

If the Establishment Clause protected against compulsory support
of organized religion, and the Free Exercise Clause protected worship, what did the Constitution say about religious symbols and
their use in the public realm? Such symbolic questions are, after all,
often the focus of our contemporary church-state debates. The
framers are invoked on both sides of the debate about religious
symbolism. What, for instance, would the framers' Constitution
have had to say about the fifty-two-hundred-pound block of granite, inscribed with the Ten Commandments, that Judge Roy Moore
erected in the rotunda of the Alabama Supreme Court in the summer of 2003?

The answer is that the framers were not especially concerned
with public religious symbolism one way or the other. They would
certainly not have approved of the use of federal public funds to
erect churches or support religious teaching, because they would
have understood the taxes involved to be obtained through coercion of conscience. But they were supremely untroubled by norms
like the opening of legislative sessions with symbolic prayers. The
framers would no doubt have thought it odd to erect a monument
to the Ten Commandments in a government building, since government had no authority in religious affairs. But the framers
would also probably have been perplexed by the legal secularists'

vociferous opposition to the monument, so long as its presence did not expend government funds and therefore coerced no one to act in contravention of his own beliefs.

The main reason the framers did not react with horror to public symbols of religion is that they were not secularists in the modern sense. They did not think that the state needed to be protected from the dangers of religious influence, nor were they particularly concerned with keeping religious symbolism out of the public sphere. For that matter, American religion, too, was very different than it is today. Church attendance was low, at least by today's standards. There was no national movement devoted to promoting the role of religion in public life. A monument like Judge Moore's, if anyone had been able to imagine it, would have had an entirely different meaning than it did in 2003, when it was erected in large part as a symbolic rejection of legal secularism. At the same time, there was no great danger that government would give offense to religious minorities when public prayers were offered or God's name invoked as a symbol of the fledgling republic. In the framers' America, almost everybody was a Protestant of some kind, and atheism as a publicly acknowledged stance was essentially unknown. The remaining orthodox Calvinists still adhered to the doctrine of the predestined salvation of only a small elect, while more liberal Protestants increasingly opened the doors of possible salvation much wider, and deists like Jefferson rejected the very idea of a personal God. But these different ideas swam in a sea of Protestant assumptions, and the framers' generation argued politics in the light of ideals connected to their common Protestant legacy. Rather than insisting anachronistically on "Judeo-Christian values," it would be more accurate to say that the framers assumed a whole set of principles that grew out of Protestant Christianity as interpreted by English liberals such as John Locke.

Where contemporary values evangelicals go wrong historically is in assuming that those Protestant-originated principles required that Christian values infuse all the activities of the state. Rather, the framers' Protestant-inflected worldview included a crucial distinction between the religious realm and the civil. As Locke bluntly put it, "there is absolutely no such thing, *under the Gospel,* as a Christian Commonwealth."[79] Locke, in this formulation and elsewhere in his writings, offered a religiously grounded explanation for why government lacked authority in religious matters. According to Locke and the overwhelming majority of Americans who accepted some version of his views, there was no basis either in religion or in reason for allowing government to exercise coercive power in affairs of religion. The individual's conscience must be left free in order for religious faith to have any meaning at all.

In America, the establishment of religion by the government came to be seen as posing a fundamental danger to the liberty of conscience by threatening dissenters with the possibility of coercion. The constitutional guarantee of nonestablishment sought to protect conscience from coercion by guaranteeing a division between the institutional spheres of organized religion and government. It is therefore not anachronistic to say that the Constitution separated the church, in its institutional sense, from the state, even though the framers' views certainly grew in Protestant soil. The removal of government from the sphere of religion was itself a product of an important strand in Protestant political thought, and the framers were extending the idea of separate spheres of religion and government by rejecting an established church. "Establishment" stood for the institutional merger of church and state; nonestablishment was a distinctively American experiment in the separation of the two most important institutions in society.

This institutional experiment had little to say about religious symbolism. It was concerned with avoiding actual coercion and with disentangling church and state, which had been historically intertwined in the Christian West. So secularists do not really get the better of the argument about symbolism when they point out that the Constitution does not mention God or Jesus. The reason the Constitution does not mention Christianity is that the framers were creating government institutions that had no authority to pronounce on matters of religion, not because the framers themselves were secularists.

CHURCH AND STATE IN THE EARLY REPUBLIC

The framers believed that the federal government could actually separate itself from the realm of religion and, in good Lockean fashion, restrict itself to the realm of civil affairs. That belief turned out to be naïve, but this was not immediately obvious when the First Amendment was drafted. Washington issued a religiously inspired declaration for a day of thanksgiving on November 26, 1789, and the second president, John Adams, issued a call for a day of fasting, prayer, and humiliation before God in 1798.[80] Neither elicited much comment or objection, and neither coerced anyone or involved the expenditure of any taxpayer funds in support of religious teaching.

Yet Jefferson declined to follow the practice on the theory that such proclamations too closely resembled the acts of an established church. In his own rough draft of his letter to the Danbury Baptists, Jefferson explained that, because of the constitutional ban on establishment, it was outside the authority of the federal government to take any actions that in any way interfered with or engaged in religious practice or exercise: "Congress thus inhibited from acts respecting religion, and the Executive authorised only to execute their acts, I have refrained from prescribing even those occasional performances of devotion, practiced indeed by the Executive of another nation as the legal head of its church, but subject here, as religious exercises only to the voluntary regulations and discipline of each respective sect."[81] Jefferson, then, initially planned to use the letter to offer a public constitutional reason—his own lack of authority—as his justification for declining to declare days of thanksgiving, but he was adding a strong symbolic reason as well. If the Church of England was the archetypal establishment, the president should avoid acting as the king at the head of the national religion.

But before sending the letter, Jefferson deleted this explanation, in the process minimizing the draft's reliance on the theory that government had no authority of any sort even in noncoercive matters of religion and focusing instead on the fact that in the federal Constitution, the people had protected the rights of conscience. He was being politically prudent, his correspondence with his advisers shows, fearing that in New England, where days of thanksgiving were commonplace, his views would be seen as confirming the reputation for atheism that Jefferson already enjoyed.[82] Jefferson's bind suggests that keeping religion and government separate was not so easy as had initially been imagined. Madison himself, when he got his turn as president, either found Jefferson's argument unconvincing, or discovered that realistic politics outweighed principle. He declared a national day of thanksgiving in 1815, though his diaries reflect that he regretted the decision twenty years later.[83]

Another early indication of the difficulty of avoiding some engagement between religion and the federal government involved the delivery of mail on Sundays. When in 1810 Congress brought the national postal system into existence, it legislated for seven-day mail delivery without anyone initially raising the problem of Sabbath violation.[84] By 1828, however, with national religious consciousness growing, local religious leaders began to complain that post offices, which doubled as gathering places in small towns, were diverting the faithful from attending church on Sunday. Committees were formed in both the North and the South to demand that mail on Sundays be stopped.

What followed was the first major national discussion of the proper relationship between the federal government and religion since the ratification of the Constitution. Stating that "our Government is a civil and not a religious institution," Kentucky Senator Richard M. Johnson took the lead in arguing that the law should not be changed.[85] Johnson made the pragmatic argument that ending Sunday delivery would delay mail service on the other six days and slow the growth of the national economy. But he also emphasized the principled claim that changing the law would require the government to take a stand on what day, Saturday or Sunday, was the Sabbath. Once the government began to "determine what are the laws of God," Johnson warned, there would be no stopping the rise of religious oppression. What was more, worried Johnson, the fact that religious groups were acting in concert to end Sunday mail service presaged further political activity by "religious combinations," which could eventually come to dominate the civil sphere. Here was a political concern that Madison would have found familiar: religious diversity might cease to protect nonestablishment when different religious denominations could form alliances.

Ultimately, Johnson persuaded both the House and the Senate to adopt committee reports in which he argued that the "spirit of the constitution" regarded the government as "a civil institution destitute of religious authority." (Johnson switched jobs from the Senate to the House of Representatives in 1829, so he had the rare chance to convince members of both bodies of his views.) Passing a law that decided a religious controversy, Johnson maintained, exceeded Congress's "legitimate bounds." Government's job was to protect the exercise of religion; the job of religion was to do good deeds, preach the faith, and exercise a "moral influence," not to call on Congress to enact laws. The measure to end Sunday mail service ultimately failed, and the mail was delivered in the United States on Sundays until 1912.[86]

Those on the losing legislative side in the Sunday mail controversy, however, got their voices heard. They agreed with Johnson that the federal government "was formed for civil, and not religious purposes," and they denied that stopping Sunday delivery tended "to form the justly odious combination of church and state." The congressional committee in charge of the Post Office, after observing that petitions against Sunday delivery had more respectable signatures than any other petitions ever directed at Congress, argued that a day of rest was "calculated to elevate the moral condition of society." The Sabbath had made "better citizens, and better men in all the relations of society, both public and private."[87] The advocates of ending Sunday delivery were saying that even though they embraced separation of church and state, they believed that religion, and the moral values that it promoted, could not easily be disentangled from the government's legitimate goals of improving society.

Their argument did not carry the day in the mail controversy, but it was soon to become directly relevant to a much more profound controversy about the proper relationship between government and religion. This controversy raged, and still rages, in an area the framers never expected government to enter, but that has, ironically, been the single most important battleground for church-state affairs in the United States for most of its history: the education of children.

2

SCHOOLS AND MORALS

Public schools are quintessentially American. Attending public school is probably the most important common experience undergone by people all over our diverse country. Some forty-eight million children attend today, and the roughly five million[1] who are educated in parochial or private schools can take in the public school experience vicariously through countless movies, television shows, and books. Yet at the time of the American Revolution, there were no public schools in the modern sense anywhere in the United States—or anywhere else, for that matter. When the Constitution was drafted a decade later, not much had changed in this respect. The Northwest Ordinance of 1789 proclaimed that "religion, morality, and knowledge, being necessary to good government and the happiness of mankind, schools and the means of education shall forever be encouraged,"[2] but did not allocate funds for schools in the federally administered territories, and government-supported education in the territories was limited to some scattered Indian schools. Anyone bothering to check again during the War of 1812 would have found a single school built by the Free School Society of New York three years earlier[3] but little formal public primary education elsewhere. Not until the 1820s did so-called common or public schools begin to be founded in big cities, promoted by old elites reacting to the gradual urbanization that accompanied industrial growth.

The well-off gentlemen in New York or Boston who took an interest in public schooling had different motivations from those of the patrons of the boarding schools and colleges—such as Philips Andover and Exeter, Harvard and Yale—that until then represented the most important vectors of formal education in America. These elite institutions had at first trained ministers and were now slowly shifting their mission to educating lawyers, political leaders, and businessmen.[4] By contrast, the new public schools aimed to educate ordinary working people, who might in the past have lived in the countryside and deferred to large landowners when it came to politics but who increasingly demanded a voice in public affairs as they began to make their way to the growing cities of the North. The unwelcome prospect of living alongside large numbers of uneducated workingmen in what was becoming a more broadly based democracy encouraged the educated class to think about preserving the republican character of their society.

Education was the answer. For men (still the only bearers of political rights) to deliberate about public affairs and vote responsibly, they must be educated enough to read about the issues of the day, and they must be committed to the unifying process of debating and voting, not to mob rule. Jefferson had earlier argued for the necessity of education to maintain republican government, and he had founded the University of Virginia to that end, but the new theorists of public education cared more about primary school than about college. The common purpose necessary to sustain a republic called for shared knowledge and common moral values, neither of which could be taken for granted in a changing America.

Today education advocates often argue that good schools enable us to compete globally; in his day, Benjamin Franklin also thought that education should prepare students for business and the professions.[5] In the 1820s and '30s, though, political concerns drove the common school movement more than economic ones. Newly emerging factory jobs did not necessarily require literacy; that would soon be demonstrated by the influx of unskilled workers who would be hired to operate those factories as the demand for labor grew. The reason to educate the workers was primarily to domesticate them for participation in the civic life of the American republic. The election of the unpolished frontiersman Andrew Jackson in 1820 heralded the expanded political influence of non-elites. Only education, it was thought, could save the republic from collapsing into a mere popular democracy in which competing social forces fought for the resources of the state, with the more numerous poorer classes inevitably victorious.

From the very start, the common school movement had to confront the question of religion. The older, private schools in America had uniformly incorporated religious instruction. Formal education—as opposed to basic reading and writing, taught informally in a range of contexts—had long been seen as a social function belonging to the sphere of religion, with schools founded by and for ministers. Not only did religious education seem like a familiar component of education more generally, it served the all-important purpose of teaching moral values to the young. If the point of the common schools was to gentle the unlettered and the ill-bred, so that they would participate in the republican project instead of subverting it, then surely the schools must give children the solid morals that they might not get at home. Teaching them to read and write without inculcating proper moral values would have been, on this theory, worse than irresponsible—it would have been a waste of money.

The notion of teaching children morality by some means that did not involve religion would hardly have entered the American mind. Morality, it was understood, derived from religion, and for even the most liberal of the Protestants who made up the northeastern elite in the 1820s and '30s, that meant morality came from the

Bible, especially the Gospels. Without religion there could be no foundation stone on which to rest basic values of honesty and rule following. None of the theorists of the new common schools advocated keeping religion out of the classroom. No religion would have meant no morality, and no morality would have meant that the schools could not achieve their society-shaping function.

Yet the impulse to teach religion in the new common schools faced a major practical obstacle: by the 1830s, Americans were hopelessly divided on which version of Christianity was right. The Second Great Awakening of the previous decades had seen extraordinary, unprecedented multiplication of new sects. Established denominations like Congregationalism were splitting up, to be replaced, in New England, by two offshoots: an old-line Trinitarian church that carried the Congregationalist banner, and a liberal, even radical Unitarianism.[6] Meanwhile, Baptists and Methodists were growing by leaps and bounds in the most "dramatic rise in religious adherence and corresponding religious influence on the broader national culture" in American history.[7] Catholic immigration from Ireland was also increasing, although it had not yet become a preoccupation of domestic politics as it would in a few short years.

This drastically increased religious diversity resulted in a paradox. The new common schools must teach religion yet must appeal to parents across the spectrum of denominations. If religion were not taught, morality would disappear and the schools would fail; if religion were introduced into the curriculum, many parents would object that it was not the right religion and might pull their children out, causing the schools to fail for a different reason. The common school movement could have been stillborn if its theorists had not come up with a creative solution to the problem.

THE NONSECTARIAN SOLUTION

The solution lay in what was coming to be called "nonsectarianism": the claim that there were moral principles shared in common by all Christian sects, independent of their particular theological beliefs. Nonsectarianism would turn out to be among the most powerful—and controversial—ideas in American public life in the nineteenth century and beyond, an idea whose resonances are still felt in our own contemporary debates over religion and values. It promised to unite Americans behind common, identifiable moral commitments, transcending their religious differences and engendering unity of purpose. It also seemed to have a basis in observed social reality. Visiting America in 1830, Alexis de Tocqueville put the point this way: "There is an innumerable multitude of sects in the United States. All differ in the worship one must render to the Creator, but all agree on the duties of man toward one another. Each sect therefore adores God in its manner, but all sects preach the same morality in the name of God."[8] Tocqueville, himself a liberal Catholic, offered this comment as an observation of American mores, but for advocates of nonsectarianism, the argument had a practical cast: if moral beliefs were truly held in common, they could be shared by all Christians and taught in the common schools without fear of offending any sect in particular.

To compound the usefulness of the nonsectarian idea, the font of common morality was said to be the Bible, which—Protestants had long held—could be interpreted by the individual and so did not need to be interpreted by the school. When Horace Mann, the great theorist of education and for a dozen years secretary of the Massachusetts Board of Education, addressed the question, he explained that, in Massachusetts schools, the Bible was allowed to do "what it is allowed to do in no other system—to speak for itself." By reading the Bible in an unmediated fashion, with no comment from the teacher, the student would be enabled "to judge for himself according to the dictates of his own reason and conscience."[9]

The invocation of the liberty of conscience was no coincidence. It tied nonsectarianism to what had been, since the founding, the dominant American principle regarding the relation of church and state. In Mann's view, the individual freedom to make decisions in matters of religion ran parallel to the individual freedom to make political choices. Nonsectarianism in the schools was therefore presented as fully compatible with the distinctive American experiment in protecting religious liberty and separating church and state, even as it promised to unite Americans in a common morality derived from religion itself. Outside the schools, liberty of conscience was also said to be essential to nonsectarian Christianity, which was by extension itself indispensable to free government.[10] The ideal American citizen, then, enjoyed dual manifestations of the voluntary principle: to choose freely in politics—the principle of republicanism; and in religion—the principle of Protestantism.

On a practical level, invoking nonsectarianism seems to have forestalled the very real concern that too much sectarian religious instruction would scare parents away from the public schools. With Bible reading a daily staple, the common schools grew, attracting students with the promise of free education. Yet nonsectarianism from the start attracted critics who alleged that it was nothing more than a cover for a highly attenuated liberal Protestantism. The cart of morality, said the critics, was being put before the horse of true faith.

Some of this criticism came from committed Protestants, like the old-fashioned Congregationalist minister Matthew Hale Smith of Massachusetts, who believed that nonsectarianism offered watered-down religion, which was worse than no religion at all. Smith argued that the decision not to teach basic Christian doctrine like the Trinity amounted to a sectarian religious preference for Unitarianism, the dangerous new heresy shared by many elite New England liberals, Horace Mann among them. Moral decline, Smith suggested, resulted precisely from treating religious morality as separate from religious doctrine. To make such a separation was "to elevate the intellectual over the moral, and man above God."[11]

Smith struck close to home with his argument that nonsectarian teaching of basic morality elevated human-focused preferences and judgments above a commitment to the divine. Nonsectarian moral education indeed operated on the presumption that religion was valuable because it inculcated morals, not that morality was desirable because God commanded it—a hierarchy that always tends to crop up in arguments for the value of public religion. By implication, then, the state's need to maintain a moral populace to keep republicanism alive weighed more heavily than any inherent love of godly morals. Nonsectarian moral teaching functioned as religion in the service of the state, not the other way around.

Even as Smith and other orthodox Protestants objected to nonsectarian moral teaching as essentially irreligious, there emerged a more powerful and lasting critique that characterized nonsectarian teaching as sectarian Protestantism in disguise. The Roman Catholic leaders who developed this line of attack spoke on behalf of a Catholic population that began growing seriously in the middle of the 1820s and amounted to some 341,000 during the 1830s. Ultimately, in the years from 1847 to 1854, it would rise to 1.3 million in the wake of the Great Famine in Ireland.[12] The wave of immigration corresponded, in other words, to the growth years of the public schools in America.

From the perspective of the new immigrants, the idea that the Bible would be read, in the Protestant King James Version, and that children would be encouraged to decide on the meaning of the Bible for themselves, ran headlong into Catholic teaching that conferred the authority for biblical interpretation on the church's priests and saw the church-sanctioned Douay-Reims translation, based on the Latin Vulgate, as the only legitimate English version of the Bible. The Catholic church had never embraced Luther's position that his individual conscience came before the judgment of the church on the meaning of Scripture, and the question of who was entitled to find the true meaning of the Bible represented a crucial point of departure between Catholics and Protestants. By emphasizing individual choice in matters of faith, the common schools were revealing themselves to be Protestant. Dr. John Power, a Catholic vicar general in New York, summed up the problem succinctly in 1840: "The Catholic Church tells her children that they must be taught their religion by AUTHORITY. The Sects [i.e., Protestants] say, read the bible, judge for yourselves. The bible is read in public schools, the children are allowed to judge for themselves. The Protestant principle is therefore acted upon, slily inculcated, and the schools are Sectarian."[13] In a sense, Power was right. The theory of nonsectarianism that underlay Bible reading in the public schools was thoroughly Protestant, and liberal Protestant at that, committed to the possibility of establishing common morality without delving too deeply into religious doctrine. The emphasis on students' choice in the interpretation of the Bible did reflect a peculiarly Protestant "voluntary principle" in religion, which had come to be associated with individual choice in republican politics.

In 1840, however, this Protestant aspect of common school education was still largely unconscious from the perspective of the Protestants who had deployed the idea of nonsectarianism to deal with religious diversity, hardly taking note that, in their minds, the relevant diversity was among different kinds of Protestants, not between Protestants and Catholics. The King James Version of the Bible was read in the schools—complete with its original seventeenth-century introduction describing the pope as "that man of sin"[14]—not to score points against the Catholic Douay-Reims translation but because the King James Bible had been the reigning Bible translation in the mostly Protestant English-speaking world for two hundred years and had acquired the air of sacred inspiration. The association of voluntary choice in religion with voluntary choice in politics had also come naturally to Protestants and had not been dreamed up in a fit of anti-Catholicism. After all,

Tocqueville, himself a Catholic highly attuned to the subtleties of Catholic-Protestant differences, had described both the nonsectarian argument and the voluntary principle in 1830, and he had not seen either as anti-Catholic. The common schools were effectively nonsectarian Protestant—but until Catholics began to say so, no one had noticed it.

When they did raise the subject, Catholics ran into extraordinarily rigid opposition. Initially, they tried to remedy the problem of having their children taught Protestant ideology by founding Catholic schools. To pay for the Catholic education system that was emerging in areas of heavy Catholic concentration, they sought state funding. Starting with a letter circulated in 1829, the Catholic bishops in America had called for parents to send their children to Catholic schools that would inculcate Catholic values and teach church doctrine.[15] Now, beginning in New York in 1840, Catholics argued that the same government support available to the essentially Protestant common schools should be made available to support Catholic schools.[16]

At first the argument was pressed on the basis of plain fairness: If effectively Protestant schools received funding, why shouldn't Catholic schools receive the same? Soon, however, Catholics began to say that supporting public schools that their children could not in good conscience attend amounted to a violation of their religious liberty, and (an argument still heard today) that they were being taxed unfairly for schools they did not use. An 1853 petition submitted by Michigan Catholics to the state legislature put it this way: "our Public School Laws compel us to violate our conscience, or deprive us unjustly of our share of the Public School funds, and also impose on us taxes for the support of schools which, as a matter of conscience, we cannot allow our children to attend."[17]

When this petition was composed, the Catholic church was more than a century away from officially embracing the idea that liberty of conscience was a basic right. Indeed, the church was undergoing a period of antiliberal "ultramontane" reaction to the European revolutions of 1848,[18] and in 1864, the papal encyclical *Quanta Cura* would condemn as "insanity" (*deliramentum*) the view that liberty of conscience was a universal right that ought to exist in every well-governed state.[19] American Catholics, then, were not relying on Catholic sources for their argument. Instead, they were using the distinctly American Protestant-origin argument for liberty of conscience and voluntarism in religion to make their case.

Framed in terms of the American notion that paying taxes to support religious teachings with which one disagrees violates the liberty of conscience—an idea developed, widely embraced, and constitutionalized at the federal level by the framers' generation—the Catholics' argument seemed almost airtight. By using the voluntary principle against the common schools, Catholics had painted American Protestants into a corner. Of course it was possible for Protestants to respond, in an inclusive vein, that the public schools should make a serious effort to be not Protestant but Christian and to do all they could to accommodate Catholics. Horace Bushnell, a nationally influential Protestant minister, called for this approach in 1853.[20] But Catholics could respond that inclusiveness was precisely what they rejected as a matter of conscience. Professing faith in the truth as taught by their church, not in Christianity in general, they needed Catholic schools, and any generic Christian compromise would not satisfy their religious beliefs.

So Protestants responded in the time-honored fashion of the intolerant when faced with a claim of conscience: instead of offering an accommodation, they simply refused to acknowledge Catholics' concern and used their legislative majorities to refuse the funding of Catholic schools. At this juncture, the previously unacknowledged Protestantism of the common schools became an overt rallying cry. Catholic schools were depicted as potential agents of separatism and the subversion of republican politics. The argument against Catholic schools became part of the nativist argument against the transformation of America through the immigration of

Irish Catholics. If Protestantism was associated with republicanism through the association of liberty of conscience in religion and free choice in politics, then Catholicism could be associated with despotism through its insistence on authority. If Catholics were unprepared for republican political participation, then they needed the Protestant-inflected education of the common schools all the more.

To republicans, the patterns of Irish Catholic bloc voting that began changing politics in the urban centers of the Northeast in the 1840s and '50s were also cause for concern. By voting in concert, Catholics appeared to the native-born to be complying with authority. Instead of integrating into pre-existing political patterns, Catholic interests and their votes could be described as separate and distinct. When combined with Catholic leaders' own insistence on the importance of church authority, the immigrant response of group solidarity looked like a threat to the American way in politics as well as religion. Today, ethnic or racial interest-group voting is considered the very essence of urban politics, not a transformative challenge to our democracy—and Madison, had he lived, might have urged that diversity only secured religious liberty. But from the perspective of 1840, the combination of a sudden change in the nature of American religious diversity and an emerging new trend in group political action seemed radically new and seriously threatening.

Nativists were responding to the social dislocation of urbanization and industrialization, and Irish Catholic immigrants represented a symbol of these changes more easily attacked than the factories or the cities themselves. At the same time, the fact that the immigrants were Catholic enabled the nativists to tap into a centuries-old tradition of Protestant-Catholic polemic. Catholics unwittingly walked into the trap of this rhetorical tradition when, having been rebuffed in their call for public funding for their schools, they adopted the alternative tack of demanding that the common schools give up the offensive practice of reading from the

King James Bible or reciting the Ten Commandments in their
Protestant enumeration rather than the slightly different Catholic
count.[21]

From the Catholic perspective, eliminating Bible reading in the
common schools seemed like a sensible compromise to the problem
of their religious objection. If they could not get funding for their
own schools, they could at least send their children to the public
schools without having them subjected to an unconscionable religious practice. Again, their argument resonated with the voluntary
principle that no one should be coerced against the liberty of conscience.

But in calling for the removal of the Bible from the schools,
Catholics misunderstood both the initial purpose of the common
schools and the depth of Protestant commitment to the Bible as a
symbol. The common schools had been founded as much to teach
morals to the new urban workers as to teach them to read and
write. According to the emerging nonsectarian theory of education,
the Bible was the central means of moral education. Taking the
Bible out of the schools would therefore, in the view of the Protestants who had created those schools in the first place, defeat their
very purpose. In this sense, Catholics were unintentionally calling
for the undermining of the unifying mission of public education.
The increased presence of religious diversity in the schools was, not
for the last time, challenging the premise that public schools were
places for the inculcation of common values.

Protestants—even moderate Protestants—defended the use of
the Bible in the schools on the ground that it did not serve the for-
bidden purpose of sectarian theological instruction but only contained a message of pure morality, with which even Catholics who
objected to the King James translation could not disagree. That
morality was necessary to make good citizens out of Catholic immigrants. When a Catholic public school pupil went all the way to the
Maine Supreme Court to argue that her liberty of conscience was
violated by a school board regulation that required reading the

King James Bible in her public school, the court insisted, on the one hand, that the Bible was used "merely as a reading book," and on the other, that the complaining young woman could hardly object to the Bible itself, which was "consonant to the soundest principles of morality." The court also argued that the curriculum could not be made subject to the objections of the Catholic church, which, it said rhetorically, might seek the exclusion of other books that appeared on its official prohibited index. The court concluded that it was up to the school board to train the "large masses of foreign population [who] are among us," Catholics who must "become citizens in fact as well as in name . . . through the medium of the public schools, which are alike open to the children of the rich and poor, of the stranger and the citizen."[22] Urging the school board to follow the Golden Rule (which it pointed out was almost the same in every English Bible translation), the court nonetheless refused to require the board to allow other versions of the Bible in the schools. The Catholic bid for a constitutional right to liberty of conscience foundered on the Protestant perception that an exemption from Bible reading would undermine the schools' project of teaching a shared republican, Christian morality.

Far worse from a practical perspective, the Catholic call against reading the Bible in the public schools could be depicted by nativists as a Catholic attack on the Bible itself. Here the polemical tradition came fully into play. Historically, Protestantism, including English evangelical Protestantism, condemned the Catholic church for keeping the Bible from the masses and interposing the priesthood between God's word and man. The church had, before the Reformation, opposed translating the Bible into English; John Wycliffe's pre–Protestant reform movement in England had made his New Testament translation into a staple of popular, individual resistance to the Catholic church. The nativists, of course, did not have the fourteenth century in mind when they took to the streets in support of the Bible in the schools. But they did know one crudely stated formula that would have been familiar to their ancestors in England: the Catholic church was against the Bible, and they were for it.

Where the Catholic request to stop Bible reading in schools met strong nativist sentiment, rioting followed. In 1844, over the course of several days, nativists in Philadelphia claiming that Catholics wanted the Bible out of the schools killed thirteen people and burned a Catholic church to the ground.[23] The so-called Bible riots in Philadelphia constituted one of the worst instances of nativist violence touched off by the controversy over the Bible, but they were not the only ones. Rioting in dozens of cities in the 1840s and '50s could be connected to the fight over the Bible in the schools.

The Bible wars of the mid-nineteenth century did not reflect any particularly deep religious faith on the part of the nativists who took to the streets. The Bible mattered as a symbol of American Protestantism and the republican ideology connected with it. The nativists' anti-Catholicism was more political, economic, and cultural than religious. Yet unquestionably the fight over the curriculum in the public schools mattered so centrally because those schools, still in their infancy, were already understood as sites for the creation of American identity, with which nativists were obsessed. This was true as a practical matter, since compulsory public schooling was the only time in an American's life when one was subjected, like it or not, to the propaganda of the state. But the public schools were also centrally important symbolically, because there the government revealed what values it intended to support. Loss of control over what was taught in the schools would be evidence of lost control over the public meaning of American life.

Both the practical and symbolic centrality of the public schools to the creation of American values has remained consistent through the rest of American history. If the framers had anticipated a forum in which the government would state, promulgate, and embody American values while teaching children its version of the good life, they might have given constitutional attention to the role of religion in such a context. (Of course, they might also have left the issue to the states.) But because common schools were a thing of the future, the framers gave us little guidance. Instead we must deal with what later generations thought and did. In the 1840s and '50s, the question of the Bible in the schools was understood as social and political, not legal or constitutional. Only after the Civil War did the question of religion in the schools move into the realm of constitutional decisions—and it is to that development that we now must turn.

THE PROPOSED BLAINE AMENDMENT: NONSECTARIAN SCHOOLS AS A NATIONAL ISSUE

The years leading up to the Civil War saw no significant reduction in Protestant-Catholic tensions. Indeed, the old nativist-Irish conflicts of the 1840s expressed themselves in the draft riots that accompanied the first efforts at conscription once the war had begun, as conscripted Irish came to believe that they were being forced to fight the Yankees' war. But during the war years themselves, national attention was so focused on what was called the Negro question and the progress of the fighting that disputes over the Bible in the schools faded from direct public attention. The Civil War mattered in the history of religious thought in America, and Abraham Lincoln's second inaugural address arguably represented a crucial step in the development of a distinctly American theology, but the war brought little significant new thinking about the relationship between church and state. More pressing matters were at hand.

With the end of the war, however, the twin issues of Catholic education and the Bible in the schools began to resurface. Between 1869 and 1874, New York, Missouri, and Ohio all saw significant debates over state support for Catholic educational institutions. All three adopted state constitutional amendments blocking distribution of state common school funds to "sectarian" schools. In New York and Ohio, as in most of the rest of the country, this meant in practice that the state would not support Catholic education. In Missouri, home to a large community of Reformed Lutherans with their own German-language school system, the ban extended to another immigrant minority that sought state support in educating its children according to its own particular religious beliefs.

The debates over the state constitutional amendments were intense. In June 1872, "Bible wars" sprang up in Brooklyn and Long Island City, New York, after schools expelled Catholic students for refusing to attend Bible reading. The Catholic community called on the school boards to retract the expulsions, and when the school boards refused to back down, crowds gathered around the homes of the school board members. *The New York Times* reported "bonfires blazing through the streets."[24]

In Ohio, the dispute was less violent but even more politically polarizing. In 1869, in response to Catholic objections, the Cincinnati Board of Education voted to stop Bible reading, religious instruction, and hymn singing in the city's public schools. (In Cincinnati, the Catholic population was heavily German, and there was also a significant German Protestant population as well as a small but important community of German Jews.) The Ohio Supreme Court upheld the board's decision in a lengthy and impassioned opinion that quoted Madison to the effect that religion and government must exist in separate spheres, and cited Buddha for the proposition that truth should be spread by love, not state coercion.[25]

In an early invocation of social Darwinism, the court urged that different religious doctrines should be allowed "a fair field" for conflict in which "the best will triumph" while "the intellectually, morally, and spiritually weakest will go to the wall."[26] Yet it soon became clear that the arena of conflict would be electoral, not spiritual. Republicans strongly opposed both the removal of religion from the public schools and state support of alternative Catholic education. After proposing and successfully ratifying a state constitutional amendment prohibiting government support for sectarian education, they rode statewide Protestant support for these issues to subsequent electoral victory. Democrats found themselves in the difficult position of either opposing an amendment popular among Protestant voters or abandoning their Catholic constituents.

Ohio's governor, Rutherford B. Hayes, struck on the idea of trying nationally a strategy that had worked for the Republicans in Ohio. On June 16, 1875, a year and a half before circumstance (and a bizarre one-off special Electoral Commission) was to propel him into the presidency, Hayes wrote to Congressman James G. Blaine of Maine, already a presidential hopeful, that "the secret of our enthusiastic state convention is the school question."[27] If the issue of Catholic education could fire up Ohio Republicans, perhaps it would prove useful elsewhere as well. By July 8, just three weeks later, the newspapers were reporting that Republicans would find a way to raise the question of government support of Catholic education in the 1876 national elections.[28]

The advantages to the Republicans of making the funding of "sectarian" education into a national issue were considerable. The Democratic Party relied heavily on Catholic votes but was acutely sensitive to the charge that it was the party of rum, Rome, and rebellion. Democrats could not win a national election by relying on Catholic votes alone, and many Protestant Democrats, especially those in Southern states, had no sympathy for Catholics. If Republicans could put a ban on government funding of religious institutions onto the national agenda, Democrats would have little choice but to oppose it in order to placate Catholic constituents. That in turn would alienate potential Protestant swing voters who themselves harbored anti-Catholic sentiments, by allowing Republicans to paint the Democrats as beholden to Catholic interests.

The unscrupulousness of this strategy of driving a wedge between Democratic-leaning Protestants and Catholics seems not to have disturbed Republican politicians. But they faced a serious problem in making school funding seem like a national question: then, as now, public schools were funded from taxes collected at the local level, not by the federal government. It had been possible for Ohio Republicans to create a statewide issue by proposing a state constitutional amendment prohibiting localities from supporting sectarian education, because under American law, cities and towns were creatures of the state government.[29] But on what theory was it necessary or appropriate to make local funding of sectarian education into an issue of nationwide import? What business had the federal government with such a purely local question?

Republicans had trouble finding a plausible answer. The solution they ultimately adopted was to go back to the theory of nonsectarianism and argue that this value was necessary to create a national, unified political culture. President Ulysses S. Grant, who was still contemplating an unprecedented run for a third term as president, made the first public attempt to articulate the Republican position at a meeting of the Society of the Army of the Tennessee on September 30, 1875. Ignoring—or perhaps trying to rise above—the scandals that had engulfed his presidency, Grant invoked the spirit of revolutionary Lexington and insisted on the necessity of "strengthening the foundations of the structure" that the heroic revolutionary generation had laid. The bases of that structure, Grant asserted, were "free thought, free speech, pure morals, [and] unfettered religious sentiments."[30]

Then Grant turned to the concrete proposal nominally intended to make these foundations of republicanism strong: "Encourage free schools, and resolve that not one dollar, appropriated for their support, shall be appropriated to the support of any sectarian schools. Resolve that neither State nor Nation, nor both combined shall support institutions of learning other than those sufficient to afford every child growing up in the land the opportunity of a good common school education, unmixed with sectarian, pagan, or atheistical dogmas. Leave the matter of religion to the family altar, the Church, and the private school, supported entirely by private contributions. Keep Church and State forever separate."[31] Insofar as Grant was calling for more common schools, the proposal could not be gainsaid. The coded language of education "unmixed with sectarian . . . dogmas" suggested clearly, however, that the president had in mind precluding support for Catholic education. The oddest thing about the proposal was that it resolved that neither state nor federal government ("nor both combined"—a nice rhetorical flourish) should support sectarian education. But no one was proposing that the federal government support education of any kind, whether sectarian or otherwise. By mentioning federal support, Grant was simply trying to manufacture some justification for proposing an amendment to the federal Constitution.

James G. Blaine, maneuvering for the Republican presidential nomination, immediately took up Grant's proposal. In November 1875 he released a letter dated October 20, addressed to "a prominent Ohio gentleman," in which he expressly proposed a national constitutional amendment on the school question. In order to make the case for a national amendment, Blaine began the letter by expressing his concern over the school controversy in Ohio, which he purported to fear might be repeated elsewhere. Blaine then argued that debate over the school question "inevitably arouses sectarian feelings, and leads to the bitterest and most deplorable of all strifes, the strife between religious denominations." The only "final" settlement of the question could be a federal constitutional amendment, which would represent "complete victory for nonsectarian schools." Blaine then went on to propose the draft text of a constitutional amendment that would extend the protection of the Establishment Clause and the Free Exercise Clause to the states, and would prohibit any money raised in any state for the support of public schools from being placed "under the control of any religious sect" or "divided between religious sects or denominations."[32]

Even for a politician who was later to be dubbed the "continental liar from the State of Maine," the letter displayed impressive hypocrisy. The potential "strife" Blaine claimed he wanted to avoid was exactly the controversy he hoped to produce nationally. The purpose of proposing a national constitutional amendment was not

to put an end to sectarian tensions but to create a wedge issue between religious denominations that would redound to the Republicans' benefit. Extending the constitutional protections of the
religion clauses to the states sounded reasonable enough, but it was
intended simply as cover for the main event, which was a federal
prohibition on any government support for Catholic education at
any level, state or federal.

Politics being what it was—and is—Grant, who was still running
for president, took it upon himself to bring the issue before Congress before Blaine could do so formally. On December 7, 1875,
Grant delivered a centennial message to Congress in which he proposed a constitutional amendment along the lines he had spoken of
to the veterans three months before. Grant seems to have realized
that such an amendment should have some affirmative message in
addition to merely the prohibition on state support for religious
schools. He therefore proposed requiring each state (still without
national funding) to establish free public schools for all children,
"irrespective of sex, color, birthplace, or religion." For this proposal
Grant offered the same republican rationale that had been offered
for the first common schools nearly half a century before. In a republic, he said, "it is of the greatest importance that all should be
possessed of education and intelligence enough to cast a vote with a
right understanding of its meaning." Education was to serve the
purposes of sustaining republican government against the threat of
uneducated popular politics. In a "republic whereof one man is as
good as another before the law," Grant said, "the education of the
masses becomes of the first necessity for the preservation of our institutions."[33]

In 1875, the "masses" in question were probably Catholic. Grant
made that clear by specifying immediately that the same amendment should forbid the teaching of "religious, atheistic, or pagan
tenets." States must not provide school funds to "any religious sect
or denomination."[34] The overall effect of Grant's proposal was to
identify common school education as a national priority and

to couple that symbolic move with a generalized opposition to Catholic education.

Grant left unspecified the implication of his proposal, namely that Catholicism still had the capacity to undermine American republicanism. An article in the *Universalist Quarterly*, though, explicitly connected Catholic opposition to use of the Bible in the common schools with the Catholic goal of subverting American republicanism: "And the reason [for the opposition] is: *that the Bible represents unsectarian Christian religion.* It brings all men to God without the intervention of the priests; it is the great charter of spiritual freedom the world over. The priest drives at the Bible in the school, knowing that if he can cast odium on that great symbol of American, republican society he may confuse and divide our people and more easily accomplish his purpose to make this a Roman Catholic country, bound in spiritual obedience to his holiness, the Pope of Rome."[35] The article's paranoia toward the Catholic church, and its corresponding elevation of the Bible to the foundational text of American republicanism, represented a strand of American thought that was as strong after the Civil War as it had been before it. Only the sophistication of the argument had increased, as Protestant Americans now sought to explain why the Bible must be maintained in the schools even as they simultaneously denounced Catholic "sectarianism." The core of the argument turned on the connection among Bible reading, morality, and successful participation in republican government. The United States Senate was soon to become the venue for a comprehensive public discussion of this chain of logic.

THE BLAINE AMENDMENT IN THE SENATE

The proposed amendment came to the Senate only after some delay in the House of Representatives, where the Democrats wanted to do all they could to make the problematic school question disappear. Blaine introduced his proposed amendment to the House on December 14, 1875, and the Democrats quickly buried it in committee. Nothing happened through the course of the spring as both parties turned to the nomination of presidential candidates for the upcoming election. In June, both parties held their conventions. Blaine failed to gain the nomination when neither he nor his opponent, New York senator Roscoe Conkling, could garner enough delegates. The divided convention then turned to Ohio governor Rutherford B. Hayes, whose letter to Blaine almost exactly a year before had set the amendment ball rolling. When the Democrats nominated Governor Samuel Tilden of New York—a state in which, like Ohio, the school question had been most pressing for the previous five years—a return to the subject of what had come to be called the Blaine amendment became inevitable.

House Democrats had another trick up their sleeves to try to neutralize the school question. In August, they altered Blaine's proposal to render it toothless. Their new version prohibited support of sectarian schools from money raised specifically for schools, while leaving open the possibility that states could still support Catholic schools from general treasury funds. Having created a purely symbolic draft text that would have no practical effect at all, the House Democrats voted almost unanimously for it. The clever strategy immunized the Democrats against the claim that they were failing to act on the school question, while simultaneously enabling them to tell Catholic constituents that their interests had not been harmed. The House then passed the buck to the Senate.

The Senate of 1876 was no longer the great forum for profound discussion of national questions that it had been in the antebellum days of Webster, Clay, and Calhoun. But it was still capable of putting on a good show in set-piece debates featuring rhetorical flights almost unimaginable today. The Republicans decided to make a stand for the Blaine amendment. They reintroduced language that would give the amendment actual effect and set about making the case that America was in need of a federal amendment prohibiting state support of sectarian schools.

The Republicans framed their argument by calling for an extension to the states of the principles of religious liberty already found in the federal Constitution. The idea that federal constitutional protections should be made to apply to the states as well had a certain logical resonance. The Fourteenth Amendment, enacted in 1868 by the Reconstruction Congress and ratified by the states (some at the point of a gun), had done just that by extending due process protections to cover actions taken by state governments.

The basic principles of religious liberty were by now so well settled in American thought that it would have been impossible to argue against them. Religious liberty meant, according to the senators, that government could not coerce individual conscience, and that citizens could not be made to pay taxes to support religious institutions with which they disagreed. There was, according to Senator Frederick T. Frelinghuysen, Republican of New Jersey, "no room for two opinions on the two propositions that religion and conscience should be free, and that the people should not be taxed for sectarian purposes. The whole history of our country, from its origin to the present day, establishes and fortifies these positions."[36] Frelinghuysen was right. The framers' generation had indeed identified these two propositions as the content of religious liberty, and it had constitutionalized them with the Free Exercise Clause and the Establishment Clause, respectively. If the amendment simply extended these protections to the states, it would be difficult for Democrats to explain what was wrong with it. How could they maintain that Protestants should be taxed and the funds expended for the education of Catholics?

The trouble with this apparently foolproof religious-liberty justification for the amendment was that it might lead to the conclusion that the states would not be permitted to support any religious teaching at all, including use of the Bible in the schools. After all,

Catholics had been using the religious-liberty argument to claim that the common schools should not require the reading of the Protestant Bible. They had further pointed out that requiring them to support what was in essence a Protestant practice of Bible reading violated their own liberty of conscience. Senate Republicans were on the horns of a dilemma. If religious liberty must be strictly enforced in the states, then how could state schools, with their now religiously diverse student population, continue to require what was in effect religion? Yet religion must be taught, or the schools would be unable to teach morality and would therefore fail to train useful republican citizens.

Only one answer was available to Republicans, and that was the justification for common schools first developed by their earliest advocates: the ideal of nonsectarianism. Relying on rhetorical bombast where careful logic might have faltered, Senator Frelinghuysen argued that the proposed amendment protected religious liberty but did not prohibit the teaching of nonsectarian religion in state schools:

> That pure and undefiled religion which appertains to the relationship and responsibility of man to God, and is readily distinguishable from the creeds of sects; that religion which permeates all our laws, which is recognized in every sentence against crime and immorality, which is invoked in every oath, which is reverentially deferred to every morning at that desk [here the senator must have pointed to the desk from which the Senate chaplain gave the daily prayer] and on like occasions at the capitol of every State of the Union . . . that religion which is our history, which is our unwritten as well as our written law, and which sustains the pillars of our liberty, is a very, very different thing from the particular creeds or tenets of either religionists or infidels. And this article [i.e., amendment] places no unhallowed touch upon that religion.[37]

Frelinghuysen's argument faced the serious challenge of distinguishing the "pure and undefiled religion" compatible with religious liberty from the sincere beliefs held by adherents of particular religious denominations—a problem faced by all theories of nonsectarian religion. Yet the argument also had great force, because it relied on the basic truth that nonsectarian religion permeated American public life. Criminal laws and laws prohibiting adultery did rest on the bedrock of religious Christian values. Citizens did invoke God's help when they took their oaths as witnesses or public servants. Public prayers opened legislative sessions everywhere in America, as they still do. All these practices were broadly understood by Americans of the nineteenth century as fully compatible with the preservation of religious liberty.

It followed that reading the Bible in the schools was not a sectarian act, to be regulated by the proposed amendment, but an act of the "pure religion" that the amendment apparently did not "touch." The Bible, Frelinghuysen asserted, was "a religious and not a sectarian book." There were, of course, different translations of the Bible, each associated with different denominations. "True, and yet there is but one Bible; that is the revelation from on high." (How to read that one Bible in the schools without relying on one of the sectarian translations was left unexplained.) In any event, the Bible was absolutely necessary in the public schools, because without it, there would be no way to teach morality: "Mr. President, where [else] shall we go for public morals? . . . To the Koran? To Confucius? To the Mormon book of their lord? To the vain philosophy of the ancients? To mythological fables? No sir; the people of this country want that book let alone. The Constitution must not touch it."[38]

The ideology of nonsectarianism here reached its most perfect form. Common morality, derived from the "pure" Bible, undergirded the fabric of American republican life. Without a shared morality, collective political life would be impossible. Public institutions and American customs acknowledged the importance of this common public morality, rooted in biblical values and shared by all denominations. Most important, nonsectarian morality and the Bible that went with it were embraced by popular opinion. The "people of this country" would not stand for government tampering with their use of the Bible any more than they would allow the removal of true nonsectarian religion from schools or other public institutions. Thus presented, nonsectarianism amounted to a theory about the relationship between government and religion. Government must not promote particular, sectarian religious values, but government rested upon and should acknowledge that nonsectarian faith on which the nation's morals rested.

Faced with this powerful argument, which they could not directly contradict, Senate Democrats searched for objections that would enable them to oppose the amendment without seeming to reject a common national morality. Some seized on the fact of local control of education to try to defuse the school issue without addressing its merits. Essentially they argued that control of schools, and indeed of religion, was reserved in the Constitution to the states, and that there was no reason for a federal constitutional amendment on the topic.[39] The emphasis on local control both followed and prefigured similar states' rights arguments made to justify local racial segregation laws, but this was no vice for Democrats in 1875.

Other Democratic senators raised a range of practical problems. The amendment, they warned with more confidence than was warranted, would end state support of hospitals, many of which were religious, and it would keep chaplains out of orphanages, veterans' homes, and prisons—results that were presumed to be undesirable because they would undercut public morality. The Senate Democrats, however, apparently understood that these arguments did not adequately counteract the Republicans' position, derived from nonsectarianism. As the debate progressed, the Democrats found themselves turning to the heart of the matter and insisting that the amendment amounted to Catholic bashing.

Although largely Protestants themselves, the Senate Democrats had Catholic constituencies, and they were prepared to defend Catholics from the implicit charge that they were unsuited to republican self-government. Senator William Whyte of Maryland, after first identifying himself as the scion of the "straightest sect of Irish Presbyterians," went on to accuse the amendment of anti-Catholic bias. "To use plain words," Whyte alleged, the amendment was "nearly an accusation against a large body of fellow-citizens as loyal to republican liberty as we proclaim ourselves to be."[40] Senator Lewis Bogy of Missouri argued that, having exhausted the race card with the end of Reconstruction, the Republicans were now playing the Catholic card to gain advantage in the 1876 election.[41] This argument, which did not directly address the merits or demerits of the amendment, changed the topic of the debate in a way that Democrats may have gambled would be to their advantage. Instead of contesting the value of nonsectarianism, the Democrats would assert the patriotism and republicanism of Catholics and put the Republicans in the position of making their attacks on Catholics explicit.

Whether the Democrats expected that they would or not, Republicans rose to the bait. Republican senator George Edmunds of Vermont flatly contradicted Whyte, invoking the papal encyclical of 1864, later read into the record, which had condemned the idea of liberty of conscience as "insanity." Whyte responded that the encyclical was twelve years old, and, in a further reference to the race question, he said he was "happy to add" that "a good many things which people did in 1864 they do not do to-day." Furthermore, Whyte insisted, Archbishop John Baptist Purcell's recent letter on the same subject had in essence modified the teaching of the encyclical. But Whyte was on very shaky ground. The Vatican had not modified its teachings on the liberty of conscience, and the church in Europe still strongly opposed separation of church and state. American Catholics found themselves in the awkward position of trying to justify to hostile Protestants aspects of church dogma that they themselves did not much like and were prepared to ignore in practice. When Senator Bogy, an able critic of the amendment, was confronted with the encyclical, he was forced into the rather lame apology that it was "very hard to explain, very hard to vindicate these things, which when well understood have received the approbation of the enlightened Catholics of the world as not being subversive of the rights of conscience."[42] It was indeed very hard for Americans, Catholic or Protestant, who believed in the liberty of conscience, to vindicate the church's condemnation of that right.

The Republicans would not let the point drop. Liberty of conscience, said Edmunds, "is universal in every church but one." The public schools were necessary to inculcate "true principles of liberty and individual conscience and freedom of opinion, upon which alone a republican government can rest."[43] If Catholics came to control a political majority, they would institute Catholic education, which would be necessarily incompatible with liberty of conscience, and hence with republicanism. The future of the republic was in jeopardy. Because the Catholic leadership had encouraged its flock to send their children to Catholic schools, Catholics could also be depicted as fundamentally rejecting the option of public education. According to Senator Oliver Perry Morton of Indiana, "there is a large body of people in this country, sincere, earnest, and pious, I have no doubt, who believe that our public schools in which religion is not taught are infidel and wicked, and who are not in favor of any school that does not teach religion."[44] Using Catholic education and official Catholic teaching on the liberty of conscience as leverage, the Republicans were in essence charging that Catholicism and democracy were incompatible.

The Democrats did the best they could to fend off the anti-Catholic rhetoric that permeated the Republican side of the debate. Senator Eli Saulsbury of Delaware called for Christian unity in the face of the Republican attempt "to array the Christian brotherhood in deadliest hate against one another" and invoked the history of "religious persecutions and appeals to religious prejudices," which had "stained the earth with blood and wrung from the hearts of millions the deepest agonies."[45] But even Saulsbury's plaintive call for Christian brotherhood underscored the degree to which invocations of religious values formed the lifeblood of American thinking about church and state in 1876. When Senator Francis Kernan of New York (one of the only Catholics on the floor at the time) pointed out that the consciences of Jews would be violated even by nonsectarian Christianity, and that the only truly nonsectarian schools would be those that avoided moral teaching altogether,[46] no one bothered to disagree. It was obvious to the senators that such schools would fail to satisfy the objectives of educating children in republican values.

The remarkable Senate debate over the Blaine amendment illustrated the paradox at the heart of nonsectarianism. By 1876, any reasonable person would have had to acknowledge that many Americans believed that the common religion was not nonsectarian. The senators were told that Catholics opposed the public schools "for the reason that they were sectarian. Even the very Bible which was used in the schools was a sectarian book."[47] They were even reminded, by the Catholic senator from New York, that not every American was a Christian. Yet these basic facts did not deter Protestants from insisting that the common schools were indeed nonsectarian, no matter what anybody else said. There was an inexorable logic to the insistence on keeping nonsectarian religion in schools: "we cannot de-humanize; therefore we cannot demoralize; therefore we cannot de-religionize; therefore we cannot dechristianize them," editorialized the *Princeton Review*. "Not to give us any religion, or morality radicated [i.e., rooted] in religious sanctions, is to give us immorality and irreligion. Here neutrality is impossible."[48] Catholic objections that nonsectarianism did not include them were met with little more than the naked insistence that it did. Nonsectarianism, in other words, was an ideology of inclusiveness that was fully prepared to exclude.

THE TRIUMPH OF NONSECTARIANISM:
THE SCHOOL "SOLUTION"

Protestant Republican intransigence on the nonsectarianism question turned out to have enormous practical consequences. Not, as it
turned out, at the federal level—the Blaine amendment, intended
from the start more to stir up anti-Catholicism than to become law,
fell just short of the two-thirds vote necessary to get it out of the
Senate and pass it on to the states. But as a direct result of the public attention paid to the question of government funding of religious schools, states that might otherwise never have bothered to
address the topic did so. In 1876, according to one scholar, fourteen states had laws or constitutional amendments on their books
restricting government funding of religious schools. By 1890, fourteen years later, twenty-nine states had adopted some sort of state
constitutional amendment or statute barring such funding.[49]

In some states, such as Minnesota, the issue played itself out
through a partisan debate followed by a referendum that Catholics
were sure to lose. In others, the impetus came from Congress,
which made it a condition of statehood for North and South
Dakota, Washington, and Montana that they adopt amendments
prohibiting state support of religious education.[50] Where Catholics
were plentiful, such constitutional requirements were understood as
concessions to national politics. A proposed New Mexico constitution contained such a prohibition, apparently included by drafters
hoping to secure the admission of New Mexico to the Union, but
New Mexicans rejected that constitution by a two-to-one ratio, at
least in part because of the unpopularity of the provision.[51]

In the aftermath of the Blaine amendment, then, the nonsectarian ideal, widespread among Protestants but to that point contested
by Catholics, became the law almost everywhere in the United
States. The legal treatises recognized the fact. The 1868 edition of
Thomas Cooley's influential, laissez-faire-oriented *Constitutional*

Limitations stated that the federal and all state constitutions prohibited "compulsory support, by taxation or otherwise, of religious instruction," adding that "all support of religious instruction must be entirely voluntary."[52] Later editions added that some, though not all, state constitutions went further, prohibiting government from contracting with religious entities to provide services.[53] Another influential treatise noted that "it has been held that the school authorities may compel the pupils to read the Bible in the schools, even against the objection and protest of the parents." The author, the rights-oriented Christopher Tiedeman, expressly derided this judicial holding as "erroneous," because it created unequal privileges for those who did not object to Bible reading, but he correctly described it as the norm.[54]

To put it plainly, Catholics in the nineteenth century lost the fight. They failed to replace nonsectarianism with a different, more pluralist conception of the relationship between government and religion, in which Catholic religious schools would have received governmental support alongside the schools they characterized as sectarian Protestant. But Protestants, who understood the public schools as machines for teaching common republican values, were unprepared to fund schools in which they imagined that some form of religious separatism would be taught. Catholics were alternatively willing to accept public schools devoid of religious content, and to provide religious education for their children in after-school or Sunday-school environments, so long as their children would not be subjected to obligatory Protestant Bible reading and prayer. Yet Protestants rejected this option as well, on the theory that schools without religion would be schools without morality.

The basic ritual practices in these schools, to which Catholics had objected, were to remain essentially unchanged until after World War II, constituting an important part of the "public Protestantism" of the period.[55] In most of the country, brief passages of the Bible continued to be read daily (and the Lord's Prayer in its Protestant version recited) even after both were joined by the

Pledge of Allegiance, composed in 1892, without reference to God. Yet in the years after it became clear that state-funded Catholic education was not to become a reality in America, Catholic attitudes toward the nature of the public schools underwent an important shift. Without giving up the aspiration of universal Catholic education, Catholics gradually ceased to see the public schools as oppressively sectarian and began to see them as acceptable environments for an education that must still be supplemented by out-of-school religious instruction. Slowly, subtly, and with difficulty, Catholics came to see nonsectarianism as an American ideology that included them.

The background for the ideological shift was economic necessity. In the absence of government funding, many Catholics still chose to educate their children in Catholic schools, both out of a desire to teach their children Catholic beliefs and to protect them from the encroaching Protestantism of the public schools. But tuition could be expensive even when it was subsidized by the church, and in some places Catholics were not concentrated enough to maintain their own schools. As a consequence, millions of Catholic children attended the nonsectarian public schools in the years between the passage of the Blaine-inspired state constitutional amendments and the eventual disruption of nonsectarian religious practices in the 1950s and '60s. In 1880, just over 400,000 Catholic children attended America's 2,246 Catholic schools.[56] By 1892, the great liberal archbishop John Ireland of St. Paul, Minnesota, estimated that of 2.2 million Catholic children in America, 1.5 million—68 percent—attended public schools.[57] In fact, at no time in American history did a majority of Catholic children attend Catholic schools.

The change in attitude toward the public schools did not come about without significant dissension and trauma within the church. In the late nineteenth century, the Catholic church in the United States was riven by an internal debate that, while in some ways an outgrowth of contemporary disagreement within the European church, also had a distinctively American character.[58] On one side were conservative Catholics, many in the church hierarchy, who believed that the church must stand as a bulwark against encroaching modern ideologies, especially socialism but also liberalism. The conservatives had championed and now embraced the new doctrine of papal infallibility, declared by the First Vatican Council in 1870, which they saw as strengthening the church by enhancing the central authority of Rome.[59] Strongly committed to keeping the faith and the faithful pure, the conservatives bitterly rejected public schooling as an acceptable option for Catholic children. The refusal of government funding, they argued with some justification, was evidence of a self-conscious Protestant plan to undercut Catholic belief. With the deceitful Protestant rhetoric of nonsectarianism there must be no compromise. Some even advocated denying the sacraments to parents who sent their children to the public schools.[60]

On the other side of the divide was a newly emerging class: American liberal Catholics. Drawn from within the church hierarchy, but also from educated laypeople, the liberals sought a deeper engagement with American society, both to serve the interests of American Catholics and to contribute their distinctive vision of the faith to all Americans. The liberals were second to none in their advocacy of helping Catholics in need—indeed, the aim of the Paulist order, founded in 1858 by Father Isaac Hecker, a New York–born convert to Catholicism, was to demonstrate to Protestant America the superiority of Catholicism precisely through an inspiring social mission to poor Catholics.[61] But liberal Catholics also believed, like Protestant educators, that "universal suffrage demands universal education"[62]—and they were prepared to make compromises with the public education system if doing so would keep young Catholics in school.

The best known of these compromises was the so-called Poughkeepsie Plan, created in 1873 by agreement of a local priest and the Hudson Valley town's school board, and imitated elsewhere.[63] Existing Catholic schools were leased for a dollar by the town, which then rehired the nuns who had taught there, this time as public school teachers. Religious instruction took place before and after school and during lunch hour, instead of throughout the day. To the liberals, the arrangement looked like a plausible solution to the public funding problem, but conservatives saw this compromise with the Protestant-dominated public school system as dangerous. Conservatives suspected that in the long run the Protestant majority would reject such arrangements. Meanwhile, Catholics would have become accustomed to free education, and when the compromise arrangements became unavailable, as they must, lay Catholics would settle for ordinary public schools for their children. The conservatives urged the laity to continue protesting the injustice of denying them full public support for their schools, and simultaneously tried to build an ethic of sacrifice that would encourage Catholics to send their children to parochial schools whatever the cost.

The conservatives' predictions were at least in part accurate: the Poughkeepsie Plan did not outlast the enactment of a state Blaine amendment in New York in 1894, nor did clones survive in other states. Whether it was because they were acclimated to free education or just could not afford to pay tuition alongside their property taxes, many Catholics accepted the reality of public education for their children. Eventually, after the internal Catholic debate in America became especially heated, Rome intervened on the side of the liberals, barring priests from withholding the sacraments and acknowledging the permissibility of public education for Catholic children alongside attendance at afternoon and Sunday schools.[64] Later, starting in the 1920s and '30s, there would be creative new efforts to introduce religious instruction to students who were released from the public schools during certain specified hours. In the short term, however, through a combination of externally imposed economic incentive and outward-looking American thinking, the liberal Catholics won the day.

Perhaps unsurprisingly, the phenomenon of Catholics sending

their children in large numbers to the public schools seems to have been accompanied by a gradual change in attitudes among lay Catholics toward the nonsectarian religion of the schools. What had once been staunch objection came to be implicit acceptance. If the schools claimed to embody a shared vision of what it meant to be Christian and American, Catholics could recognize themselves within that description. Reciprocally, the schools themselves, without much changing the practices that had long been condemned by Catholics as sectarian Protestant, came also to be accepting of Catholic identity as an integral part of American nonsectarian Christianity. The presence of Catholic children in the nonsectarian schools therefore played a major role in the process of incorporating and assimilating Catholics into the ideology of Americanism.

A two-way process was at work here, at once coercive and voluntary. By condemning the funding of the Catholic schools as a merger of church and state, nonsectarian ideology forced Catholics to choose between entering the "nonsectarian" environment of the public schools or paying for schools of their own. Faced with these two unattractive options, most Catholics chose the educational mainstream, but in so choosing, Catholics could rely on the reasoning of the new liberal Catholicism to make the choice their own. Liberal Catholics believed the public schools were not second best, but in fact offered great benefits—including the civic education necessary for active citizenship. As Catholics entered the public schools, however, those schools were faced with the challenge of expanding Christian nonsectarianism to include Catholic difference, and this they gradually began to do.

It would be too simple, therefore, to depict the triumph of nonsectarianism as the simple application of state force to Catholics. Catholics could resist, as many did, by resorting to Catholic education despite the financial burdens associated with it. Particularly after Catholic immigration slowed in the 1920s, the church began devoting more resources to building parochial schools; in the period from 1940 to 1965, the percentage of American children who attended Catholic schools doubled, to a high of 12 percent.[65] (The figure today is closer to 5 percent.[66]) But Catholics also could and did develop their own internal justifications for the choices they were called upon to make, and Catholics could influence the American ideological environment in which they were participants. Even if it did not disappear, anti-Catholicism in America declined markedly during these years of Catholic assimilation.[67] The reasons for that decline had much to do with the expansion of the ideal of Christian nonsectarianism to include Catholicism—from the start the aim of Protestants who had always sought this outcome, dictated on their own terms.

CHARITIES AND CHURCHES IN THE PRE–WELFARE STATE

Compared to the firm legal line drawn around government funding of Catholic education, the nonsectarian ideal turned out to be relatively pliant when it came to sectarian charities. In the years before the Civil War, the poorhouses that had in American cities served as a kind of last resort for marginal figures from orphans to alcoholics to the mentally ill were beginning to be supplemented by orphanages and schools for juvenile delinquents, founded by voluntary charitable associations and by direct grants from states and municipalities. Like the earliest common schools, founded around the same time, these new institutions sought to transcend denominational difference and so taught their charges a kind of nonsectarian Christianity that the well-meaning Protestant elites who founded them believed necessary to inculcate basic morality.

Responding to the threat of Catholic children being subjected to coercive Protestant instruction, the larger Catholic dioceses founded parallel institutions of their own. By the 1820s, New York State already had three Catholic orphanages, in Manhattan, Brooklyn, and Albany; and in 1863, New York Catholics organized the Society for the Protection of Destitute Roman Catholic Children, which ran a home for vagrant or delinquent Catholic youth.[68] These Catholic institutions received direct state support no differently than their nonsectarian Protestant equivalents, without generating the sort of controversy associated with the schools. Indeed, during the Senate debate over the Blaine amendment, one of the pragmatic arguments made against a national ban on sectarian instruction, by Senator Francis Kernan of New York, was that it would prohibit religious instruction in orphanages and soldiers' homes, as well as in juvenile reformatories, where it was needed most.[69]

The urbanization and industrialization of the post–Civil War years, and the growing poverty that accompanied them, called for a more thoroughgoing response from Protestants and Catholics alike—and that response turned out to have important consequences for government funding of charitable religious institutions and the way those institutions came to understand their mission. Put simply, the ameliorative charities of the prewar years increasingly came to seem insufficient to deal with the scope and horror of urban poverty. For Protestants, this was a challenge to the "social program" of American organized religion, which had long emphasized self-reliance.[70] The same could be said, to a lesser degree, for American Catholics, who had imbibed the American ethos of inexorable economic progress: one Catholic lay leader assured his audience in 1865 that "our poor, for the greater part, are only so temporarily. Where there is health, temperance and industry, there cannot be poverty in this country."[71] In the decades that followed, the persistence of urban poverty made this optimistic view more difficult to sustain.

It took time to develop sophisticated theological responses to this growing crisis. The term "social gospel" did not come into use until sometime after 1900, and Walter Rauschenbusch's famous essay of that name was not composed until 1908. Well before then, however, Catholics dealt with the realities of urban poverty—which affected them disproportionately—by setting out to build a network

of social services. By 1885, Sadlier's *Catholic Directory* showed nationwide "37 homes for the aged, 154 hospitals, 272 orphan asy-
lums, and 46 industrial schools and related agencies for needy
youth,"[72] all under Catholic auspices. Thousands of small Catholic
benevolent associations provided direct charity to the needy, and
larger unions and associations even began to provide life insur-
ance.[73] Thus American Catholics of the nineteenth century were,
like some of their Protestant brethren, developing the infrastructure
of faith-based support organizations that many people today experience as the core of the religious mission of feeding the hungry and
clothing the naked.

The Catholic charitable institutions operated in parallel to private hospitals, old-age homes, and orphanages that were not associated with any particular religious denomination and that bore,
statistically speaking, the brunt of the burden of providing social
services for Americans in need. Where possible, Catholics also
sought access for their clergy to minister to patients or residents in
these nonsectarian institutions.[74] The key fact about the full range
of charitable institutions in this period, though, is that almost none
were state-run, but nearly all, whether nonsectarian or Catholic, received significant government assistance. Before the rise of the welfare state, government dealt with the problems of poverty largely by
relying on private institutions and supplementing their financial
needs when it became obvious that it was in the public interest to
do so. "Voluntary hospitals were always seen as clothed with the
public interest even when their legal character was entirely private
and their governing boards private and self-perpetuating . . . the
great majority of hospitals in the 1870s and 80s pieced together annual budgets with an eclectic mixture of contributions from local
government, endowment income, the proceeds of community
fundraising, and the fees of occasional private patients."[75]

Where machine politics operated, as they did in Boss Tweed's
New York, government support of charitable organizations also
functioned as a way to pay off political allies. Tammany Hall di-

rected $1.25 million of city funds to institutions associated with the Catholic church in 1869–71, and another $300,000 to charitable institutions that were Protestant, Jewish, or unaffiliated.[76] Less bashful than today's political operatives, Tweed asserted his credo of open-ended, equal-opportunity redistribution on the Senate floor in Albany. As *The New York Times* reported it, Boss Tweed endorsed "supporting all deserving charities, without asking what denominations control them." He proposed to cast aside opposition by acquiescing in whatever logrolling the Republicans wanted: "We, on this side, are in favor of aiding all the charities. So now, gentlemen on the other side, offer your amendments, inserting deserving charities, and we will accept them."[77]

The fact that government funding of charitable institutions was interconnected with the combination of wealth redistribution and corruption that machine politics entailed helps justify the Republican political voices that were frequently heard calling for reduction or elimination of the subsidies. Then, as now, the consequence of such direct state aid to religious charities was likely to be open political debate about which religious institutions deserved funding and which did not. Yet there was also an important element of anti-Catholicism in this reform message, especially in places like New York, where state subsidies to urban Catholic charities far outpaced any others. So it should not be surprising that, at the same time the schools question was eliciting strong arguments against the funding of sectarian religious schools by the states, some Republicans extended the arguments to noneducational Catholic institutions. At New York's state constitutional convention in 1894, the anti-Catholic National League for the Protection of American Institutions put forward a constitutional amendment that would have banned any kind of government support to any sectarian institutions, whether educational or otherwise.[78]

In New York, the call for the prohibition of state aid to any sectarian institutions was received differently from the narrower formulation that would ban state assistance only to Catholic schools:

unlike its school-focused counterpart, it failed to pass. This result came about at least in part as a result of a compromise. Prominent Catholics, apparently authorized to speak on behalf of the archdiocese, expressed a willingness to abandon their claims to support of Catholic schools if funding for charities would remain untouched.[79] (One of the most effective Catholic spokesmen was the New York Catholic lawyer Frederick René Coudert, a founder of the Coudert Brothers firm.)

Evidence from other states, though, is more complicated. It shows that the states had come to rely on Catholic institutions to deliver much-needed services, but it also reveals that the theory and practice of nonsectarianism affected the way Catholic social services came to be delivered. Many of the state Blaine amendments adopted all over the country included broad language that banned state aid to any sectarian institution of any kind. In a few places, like Nevada[80] and South Dakota,[81] courts in the 1890s struck down state legislatures' appropriations to Catholic orphanages as violations of state Blaine amendments. In the Nevada case, which was frequently cited by other courts, there was just a single Catholic orphanage in the state, and so it may have been relatively easy for the state to stop supporting it; the same may also have been true in South Dakota.

Where Catholic institutions were more prevalent, though, other solutions were found. The Illinois Supreme Court in 1892 held that the Cook County Industrial School for Girls was a front for two Catholic girls' orphanages and therefore could not receive state funds.[82] But in the wake of the court's decision, the Industrial School bought its own buildings—previously it had farmed its charges out to the Catholic girls' homes—hired nuns to run its facilities, and went about its business. It was now nominally a nonsectarian institution, even if it was Catholic in practice, and when the Illinois Supreme Court considered the issue a second time some years later, it approved the new arrangements, holding that because the school was being paid less money than the total cost of educating and supporting the girls, there was no state "aid" to religion.[83] The legal reasoning may have been tenuous, but the policy logic was strong. The church was saving the state money and fulfilling a necessary function, and that was enough to justify allowing continued state funding. The Supreme Court of the United States, ruling on the permissibility of funding a Catholic hospital in Washington, D.C., with federal dollars, held that the hospital corporation was technically secular even though it was organized and run by nuns.[84]

Across the country, then, state support for Catholic education was roundly rejected, but one way or another, state support of Catholic charities such as hospitals and orphanages was often maintained. Continued government support of Catholic social service organizations nationwide reflected a widespread recognition that their activities were serving the public interest by providing a service that the government was unable or unwilling to do without. The situation of the Catholic hospitals and orphanages, in other words, differed from that of Catholic schools. Because government had already undertaken to support public education on a broad scale, and because those schools were fully prepared to accommodate Catholic students, Catholic schools did not seem, from the Protestant perspective, to be filling an unmet need. It is therefore possible to explain state governments' willingness to support Catholic charitable institutions in functional terms: with the modern welfare state more than half a century in the future, state governments simply had no choice. In the 1920s, the Pennsylvania Supreme Court struck down municipal funding for Philadelphia's various religious hospitals as illegitimate aid to sectarian bodies. But by then, the public hospitals of Philadelphia had added capacity, and the religious hospitals were arguably no longer as necessary to public health.

Beyond necessity, however, there was another all-important difference between Catholic schools and Catholic charities. Unlike charities, which Americans saw as unfortunately necessary to deal with temporary poverty, schools were, by design, devoted to teaching young people the republican values that Protestant Americans believed necessary for citizenship. For the state to fund separate Catholic schools was to encourage the development of morals that were imagined to be separatist and of citizens who might not be united in the goal of continuing the common American enterprise. Although nonsectarianism had begun as a compromise among Christian denominations, teaching as much morality as was necessary for good citizenship, it had developed into a crucial facet of American ideology. Catholic schools were threatening in a way that Catholic charities were not, because they called into question the centrality of nonsectarianism to the meaning of being American. A major reason the Catholic charities could be supported was that their main function, in the eyes of Protestants, was not the teaching of Catholic values or the enrichment of Catholic souls so much as the sustenance of Catholic bodies.

Over time, Catholic social service institutions developed a dialogue with this external understanding of them. From a relatively early period, Catholic hospitals opened their doors to all, regardless of religion.[85] Nuns did much of the nursing, and priests were on staff, but the hospitals operated much as did nonsectarian institutions in the same areas. This, too, was an indirect effect of nonsectarian ideology. Catholic orphanages were another matter: their school-aged charges got the same sort of Catholic education as pupils in Catholic schools, a practice tolerated probably because of the difficulty of separating the cost of education from the costs of housing and maintenance. But apart from institutions that had to educate as an inseparable part of their central mission, Catholic charities in this period began to develop a view of their activities that distinguished the religious component from service delivery. This attitude was an indirect result of the nonsectarian ideology that justified government support of Catholic charity but not of Catholic education.

In a later period, the division between the religious and nonreligious activities of charitable organizations would come to be formalized in the law, with a prohibition on state support of the former. In the nineteenth century, however, the distinction was not explicit and legal but implicit and cultural. The theoretical explanation for why the government could support religious institutions but not religious schools had not yet been fully worked out. Everyone agreed that the union of church and state must be condemned. But if the churches performed activities that the state needed, then government funding was understood not to represent such a merger—nonsectarianism could give way to practical reality.

NONSECTARIANISM AND SEX: THE MORMONS AND THE MARRIAGE PARADIGM

The triumph of nonsectarian Christianity as a national ideology went beyond the schools. It extended even to the family structure itself, the flashpoint of conflict for the most controversial religious group in nineteenth-century America: the Church of Jesus Christ of Latter-day Saints, known colloquially as the Mormons. Founded in 1830 by Joseph Smith, the Mormons came under intensive criticism almost from the beginning, especially for the practice of plural marriage—a practice that emerged quietly in the Mormons' first decade and was formalized in a revelation dated 1843, the year before Smith was murdered by a mob at Nauvoo, Illinois.

Bigamy, a crime under the English common law, violated the laws of all the states, and Mormons would not have had the political or legal clout to convince any state legislature to allow plural marriage. But spurred by the antagonism that Mormon communities had encountered in Ohio, Missouri, and Illinois, Smith's successor, Brigham Young, led the Mormon vanguard westward to the Great Salt Lake Basin, beyond the reach of the state laws that banned polygamy. Young hoped to create the state of Deseret, in which Mormon principles of "theo-democracy" would have held sway. Congress chose not to admit Deseret as a state, instead keeping federal legal control over the Territory of Utah, organized in 1850. Territories had their own legislatures, though, and the Utah legislature, dominated by Mormon representatives, conferred on the Mormon church the power to regulate its members' marriages.[86] Plural marriage, practiced especially by well-off senior members of the church, became not only official church doctrine but legally permissible within the Territory of Utah as well.

So the matter might have stood were it not for the steady stream of antipolygamy writing and political argument that began in the middle of the 1850s and peaked twenty years later with a national series of dramatic public lectures delivered by Ann Eliza Young, who had divorced Brigham Young, left the Mormon church, and re-created herself as an antipolygamy advocate. Republicans had always seen themselves as natural enemies of polygamy, which they associated with slavery. As early as 1856, the Republican platform dubbed these evils "the twin relics of barbarism." In 1860, congressional Republicans passed a federal law banning its practice in the Utah Territory. But the law—difficult to implement over Mormon resistance under the best of circumstances—had gone essentially unenforced in the turmoil of the Civil War years. With the reemergence of more ordinary domestic concerns, Young, "the Rebel of the Harem," took the national spotlight. In the spring of 1874, a successful lecture tour brought her to Washington, D.C., where her audiences included not only the expected assortment of politicians but also President Grant and his wife.[87]

Republicans, inspired both by sincere outrage at the mistreatment of women that Young depicted and by the opportunity to put at least some Democrats in the difficult position of having to support polygamy, quickly proposed new legislation that strengthened the polygamy ban—and by the end of the summer, they had passed it. The Mormons' lobbyists and political allies put up a fight, but ultimately their argument, based on the value of local control over domestic affairs, could not stem the Republican tide.[88] As part of their case, the Republicans emphasized the enormous power of the

Mormon church in Utah, which they condemned as a theocracy. As Sarah Barringer Gordon shows in her fascinating book on the subject, Republicans used this rhetoric to associate Mormon domination in Utah with the despotism they ascribed to the Catholic church.[89] The passage of the antipolygamy law in 1874 can be seen as a dry run for the Blaine amendment fight two years later. Republicans in both cases were setting out to vindicate the principle of federal control over local practices that offended their moral sensibility; in different senses, Mormons and Catholics represented significant religious diversity, and in both cases, Republicans could present themselves as advocates of the separation of church and state. But if Catholics could block Blaine at the federal level, the Mormons lacked comparable political clout.

The Mormons, though, were not yet prepared to give up the fight—and because Congress was prohibiting their local practices through a law, not a constitutional amendment, they had a last arrow in their quiver: an appeal to the U.S. Supreme Court, guaranteed by a special provision of the new law. The Mormon leadership negotiated with the Utah U.S. Attorney to create a test case in which they would put forward one of their own to be convicted of polygamy, then argue to the Supreme Court that the antipolygamy law violated the Constitution.[90] The Mormons' lawyers sought to argue that Congress lacked the power to interfere with the purely local government of the territory. But the Supreme Court reframed the issue to ask whether Mormons' religious belief in polygamy meant that the law in question violated their free exercise of religion under the First Amendment.[91]

Never before had the Supreme Court so much as considered a claim that Congress had passed a law prohibiting free exercise. Since 1791, Congress had steered clear of any law that might have given rise to such an objection, and it would be another seventy years before the Supreme Court came to believe that the First Amendment applied to the states, not only Congress. But because of the anomaly that Congress, exercising its control over territorial

Utah, had passed a law regarding the otherwise purely local issue of marriage, the constitutional question was arguably necessary to a decision.

The Supreme Court decided the constitutional question unanimously, and Chief Justice Morrison Waite issued an opinion that inaugurated the judicial custom of delving into constitutional history in church-state cases. Waite's opinion correctly identified the debate over taxation for the support of religion as the central controversy over church-state relations in the immediate preconstitutional period. Using documents provided to him by his neighbor, the great American historian George Bancroft,[92] Waite zeroed in on the Virginia debate over the 1784 general assessment bill that would have provided nonpreferential funding for religion. He quoted Madison's *Memorial and Remonstrance* and Jefferson's religious freedom statute; then, for good measure, the Chief Justice threw in a long quotation from Jefferson's presidential letter to the Danbury Baptists—the passage introducing the metaphor of the wall of separation between church and state.

Having set the stage by invoking the wall of separation, Waite might have gone on to find that Congress lacked the authority to prohibit the Mormons' essentially religious marriage practices. Indeed, as Waite had to acknowledge, for hundreds of years of English legal history, "until the time of James I,"[93] bigamy had been punished by the ecclesiastical courts, not simply because religion was offended by bigamous acts, but because religious, not civil, courts regulated *all* aspects of marriage. This would seem to have provided strong evidence that marriage was a religious area of the law and therefore unsuited to congressional regulation. Such a holding would have had far-reaching consequences, because modern courts then might later have concluded that the states could not regulate marriage, either.

Yet here the norm of Christian nonsectarianism came into the picture. Chief Justice Waite observed that, beginning with James's reign in the early seventeenth century, bigamy became punishable by civil courts, a rule subsequently adopted by the American states. Even Virginia, after enacting its religious freedom statute, had passed an antibigamy law. It followed, said Waite, that it was "impossible to believe that the constitutional guaranty of religious freedom was intended to prohibit legislation in respect to this most important feature of social life." The reason was that, although marriage was "from its very nature a sacred obligation," it was also, at the same time, "in most civilized nations, a civil contract, and usually regulated by law."[94]

If the idea that marriage was both sacred and simultaneously regulated by civil law sounds strange to our ears, there is reason to think that American lawyers of the nineteenth century also sensed the tension. The source of the problem was that the roots of American law—including marriage law—lay in England, where church and state were united, not separate. Not until 1753 had marriage in England finally been taken away from the religious courts, and except for a brief period under Cromwell's Puritan revolutionary rule, civil marriage was not fully available there until 1836.[95] The basic legal theory of marriage in England until then was that individual men and women had the legal capacity to marry each other by a simple act of consent, but the church must solemnize the marriage, and the state was entitled to insist on the church performing this role before it would recognize the union as binding.

The option of getting married without a priest's blessing came to America with the Puritans of Massachusetts Bay Colony, who were second to none in their religious commitment and zeal but whose Congregationalist faith was animated by a strong dose of anticlericalism.[96] More aggressively Protestant than the Church of England, which they condemned for clinging too much to the old Catholic ways, the Massachusetts Puritans in 1646 passed a law making it a crime for anyone other than a magistrate—that is, a government official—to bring persons together in marriage.[97] To prohibit clergy from officiating at marriages was a radical move, but the Massachusetts Puritans were radical people, religious experimentalists living in a quasi-theocratic community at the frontier of the known world.[98] The religious basis for this civilly sanctioned marriage was that an Anglican priest was not necessary to form a good marriage, either before the law or before God. By taking marriage away from the priests and the Anglican hierarchy, the Puritans flouted the established church whose reach they had fled, in the process reducing the power of the priesthood relative to the congregations.

Parliament was not prepared to endure the snub indefinitely but was willing to reach a compromise with the unruly colonists. When issuing a new provincial charter to Massachusetts Bay in 1691, Parliament superseded the old rule and authorized "every justice of the peace within his county, and every settled minister in any town" to solemnize the marriages of persons who had obtained a certificate from the local government.[99] This restored to clergy the right to perform marriages but also preserved the option of being married by a justice of the peace, without clerical participation—an option that, although unavailable in England at the time, continued to be a basic element of Massachusetts marriage law, which soon spread to other colonies.

In the minds of those who first introduced civil marriage to America, then, it was possible to bifurcate the formalities of marriage between consenting adults from the judgments of heaven. The legal requirement that a marriage be solemnized before an authorized person, whether government official or minister, simply reflected the practical requirement that the government keep records of who was married to whom, especially for purposes of establishing descent and property ownership. The state demanded a monopoly on the authority to solemnize marriages in order to ensure that the legal protections of marriage applied—not because the state claimed to have any special authority in matters spiritual. Writing in 1810, the chief justice of Massachusetts warned that "every young woman of honor ought to insist on a marriage solemnized by a legal officer, and to shun the man who prates about marriage condemned by human laws, as good in the sight of Heaven."

This cant, she may be assured, is a pretext for seduction."[100] The advice was practical, not moral or religious: women should insist on legal marriage to make sure they were not denied the associated legal rights.

With the rise of nonsectarian ideology, however, the option of civil marriage in America came to be infused with a quasi-religious character. The same government that taught morals through nonsectarian religion in the public schools could be said to uphold the morals of a good Christian life through the institution of marriage. As marriage became central to the American conception of home over the course of the nineteenth century, words like "sacred" increasingly attached to the legally sanctioned institution, not to the formal religious solemnization of marriage. The mutually reinforcing ideals of nonsectarian morality and American republicanism were undermining the framers' idea that religion belonged in one sphere and temporal government in another. The key to the erosion lay in the government's engagement with morality. So long as citizens naturally displayed virtue of their own, government could avoid taking moral stances, and Jefferson's wall of separation could seem largely impregnable. But if good government depended on creating good citizens, then there could be no escape from moral undertakings, and so no escape from the nonsectarian religion that gave morality its basis. If marriage was a moral bulwark for republican society, then it had a religious component, even if it could be administered by a justice of the peace or a city clerk.

So the observation of Chief Justice Waite in the Supreme Court's polygamy decision that marriage was simultaneously religious and regulated by states' civil law was correct, but it did not follow that Congress could constitutionally regulate marriage in the Utah Territory. Unlike the states, which could in principle draw the line between church and state wherever they chose, Congress was bound by the First Amendment, which prohibited establishment of religion and protected free exercise. The State of Virginia had indeed banned bigamy after passing its religious freedom statute, but if there was any contradiction between these two state laws, that would have been a matter for the Virginia courts to resolve. Waite needed more evidence to explain why, despite the First Amendment, *Congress* had the authority to prohibit the Mormons from implementing their own interpretation of the "sacred obligation" of marriage. He found it in a passage from the early writings of the distinguished German-born political theorist Francis Lieber, a passage that had already been cited in an influential legal treatise in a discussion of bigamy.[101]

According to Lieber, polygamy was the essence of patriarchy, and patriarchy in turn was associated with despotism, not republican democracy. Waite used Lieber's argument to highlight the relationship between the social institution of marriage and the type of civil government that would prevail in a given country. If the kind of marriage allowed would actually determine the shape of the government, then it surely followed that the government must be permitted to regulate marriage. The thrust of this argument was that the normal marriage practices of the citizens of nonsectarian Christian America were connected to the republican form of government that they enjoyed. Marriage of two persons on equal terms was analogous to government of equals under conditions of consent, whereas marriage of a single man with multiple women was being compared to the rule of one man over many subjects. Imprecise though the analogy may have been, it did its work of connecting marriage practices to political structure. For good measure, Waite noted that "polygamy has always been odious among the northern and western nations of Europe"—a comment that, drawing on Lieber's theories, associated the Saxon lands where democracy was imagined to have been born with the practice of ordinary two-person marriage. (The association of monogamy with Northern and Western Europe was also intended to distance Christianity from the polygamy of the Old Testament and its association with the Jews. The Mormons, of course, drew heavily on this Old Testament source for polygamy.)

Once the Court had ascertained that Congress could legislate on the subject of marriage, it remained only for the Court to ask whether the Mormons were entitled to a religious exemption from a law that Congress was authorized to make. Waite dismissed the notion as unprecedented. While laws could not prohibit religious beliefs or opinions, they could certainly prohibit religiously motivated practices: "Suppose one believed that human sacrifices were a necessary part of religious worship, would it be seriously contended that the civil government under which he lived could not interfere to prevent a sacrifice? Or if a wife religiously believed it was her duty to burn herself upon the funeral pile of her dead husband, would it be beyond the power of the civil government to prevent her carrying her belief into practice?"[102] To allow religious exemptions from the laws would make the individual believer "superior to the law of the land." It would "permit every citizen to become a law unto himself."[103] The possibility that the Constitution might have created a right to religious exemptions under at least some circumstances was never discussed. The Mormons had gotten their day in court, and they had lost.

What happened next showed that the norms of Protestant nonsectarian Christianity were not to be avoided by religious minorities like Mormons. For a decade after the 1878 decision of *Reynolds v. United States*, the federal government vigorously prosecuted Mormon men and women for violating the federal antipolygamy laws, which were strengthened yet again in 1882 under Republican congressional leadership. (The bill's sponsor was the avid antipolygamist George Edmunds, who had been such a stalwart supporter of the Blaine amendment in the 1876 Senate debates. Edmunds would go on to cosponsor the Edmunds-Tucker Act of 1887 that disincorporated the Mormon church and rescinded the suffrage of women in Utah.) Hundreds went to jail for their faith. The Supreme Court upheld a law banning polygamists from voting or holding office in Utah[104] and another that required voters in the new Idaho Territory to swear they were not members of any group that advocated polygamy.[105] In effect, the government of the

United States made plural marriage a practical impossibility anywhere under its jurisdiction.

Eventually, not unlike those Catholics who had little choice but
to send their children to the nonsectarian common schools, the
Mormon polygamists relented. In 1890, after decades of resistance,
the president of the Mormon church, Wilford Woodruff, announced that the Latter-day Saints must no longer violate laws
prohibiting plural marriage.[106] Four years later, Congress granted
statehood to Utah, a long-sought result for the Mormons that
might never have happened without the change in the Mormon
line. Over time, the largest and most mainstream Mormon denomination expressly banned polygamy for its own members as a matter
of faith, not only as a matter of following the law. The nonsectarian
norm literally became Mormon teaching, enabling Mormons to assimilate themselves into the ideology and social reality of American
Christian nonsectarianism.

If today Mormons are often seen as archetypally American,[107]
deeply patriotic and overrepresented in the highest echelons of government service, this is a mark of both the coercive and transformative power of the nonsectarian ideal. Nonsectarianism demanded
conformity on some dimensions, but once conformity was
achieved, pluralist inclusiveness was sure to follow. An especially
delicious irony of history is that today's mainstream Mormons tend
to be steadfast supporters of legislation defining marriage as the
union of one man and one woman.[108] In the contemporary political scene, this definition has been chosen to emphasize one *man*
and one *woman*, and so preclude same-sex marriage, but just a little
more than a century ago, such a definition would have emphasized
one man and *one* woman, and been aimed at a Mormon church
that steadfastly resisted the paradigm. The historical power of nonsectarian conformity backed by state coercion could hardly be more
apparent.

In the wake of the polygamy debates, then, as well as the national debate about government support of Catholic schools that

took place in the 1870s, it was clear that Christian nonsectarianism functioned as the quasi-official American religion. From the Bible in the schools to public prayers to the monogamy norm, nonsectarianism set the tone. In the minds of most Americans, this nonsectarian religion posed no conflict with liberty of conscience, and indeed incorporated it. Protestants insisted that nonsectarian religion did not coerce anybody to perform religious actions to which they objected, and non-Protestants were free to worship as they wished, so long as their public conduct did not challenge the laws.

Nonsectarian religion of this sort was both traditionally American and, in a certain sense, an innovation. Public oaths, whether taken by officeholders or witnesses, had always invoked God's help. Legislative prayers were commonplace, as they had been since colonial times, and indeed today these well-established customs remain unchanged, an unbroken link to our English past. On the other hand, the formal theory that nonsectarian Christianity united Americans in common moral bonds had not existed in America at the founding. It had been invented in the 1820s and '30s, and used to solve the problem of providing moral education to diverse denominations in common public schools. Nevertheless, the new idea that nonsectarian Christianity was the American national religion took hold very effectively in the half century between the rise of the common schools and the failed Blaine amendment. Most Americans by 1876 took nonsectarianism for granted and would have been surprised and perhaps outraged to hear that the generation of 1776 did not share their vision of an America united by common religious-moral values.

Yet in the past as today, religion used in the service of national identity need not be religion deeply felt. The fact that Americans in the nineteenth century relied on nonsectarian religion as a nationally unifying force did not spare them from serious challenges to religion as an organizing principle of life. The Civil War itself, with its surfeit of theological justification and massive slaughter, stood as a challenge to religious certainties. After theology had played such an important part for both sides in justifying the war, the destruction wrought on North and South alike must have seemed to some a mute condemnation of the redemptive power of faith. Nonetheless, the postwar years' greatest challenge to religious faith, and to the accepted nonsectarian model of church and state, did not stem from the exhausting effects of the war itself. It came from a new source altogether, a new force in American thinking that was to pose a powerful challenge to the nonsectarian project. Its name was secularism—and, in different forms, it would become a perennial rival to religion in the struggle to forge national unity in the face of religious diversity.

3

THE BIRTH OF
AMERICAN SECULARISM

The year 1859 saw the publication of the most important scientific work since Isaac Newton's *Principia* of 1687: Charles Darwin's *The Origin of Species*, which not only elevated biology into the realm of theoretical science previously reserved for physics and chemistry, but immediately cast grave doubt on the biblical account of the creation of life. Its sequel, *The Descent of Man*, published in 1871, further undercut the religious view that man was specially created as the pinnacle and purpose of the universe. These two books appeared just as industrialization and the spread of the railroads were transforming ordinary life. Technologies such as the telegraph, the steam engine, and eventually electric power vastly enhanced the prestige of science. Though we now take such progress for granted, each major scientific breakthrough in the modern age has challenged religious verities and led to new debates about whether traditional religion should finally be jettisoned.

If the theory of evolution was not subject to immediate experimental testing, it grew out of the same scientific methodology that made the trains run on time. The variations among species that Darwin meticulously observed, and the fossil record he set out to interpret, were facts that had to be confronted. As Darwin's ideas made their way to America, educated people could engage them and try to disagree, but they could not reject natural selection out of hand. *The Origin of Species* had its first American edition in 1860, and rapidly made its way into American academic circles despite opposition from such luminaries as Harvard professor of geology Louis Agassiz.[1] The remarkable successes of science and technology unsettled old religious truths and propelled a new movement toward religious skepticism and even materialism.

Whether America as a whole underwent a process of secularization in the nineteenth century is a controversial historical question. Indeed, even today there is debate on whether American society is secular. Given the pervasive belief in God, widespread church attendance, and the influence of religion on politics, many would deny the label. But according to another view, America is the very essence of a secular society, in which worldly economic and cultural forces drive our lives and important decisions. In light of sociologists' and historians' continuing disagreements about what counts as secularization, it pays to be cautious about arguing for or against some profound transformation of American society from "religious" to "secular."[2]

What can be said with historical certainty is that a movement that defined itself as secularist did emerge in the United States in the last quarter of the nineteenth century, arguing openly that religion should not be accorded authority in human decisions, whether individual or collective and political. This movement introduced a distinctive type of diversity into American religious life, coming not from a new Christian denomination or even from a different religion altogether, but from a relatively far-flung group of people who rejected religion itself. Instead of seeking some amorphous concept of secularization, then, let us turn to an American secularism that can be pinned down—its rise, the evangelical reaction to it, and its eventual retreat and rebirth. The new secularism called for new thinking about church and state, and the consequences of that thinking, altered by time and changed circumstances, are still with us today.

DEFINING SECULARISM

Although today's secularists like to claim those framers who believed in a watchmaker God as their intellectual forebears, the eighteenth century knew no phenomenon by the name of "secularism." The term entered the language in the 1840s in England, where it was coined and popularized by George Jacob Holyoake, a young freethinker who over the course of a long career was to become an important figure in English radicalism. Holyoake had been jailed for blasphemy after a public lecture in which he spoke dismissively of God and religion; in the course of his lengthy imprisonment, his infant daughter died of illness and malnutrition. This dreadful episode left Holyoake searching for a publicly palatable means to express his deep skepticism about religious truth. He settled on the term "secularism," which he sharply distinguished from the atheism that had gotten him into trouble.[3]

For Holyoake, secularism was the view that religion should not be taken into account in human affairs:[4] it related to "the present existence of man, and to action, the issues of which can be tested by the experience of this life."[5] To be a secularist, then, was not, technically speaking, to deny that God existed—on that question secularism purported to remain silent. But regardless of whether God existed, secularism urged the individual to focus on things of this world, not of the world to come, and to rely on empirically observed facts, not theories of the unseen. In practice, Holyoake argued that government and the schools should simply ignore religion, neither formally rejecting it nor embracing it as relevant.[6]

The thin line between the atheist's outright denial of God and the secularist's advice that one should ignore religion served a crucial rhetorical purpose. Atheism was culturally (and, for a time, legally) unacceptable in Holyoake's England. Secularism, however, stood a chance of gaining adherents among freethinkers, skeptics, and other radicals. Unlike the atheist, the secularist would be permitted to ascend the podium for public debates with the more liberal clergy who were themselves increasingly inclined toward a very loose interpretation of Scripture and Christian dogma. Perhaps most important, secularists could turn the subject of debate away from abstract issues of theology and toward practical questions such as what should be taught in schools. Within a couple of decades of Holyoake's first public statements in favor of secularism, there were self-described secularist associations all over England, loosely affiliated with radical causes and promoting skepticism in matters of religion and increased separation between church and state.[7]

Holyoake's views were noted in American religious circles, but the movement he started made no immediately appreciable inroads here.[8] When Holyoake visited the United States for a lecture tour in 1880, the newspapers focused on his later career as a leader and historian of the workers' cooperative movement, and made little or no mention of his role as the self-proclaimed father of secularism.[9] Yet the term that Holyoake invented did eventually catch on in America, though with a different demographic cast. Holyoake was a product of self-education and the working class, and his movement was designed to appeal to pragmatic workers who, he believed, had no use for the religion that was deployed to justify their oppression.[10] In the United States, by contrast, secularism started with elites and made its way to ordinary people incompletely and with great difficulty—a difference that would come to matter tremendously in the trajectory of secularism here.

American secularism, as it eventually emerged in the 1870s and '80s, was not Holyoake's movement but rather a gradually growing development in educated circles embracing rationalism and science over traditional religious belief.[11] The true aim of this strong secularism was the full replacement of religion by reason, both in the realm of belief and in the political sphere. The intellectual side of the secularist equation sought to convince Americans to form their beliefs on the basis of scientific evidence, not revelation; religious dogma (what its adherents would call faith) must be abandoned in favor of the conclusions reached by the scientific community. The political side of secularism demanded, in the words of one of its leading exponents, "that our entire political system shall be founded and administered on a purely secular basis."[12] That meant, among other things, an end to the use of the Bible in the public schools, the abolition of Sunday laws, a stop to state support of chaplains in legislatures and the military, and the elimination of tax exemptions for churches: in short, the overthrow of the practices of nonsectarian Christianity, still the basic secular political program on church and state as it exists today.[13]

SECULARISM'S SCIENTIFIC UNDERPINNINGS

Two books written in the 1870s and widely read for decades laid the scientific groundwork for American strong secularism as not just an intellectual position but an ideology: Andrew Dickson White's work, *The Warfare of Science* (1876), which grew out of a lecture first delivered at the Cooper Institute in New York in 1874; and *The History of the Conflict Between Religion and Science*, by New York University chemist-turned-historian John William Draper, published in 1876.[14] Although neither of these books used the word "secularism," both were serious, systematic efforts by members in good standing of the educational elite to promote reason to the detriment of doctrinal religious faith.

It would be hard to imagine anyone more representative of the educated American elite than White, a Yale-trained historian and student of politics who in 1868 became the first president of Cornell University. After early stints in Europe, studying in Germany and later working as a junior diplomat in the American embassy in St. Petersburg, White returned to the United States to teach history at the relatively new University of Michigan. Between 1857 and 1863—years during which the schools question loomed large in Michigan politics—White began to think about the desirability of nonsectarianism in higher education. Returning to his native New York, where he assumed a seat in the state Senate, White made the acquaintance of Ezra Cornell, a wealthy member of the same body who had made his fortune in telegraph lines. With Cornell's money and White's academic leadership, they founded Cornell University in 1865 as the first nonsectarian university in the United States.[15]

The new university's nonsectarianism was not originally intended to be secular. When it came under withering criticism from those who insisted that a religious orientation was necessary to ground cogent principles of higher education, White defended the university on the grounds that nonsectarianism was hostile not to religious teaching but only to the exclusive advocacy of one particular denomination. Sectarianism, not religion, was the enemy. But White, who always insisted that he was himself a churchman and an Episcopalian, did come to see religious orthodoxy as inimical to the free academic inquiry necessary for good science. The fact that the attacks on the new university came from supporters of theological orthodoxy no doubt confirmed White's views on this score. By the time White gave his lecture at the Cooper Institute, his exasperation had grown into the hypothesis that religion was bad for science but that free scientific inquiry could do no harm to religion: "In all modern history, interference with science in the supposed interest of religion, no matter how conscientious such interference may have been, has resulted in the direst evils both to religion and to science; and, on the other hand, all untrammeled scientific investigation, no matter how dangerous to religion some of its stages may have seemed for the time to be, has invariably resulted in the highest good both of religion and of science."[16]

This claim no longer relied on nonsectarianism as a means for defending free inquiry; instead, it acknowledged directly that religious interference had badly harmed the cause of truth. White's title, *The Warfare of Science*, left it slightly ambiguous whom science was fighting, but the greatly expanded two-volume version of the book published in 1896 left no doubt: it was titled *A History of the Warfare of Science with Theology in Christendom*.[17] Although White took pains to distinguish dogmatic theology—which he considered inherently opposed to science—from what he called "religion," the subtlety of this distinction would have been lost on most readers.

White's lecture and the book that grew from it communicated explicitly to the educated public that organized religion, with its doctrines and dogmas, stood opposed to the scientific progress to which their education had begun to accustom them. As White gave the lecture again in elite venues like Brown University's Phi Beta Kappa ceremonies,[18] it brought home an association among America's centers of higher education, the goals of free inquiry, and the need to move away from religious influence and sponsorship. During his studies in Germany, then the world leader in university education, White had been exposed to a whole range of fields in which scientific approaches were eclipsing traditional religious methodologies.[19] White was not alone in bringing that trend to the American university. When Charles William Eliot became president of Harvard in 1869 and set about the task of transforming the Congregationalist-founded college into a world university, he, too, looked self-consciously to the model of the German universities where he had studied. Although far more circumspect than White, and not himself a lightning rod for opinion on the religious character of the university, the Unitarian Eliot presided over Harvard during the years in which it changed from a sectarian institution to an essentially secular one.[20]

Shortly after White's initial New York lecture, John William Draper, another university professor, made his contribution to the intellectual program of secularism with *The History of the Conflict Between Religion and Science*. Draper began with the assumption that, on both sides of the Atlantic, the educated classes were losing their faith in religion: "Whoever has had an opportunity of becoming acquainted with the mental condition of the intelligent classes in Europe and America, must have perceived that there is a great and rapidly-increasing departure from the public religious faith, and that, while among the more frank this divergence is not concealed, there is a far more extensive and far more dangerous secession, private and unacknowledged."[21] Draper did not say that he was opposed to this development. To the contrary, it resulted naturally from a two-thousand-year-old struggle between Christianity and science. The former insisted on divine revelation that "must necessarily be intolerant of contradiction," while the latter represented the "irresistible advance of human knowledge." In this conflict between static religion and dynamic science, Draper wished to take sides. "History shows that, if this be not done, social misfortunes, disastrous and enduring, will ensue." If religion were to win its latest battle against science, Draper argued, a new Dark Age would be sure to follow.[22]

The villain of Draper's piece was the Catholic church, whose history he traced with special emphasis on the repression of dissent, both political and intellectual. One chapter held up medieval Islamic science as the ideal of unfettered inquiry, focusing on its accomplishments in mathematics, astronomy, chemistry, physics, and public education. Other chapters were organized around specific conflicts between the church and science, to devastating effect. The church was shown upholding the flat Earth and the geocentric universe against Copernicus, Galileo, and the circumnavigation of the globe. The scriptural view of Earth as only some five thousand years old (and created in six days) was shown to be contradicted by the discoveries of geology and evolutionary biology.[23]

Moving beyond pure science to epistemology, Draper rejected both the Catholic claim that truth could be measured by the authority of the pope and the Protestant idea that the Bible was the criterion of factual accuracy. The Pentateuch, Draper said, was simply spurious with respect to its historical claims.[24] Finally, Draper turned to politics. The Catholic church sought to dominate political authority in Europe with the goal of continuing to suppress science and the modern civilization that it would inevitably bring with it. This amounted to "an impending crisis" in which the Catholic church had staked out its position by the declaration of papal infallibility and the condemnation of a syllabus of scientific errors at its 1870 Vatican Council. Although Protestant evangelicals were less well organized, Draper pointed out that in 1873, a large meeting in New York of the Protestant Evangelical Alliance had, much like the Catholic church, devoted its attention to the condemnation of scientific error.[25]

Draper's book was an instant success. By 1910 it had been published in twenty-five authorized editions. Draper's sales no doubt encouraged White to expand his basic argument to two volumes, which were also regularly reprinted over the next fifty years. Buttressed by the prestige of science, which they invoked and sought to advance, these works brought out of the shadows the argument that religion was both mistaken and harmful. Although White tried to avoid attacking "religion" by focusing his attention on theology, and Draper reserved most of his contempt for the Catholic church (he considered the Reformation a partial step toward the triumph of reason), the works were read and understood as impugning the religious way of encountering the world. They generated responses and condemnations from Catholic and Protestant clerics alike, who understood that the high status of university presidents and professors, when placed on the side of science in a war against religion, would unquestionably constitute a major challenge to the religious ideology of the time.[26]

By design or not, both books became primers for nonspecialist Americans who wanted to pursue their own arguments against religious doctrine on questions like the age of Earth and the inerrancy of the Bible. The books' styles might have been inaccessible to a very poorly educated reader, but both were clearly written and could have been followed by anyone with a high school diploma and some of the reading patience that preceded the television age.

White's complete *A History of the Warfare of Science with Theology in Christendom* led the reader through topics from cosmology to anthropology, the history of language, chemistry and physics, and biblical criticism. Each section began with a presentation of the theological view, then thoroughly debunked it by reference to the latest scientific evidence and interpretation. Polemical themselves, the book's two volumes also provided a guide to conducting polemic.

In the worldview that emerges from Draper and White, the formal beliefs and doctrines propounded by organized Christianity appear as either mistaken or downright harmful. Neither book attacked personal, individual belief in God, the Trinity, or Christ's power to save, and neither expressly advocated something called "secularism" (that was left to the political side of the movement), but the works also did not treat the topic of personal spirituality as important or relevant to ordinary life. Focused on the virtue of truth, the progress of science, and the useful technology that would be promoted by free inquiry, they depicted systematic religious faith as outmoded and even foolish. These works, then, did not offer a direct Nietzschean attack on theism so much as they made God seem largely irrelevant to modern life and conditions.

The relegation of religion to the realm of personal spirituality, accompanied by a rejection of the Bible as a source of objective knowledge about the world, was to constitute the core of the American secularism of the late nineteenth century—and these views created new diversity on questions of religion at least as much as earlier denominational expansion had done through enthusiasm and immigration. To understand the impact of the refutation of the Bible's historical accuracy, recall the symbolic centrality of the Bible to the vision of American national identity that could be found in Senator Frederick Frelinghuysen's impassioned speech in the Senate debate over the Blaine amendment. Frelinghuysen was speaking in 1876, the year White's lecture was published in book form. He and White were exact contemporaries, and indeed White in his autobiography spoke warmly of Frelinghuysen's appointment as Chester Arthur's secretary of state.[27] For Frelinghuysen, the American people would brook no interference with "that book," the source of their morality and their republican strength. Yet White and Draper were leveling a frontal attack at the very text that was considered the wellspring of the nation's values. Though they might have tried to claim that their scientific attack left biblical morality intact, White and Draper were out to do nothing less than displace the intellectual sway that religion held on the minds of believers.

In pursuit of this goal, the scientist-publicists used the Catholic church, which had for so long dominated European Christianity, as a stand-in for religious belief more generally. Partly this approach made sense because much of the history of theological dogma was the history of the church. But it also reflected a subtle strategy adopted by American secularists whose main religious interlocutors were more likely to be Protestant than Catholic. Attacking the Catholic church for its authoritarian inflexibility was a familiar move guaranteed to resonate with Protestants, much like the attack on the new doctrine of papal infallibility, itself a staple both of anti-Catholic American Protestant republicanism and of the new secularist literature. By making the Catholic church the main antagonist of science, the secularists defined an enemy that their Protestant audience already loved to hate.[28]

The clever twist that White and especially Draper added to their attack on the church was that Protestant churches were joining the Catholic church in condemning science—in other words, siding with the traditional opponents of independent thought. Organized Protestantism could then be depicted as part of religion arrayed against progressive science. From the perspective of Protestants, the contemporary fight over creation and evolution was something new, the first time that a serious adversary had come forth with powerful arguments to challenge doctrines clearly stated in the Bible. But the secularists were depicting this fight as just the latest battle in a centuries-old war that predated Protestantism, and by doing so they were putting the Protestant churches into the tradition of Catholic repression of dissent.

Through this secularist maneuver, science came to take the place once occupied by Protestantism in the traditional polemic against the Catholic church. Where once Luther had insisted on the primacy of his own judgment and reason in interpreting Scripture, science now demanded the right to follow the evidence wherever it might lead, including denial of the biblical story of creation. Anyone who opposed this free inquiry would be spiritually akin to the church that had denied Luther his independent judgment and silenced Galileo. Faced with this devilish piece of argumentative sophistication, the Protestant churches found themselves in a difficult double bind. If they were to accept scientific accounts of Earth's antiquity and evolution, they would contradict their foundational commitment to Scripture. But by insisting that Scripture must be true, they seemed to be denying the possibility of individual judgment, which was equally important to their basic ideals.

The response of the mainline Protestant churches to the challenge of secularist, scientifically inspired polemic was mixed. The Bible, after all, could not be abandoned wholesale. It could, however, be interpreted, and the more modernizing, liberal clergy were willing to consider the possibility that the biblical account of creation was more suggestive allegory than literal fact. Similarly, some of the more remarkable, naturally disruptive biblical miracles—like the parting of the Red Sea or Joshua ordering the sun to stand still—could be naturalized into scientifically explainable anomalies. Yet many members of the clerical classes resisted the promiscuous reinterpretation of the biblical text that seemed to be the only choice for the believer who wanted to maintain the new truths of science and the traditional truths of religion. It was difficult for people who had grown up believing sincerely in the Bible's centrality and truth to accept the notion that man was descended from the apes, not created on the sixth day. There was a lingering sense among the shepherds of the religious flock that giving up on such basic tenets of the faith might leave no stopping point in the slide toward the triumph of science and downfall of religion. The result of this ambivalence was that the mainline churches equivocated, neither fully capitulating to the scientific interpretation of creation and evolution nor making a unified stand against it.[29]

THE LECTURERS AND THE QUESTION OF POLITICS

Into this environment of uncertainty came the lecturers, whose job in the nineteenth century was to take new and provocative ideas, often generated by the educated elite, and translate them into entertaining, informative, and sometimes convincing lectures that would be heard by middle-class audiences nationally. Riding the lecture circuit meant giving a single lecture again and again in small and medium-sized cities where a paying audience could be gotten. The lecturer's charisma counted for a lot, as Henry James suggested in his novel *The Bostonians*, which hints at the combination of celebrity, cultural influence, and occasionally heavy paydays that tantalized aspiring lecturers. A skillful speaking style was a valuable commodity, and of course a provocative message helped draw public attention. A lecture that achieved notoriety had a better chance of broad success as new audiences demanded to hear in person what others were discussing.

Secularism became a topic of public lectures, most notably through the efforts of Robert G. Ingersoll, a lawyer and politician who rose to the level of Illinois attorney general (1867–69) but was blocked from further advancement by his notorious and public agnosticism. His career in mainstream electoral politics thwarted by his beliefs, Ingersoll made lemons into lemonade and set out on the lecture circuit, where he had success for nearly thirty years with a range of lectures that eventually filled twelve volumes.[30] His most famous lecture, "The Gods" (1872), expressed religious skepticism and downright contempt for the Bible itself. That so many people paid to listen to such a lecture does not necessarily mean that they were receptive to Ingersoll's ideas. Paying good money to be shocked and scandalized is a respectable American tradition. But neither were audiences stoning Ingersoll, and the mere fact that "The Gods" was widely delivered and reported in the press suggests that some audience members may have been listening with interest, not only with horror.

"The Gods" revolved around the claim, borrowed very loosely from the German philosopher Ludwig Feuerbach,[31] that beliefs about God or gods amounted to projections of humans' own particular preferences and characteristics. From here Ingersoll went on to deny the divine source of the Bible. "As a matter of fact," Ingersoll maintained, "there never was, and never can be, an argument even tending to prove the inspiration of any book whatever . . . the instant we admit that a book is too sacred to be doubted, or even reasoned about, we are mental serfs. It is infinitely absurd to suppose that God would address a communication to intelligent beings, and yet make it a crime, to be punished in eternal flames, for them to use their intelligence for the purpose of understanding his communication. If we have the right to use our reason, we certainly have the right to act in accordance with it, and no God can have the right to punish us for such action."[32] This argument began with the traditional Protestant insistence on the right of free individual judgment in interpreting Scripture, then used it to ridicule the very idea that the biblical text ought to be assumed sacred without being proved so. The reader, once freed from the shackles of reverence, could read the Bible "as you would any other book." The text would then testify against itself. "All that is necessary, as it seems to me, to convince any reasonable person that the Bible is simply and purely of human invention—of barbarian invention—is to read it."[33]

Here Ingersoll adopted a trope that had become standard in English secularist literature and that may owe its origins to George

Jacob Holyoake, who certainly used it to great effect: no reasonable, modern person could read the Bible and find its stories or its morals convincing. Ingersoll's example was the legal text from Exodus (21: 4–6) specifying that the Hebrew slave who had been given a wife by his master could not take her with him into freedom when his term of slavery ended, but must either commit himself to permanent enslavement in her company or leave his master's house without wife or children. In 1872, with *Uncle Tom's Cabin*'s depiction of the separation of slave families fresh in all minds, this example alluded to the notable failure of the biblical text to provide a strong antislavery rationale during the Civil War. Ingersoll drove the point home: "Did any devil ever force upon a husband, upon a father, so cruel and so heartless an alternative? Who can worship such a god? Who can bend the knee to such a monster? Who can pray to such a fiend?"[34]

The formal logic of Ingersoll's indictment was that the immorality of the biblical passage could not be the work of a just God. But beyond casting doubt on the veracity of the Bible (Ingersoll also ridiculed the plausibility of biblical miracles), Ingersoll intended to shock his audience with the implicit suggestion that God's very existence was doubtful. Science would be the engine of disbelief. "We are explaining more every day. We are understanding more every day; consequently your God is growing smaller every day." The moral consequence of giving up on God was self-reliance, driven by technology. "To prevent famine, one plow is worth one million sermons, and even patent medicines will cure more diseases than all the prayers uttered since the beginning of the world."[35] The last claim was surely overstated, since prayer, at its worst, presumably does the patient no harm. But the humor would not have been lost on the audience. They were being sold secularism, just as they were accustomed to being sold religion and, for that matter, snake oil. The self-consciousness of Ingersoll's style already did much to promote secularism, merely by placing it on the same footing as religion.

Ingersoll closed his lecture—a genre that was, after all, a secular sermon—by depicting the mounting, indeed millennial progress of reason, intellectual freedom, and science against the terrible and constant opposition of organized religion. Seekers after truth were "a few brave men and women of thought and genius," locked in "deadly conflict" with "the great ignorant religious mass." But the happy few were winning. "Day by day, religious conceptions grow less and less intense. Day by day, the old spirit dies out of book and creed. The burning enthusiasm, the pointless zeal of the early church is gone, never, never to return. The ceremonies remain, but the ancient faith is fading out of the human heart." When religion disappeared entirely, it would be replaced by its opposite number, reason. On that day, "Reason, throned upon the world's brain, shall be King of Kings, and God of Gods."[36]

The brilliant conclusion to "The Gods" subverted religion literally, metaphorically, and rhetorically all at once. The triumphant enthronement that constituted the apocalyptic biblical climax would be Reason's, not God's. Not only would Reason be king, but it would be God as well. The radicals of the French Revolution who had built temples of reason would have been well satisfied with Ingersoll's peroration.

More clearly, and certainly more dramatically, than the academics Draper and White, Ingersoll combined the intellectual program of American secularism—the replacement of religious faith with reason—with the political program of getting religion out of the governmental sphere. Schools were one context in which this goal could be promoted, so Ingersoll demanded "an absolute divorce between Church and School."[37] Ingersoll wrote that "it is not fair to make the Catholic support a Protestant school, nor is it just to collect taxes from infidels and atheists to support schools in which any system of religion is taught."[38] Consistent with this view, he deployed his rhetorical talents to deliver the nominating speech for James G. Blaine at the 1876 Republican convention[39] (altogether a remarkable fact, given Ingersoll's atheism). At the time Ingersoll still harbored hopes for advancement within the Republican Party, and Blaine's stance against state support for Catholic education was desirable from the perspective of secularism, even if it did not go far enough.

The party of Frelinghuysen, however, would never have been prepared to endorse Ingersoll's anti-Bible politics. So Ingersoll turned elsewhere, participating in the creation of the first major, national secularist organization, known as the National Liberal League. The league aspired to function as the political wing of secularism, promoting a political program of perfecting the separation of church and state. But with the exception of Ingersoll, whose desire to preserve his political viability within the Republican Party made him skeptical about a full embrace of the league, it had no especially prominent politicians among its members. It was founded in 1876 by a freethinker named Francis Ellingwood Abbot, a Harvard-trained philosopher connected with the Metaphysical Club and one of the quirkiest figures one might ever hope to encounter in the annals of American history. Reading Darwin—who reciprocated Abbot's admiration—had helped lead Abbot down the path from serving as minister of a Unitarian congregation to losing the church after a court battle over whether he was still a Christian (the Massachusetts Supreme Judicial Court determined that he was not). Abbot then began publishing his own periodical, *The Index,* "A Weekly Paper Devoted to Free Religion," which served as the mouthpiece for Abbot's secularist views, which he soon labeled "liberalism" (the league, too, initially avoided using the word "secularism" in its name, although it was renamed the American Secular Union in 1884).[40]

When Ingersoll addressed the National Liberal League's convention in Cincinnati in 1879, he loosely endorsed the league's secularist, Abbot-framed program of ending use of the Bible in the public schools, tax exemptions for churches, the public employment of chaplains, oaths invoking God, and the Sunday laws. Ingersoll then connected these goals to the broader search for free inquiry and the truth: Catholics, Presbyterians, Methodists, and Baptists had the same right to their beliefs "that we have to believe that it is all superstition. But when that Catholic or Baptist or Methodist endeavors to put chains on the bodies or intellects of men, it is then the duty of every Liberal to prevent it at all hazards." The liberal political platform, Ingersoll continued, stood for "universal education—the laws of science included, not the guesses of superstition—universal education, not for the next world but for this—happiness, not so much for an unknown land beyond the clouds as for this life in this world."[41]

For Ingersoll, secularism was itself a kind of religion: it was a worldview about the superiority of science that generated its own distinctive view about the proper relationship between church and state. For the first time, some Americans were both denying the value of religion altogether and simultaneously using what they considered the foolishness of religion to argue for its removal from the governmental sphere. Unlike Jefferson, who had written that opinions about religion were just as irrelevant to politics as were opinions about geometry, the strong secularists of the league believed precisely that correct opinions about science were crucial to making correct judgments—and that the falsehoods of religion must be kept away from politics, to which they were actively detrimental.

When it came to practical politics, the league supported the basic principles of the Blaine amendment[42] and its successor, confusingly known as the Blair amendment. The league naturally wanted to go further, to ban religion completely from the schools, and so added the proviso that new constitutional amendments barring state support of sectarian education should not make special provision for permitting the Bible to remain in the public schools.[43] But the overlap between the league members' interests and mainstream Republican opposition to Catholic schools was great enough to justify their support for the Blaine amendment, and Ingersoll's Republican connections did not hurt, either. Eventually the league's differences from Republicanism drove its leaders to think of themselves as a separate political party and to urge Ingersoll to run for president on their platform. But by the time this happened, the league had been torn apart by divisions among its various factions, some of which had radical views not only about church and state but also about free love. A serious third-party candidacy was never in the cards, and Ingersoll turned them down, despite his sympathies for the league's remarkable, innovative position on church and state.

American secularism, then, began as strong secularism,[44] concerned with removing religion from the public sphere as a corollary to the general goal of removing superstitious religion from all human thought and decision making. American secularists almost universally preferred to say that they were agnostics rather than atheists—both Ingersoll and another secularist lawyer, Clarence Darrow (to whom we will come presently), gave popular lectures titled "Why I Am an Agnostic"—but this was not because they harbored some secret doubts about the possible existence of divine providence. Rather, American secularists' stance rested on a claim of intellectual openness. Denying God would have sounded like a proposition of belief without the kind of firm evidence on which scientific truths were said to rest. Describing themselves as agnostics allowed secularists to answer the question "Is there a God?" as Ingersoll did, by saying, "I do not know—but I do not believe."[45] Darrow, in his lecture on the topic, said that an agnostic was a doubter—but he dismissed religious faith as superstition and claimed it was "impossible for the human mind to believe in an object or thing unless it can form a mental picture of such object or thing."[46] It being impossible to conceive of an abstract God, it was impossible to believe in one.

Strong secularism functioned, in other words, as a comprehensive worldview that presented itself as an alternative to religious conceptions of the world. There were a handful of liberal Christian thinkers who, like the ecumenical Episcopalian William Reed

Huntington, thought that the state should be a "secular machine" so that the church could focus on its exclusive task of offering spiritual salvation.[47] But most influential secularists would have liked to see the churches wither away and scientific reason triumph. They believed that religion was not a private phenomenon but an inevitably public force to be reckoned with directly and defeated.

By the end of the nineteenth century, such strong secularism was assuming a familiar, if by no means dominant, place in the realm of American ideas. After its American birth in elite circles, secularism was beginning to diffuse to the middle classes through lectures and the popular press. William Cowper Brann's sole-proprietor magazine, *Brann's Iconoclast*, sold nearly one hundred thousand copies of each issue during its three successful years between 1895 and Brann's murder (apparently growing out of his outspoken criticism of Methodist Baylor University) in 1898. Brann was raised on a farm with little or no formal education; he worked himself up from bellboy to printer to reporter and publisher, and his satirical portrayals of organized religion, produced in Waco, Texas, where he lived, represented a more popular—and populist—strand of secularist thought than that of professors like White and Draper or lawyers like Ingersoll and Darrow.[48]

Increasingly, the figure of the village atheist was entering popular consciousness, as exemplified by Edgar Lee Masters's poem of that name in his *Spoon River Anthology* (1916). By definition, such a person lived not in a great cosmopolitan center but in some out-of-the-way spot, where his atheist views must come via books or education elsewhere. The village atheist had a little learning but need not have been the best-educated man in town—some indication that secularism was spreading beyond elites. But the village atheist was also, presumably, the only atheist for miles, so he could be gently parodied as a figure of fun, like the village idiot with whom his nickname associated him. Secularism, at the close of the century was beginning to make slow inroads into belief at the national level.

THE OPPOSITION

Some voices were soon raised against secularism and its political program. The most prominent was that of the National Reform Association, devoted to passage of a so-called Christian amendment to the preamble of the Constitution that would recognize the authority of the Christian God and the Holy Scriptures as the foundations of the nation. The association got its start in 1864, with the Civil War still raging, before secularism had found its feet. From the beginning, the group consisted of a multidenominational array of ministers who believed that the nation's moral shortcomings—including, to begin with, slavery—derived from the original sin of failing to acknowledge God in the Constitution.

The association soon began to develop nuanced positions on a range of politically charged issues. At its 1872 convention, held in the flash point city of Cincinnati at the time that the schools controversy there was coming to a head, papers were presented on such topics as "The Relation of Education to Religion" and "Neutrality of the State in Morals and Religion a Thing Impossible."[49] The association devoted itself broadly to promoting nonsectarian Christianity, and, Protestant to the core, it supported the Blaine amendment, ironically just like its nemesis, the National Liberal League, though for slightly different reasons.

What most differentiated the National Reform Association from mainstream, ordinary nonsectarianism was its insistence that the de facto reign of nonsectarian Christianity was not enough: the United States needed a formal, constitutional recognition of Christianity to set itself on the right path. In making this point, the association insisted that America's unwritten constitution already embodied the nation's Christian character; the failure of the written Constitution to do the same was the fly in the ointment, the fatal flaw that needed to be repaired. Nonetheless, the association denied absolutely that acknowledging Christianity in the Constitution would mean a union of church and state. Church was one thing and religion another. Church *institutions* must be kept separate from government, the association believed. Religion, on the other hand—nonsectarian Protestant Christianity, to be exact—was the only firm basis upon which the American polity could rest.[50] Separation of church and state was a slogan shared by all sides, then, and everyone opposed the union or merger of the two. But the application of that abstract principle was a topic of disagreement among secularists on one extreme, the Christian amendment advocates on the other, and most everyone else somewhere in the middle.

In 1872, the National Reform Association was for the Bible in the schools and promoting the morality of the nation; it had not yet discovered that its enemy was a phenomenon called "secularism." By the time the association celebrated its twenty-fifth anniversary in 1889, however, secularism had emerged as the embodiment of everything it stood against. An address at the Quarter-Centennial Convention, held that year in Pittsburgh, described and criticized "The Secular Theory of Education." A year later, David McAllister published the first edition of *A Manual of Christian Civil Government*, subsequently enlarged and republished several times until 1898. For McAllister, the very purpose of national reform was to combat the "infidelity and atheism" to which the secular theory of government must inevitably tend.[51]

McAllister freely used the term "secularism" to describe any governmental theory or institution not expressly based on religious authority. For him, the written Constitution was aptly characterized as a secular document, because it did not mention God. In this respect, argued McAllister, the Constitution deviated from an otherwise unbroken tradition of acknowledgment of divine authority that could be found in the Declaration of Independence and in every important constitutional document stretching back to the Magna Carta. Secularism stood for the absurd notion that the authority of the polity could depend on "We the People." If the state was to be a moral agent, its morality must be grounded in religion, and that grounding must be acknowledged in the constitutional text. Otherwise a man like Ingersoll, "the most notorious scoffer and atheist in America," would be right when he insisted that "the government of the United States is secular. It derives its power from the consent of man."[52]

Despite the persistence of the National Reform Association, public support for the hard-line Christian amendment position turned out to be relatively scarce. Like its twin, the National Liberal League, the association was never able to become a mainstream entity. Despite small victories, such as the introduction of the association's Christian amendment in Congress in 1894 and 1896, or the assertion by Supreme Court Justice David Brewer (an association member) in a judicial opinion that America was "a Christian nation," McAllister was forced in all honesty to acknowledge in his 1898 volume that the association was unlikely ever to achieve its stated goals. Although, as the association saw it, America was headed for either "the abyss of secularism" or "a renewal of Christian political institutions,"[53] most Americans did not share the sense of an impending crisis. Liberal Christians could agree with the separation of church and state, which was anyway a traditional American Protestant position, and confront the challenge of Darwinism by allegorical biblical interpretation. The association's differences with the league were symbolic rather than pressingly practical, with both supporting the Blaine amendment. Secularism was not yet, at the close of the nineteenth century, broadly understood to pose the kind of absolute challenge to the American way of life that its most vigilant opponents saw in it.

That was about to change. Within a couple of decades, a group of evangelical ministers, concerned by the rise of secularism and the gradual accommodation of mainline Protestant churches to modern science and biblical criticism, would coalesce into the movement known as Christian fundamentalism. It would take another seventy-five years, and the transformation of a peripheral movement into one supported by its own universities and national political organizations, but fundamentalism would eventually change the face of American religion and politics, and give its name to a broader worldwide phenomenon of enormous historical importance.

4

THE FUNDAMENTALS,
THE FUNDAMENTALISTS,
AND THE MONKEY TRIAL

THE ORIGINS OF FUNDAMENTALISM

Fundamentalists and their critics both like to depict the movement as ancient and primordial: the "old-time religion" in the here and now. In fact, fundamentalism got its name from an organization called the World's Christian Fundamentals Association, which was conceived in 1918 and held its first, six-thousand-person conference in Philadelphia in 1919, in the immediate aftermath of World War I. The notion of organizing believers around certain nonnegotiable "fundamentals" of Christian thought was hardly a decade older. The distinctive word "fundamentals" was popularized by a series of twelve slim paperback volumes—hardly more than pamphlets—privately published in Chicago between 1910 and 1915 and collectively entitled *The Fundamentals: A Testimony to the Truth.*

The Fundamentals was financed by a pair of Presbyterian philanthropist brothers, Lyman and Milton Stewart. Under their patronage, three hundred thousand copies of each volume were sent free of charge to "ministers of the gospel, missionaries, Sunday School superintendents, and others engaged in aggressive Christian work throughout the English speaking world."[1] The intellectual vision behind *The Fundamentals*, however, belonged to Amzi Clarence (A. C.) Dixon, a Southern-born Baptist preacher who spent most of his career as a pastor to large Northern Baptist congregations in places like Brooklyn; Roxbury, Massachusetts; and, most fatefully, Chicago, where Dixon served as pastor to the Moody Memorial Church beginning in 1906.

His pulpit in Chicago brought Dixon into direct contact with the faculty of the Divinity School at the recently founded, Rockefeller-funded University of Chicago, a bastion of the new scientific approach to higher education. If the University of Chicago's buildings looked as though they had been transplanted directly from Oxford, the organizational structure and much of the academic approach was imported almost wholesale from Germany, including guaranteed academic tenure and the intellectual freedom that came with it.[2] In the Divinity School, that meant that the faculty emphasized the German approach to biblical criticism, according to which the Bible was the product of multiple human authors and reflected their edits, errors, literary idiosyncrasies, and human perspectives. The Chicago theologians did not wish to abandon God altogether, but they sought to understand God through the lens of contemporary developments in science and biblical studies. The results exemplified modernist or liberal Christian thought, whose God expressed himself through an immanent presence in nature and history, not by direct intervention in human affairs or by revelation as it was traditionally understood.[3]

If A. C. Dixon knew one thing, it was that Christian modernism was deeply wrong and destructive of religious truth—worse, in fact, than the science that it claimed to accommodate. Dixon began to criticize Chicago-style biblical criticism while still in Brooklyn, but it was Dixon's particular attacks on the Chicago theologians once he arrived in their city that brought him to the attention of Lyman Stewart, who had the means and the desire to reach out to a national audience and needed an effective advocate and organizer to get the antimodernist message onto paper.[4] Dixon took up the task, presiding over and editing the first five volumes of *The Fundamentals*.

Those volumes, and indeed the entirety of *The Fundamentals*, functioned more as general defenses of traditional faith against the threat of Christian modernism than as attempts to specify particular, definitive beliefs to which every Christian must subscribe. The volumes that Dixon put together focused heavily on refuting biblical criticism. Articles by a range of writers set out to demonstrate that Moses, and not a collection of four anonymous authors, had written the Pentateuch. Just as important, the articles insisted that the faith required by the Gospels—the virgin birth, the Trinity, the nature of incarnation—remained intact in the face of the new criticism. The subject of evolution never even arose in the first five volumes; when it was discussed in later volumes, Darwinian natural selection was roundly condemned,[5] but the idea that there might have been some sort of evolution directed by divine guidance was not always rejected outright. In any case, at least one article in a later number of *The Fundamentals* took the position that the Darwinist danger had passed, and the theory of the origin of species had "quietly but firmly been labeled and shelved as merely one of the past phases of philosophic thought." The same article was willing to concede that there had been some evolution in the history of mankind, but only "entirely confined to the sphere of the activities of fallen man"—in other words, after Adam.[6] Another took the view that evolution was not an impossibility in nature, but that if it existed, it was directed by God and bore no relation to natural selection of the Darwinian type.[7]

Evolution, then, was not central to Dixon's concerns and did not dominate *The Fundamentals*, which were more exercised about Christian modernism and liberalism than about science. The same was initially true of the World's Christian Fundamentals Association, organized by William Bell Riley, another Southern-born Baptist who made his career ministering to Northern congregations. The WCFA reflected Riley's desire to combine fighting Christian modernism with promoting social activism. When Riley spoke to the inaugural WCFA conference, he did not treat Darwinism as the primary threat that the organization would have to address.

Fundamentalism began, in other words, not as a direct response to secularism itself, but as a response to liberal developments in Christian theology that were themselves influenced by the scientific worldview.[8] Yet within five years fundamentalism would be infused with profound antisecularism and would become the dramatic counterpart to secularism, locked in a national debate that remains unresolved to this day. The key to this change in emphasis was a man who was not himself a member of the fundamentalist movement, but a politician, celebrity, and super-lecturer whose government career had ended and who was looking for a populist crusade: William Jennings Bryan, the Great Commoner, then in his seventies but still sometimes called the Boy Orator of the Platte.

MONKEYS

Why the retired Bryan, a lifelong Presbyterian, turned his attention to fighting the teaching of evolution in the public schools in 1920 remains a little unclear, despite a thoughtful discussion of the subject in Edward Larson's fine book on the Scopes monkey trial, *Summer for the Gods.* As Larson notes, Bryan seems to have been affected by a 1916 study of religious beliefs on university campuses that highlighted the decline of students' faith as they progressed through college and were, presumably, influenced by the secularist teachings of their faculty.[9] The study captured the realities of American secularism, in 1916 as in 1876 a movement beginning with elites such as professors and making its way to the rest of society through mechanisms of diffusion such as the college classroom. It revealed that graduates were less likely to be believers after four years of higher education than when they entered. Yet although he clearly was looking for an arena in which to tackle secularism, Bryan did not take on the universities.

It is tempting to speculate that by challenging Darwinism in a self-described crusade, the old politician was choosing to attack secularism at what he considered its weakest link: its failure to convince ordinary people to abandon their attachment to biblical religion. As we shall see, when Bryan's audience is taken into account, this focus appears to have been prescient. Although Bryan was no expert on the details of the biological and geological arguments for or against evolution, he had a finely honed instinct for popular beliefs, and he knew that the Bible remained the centerpiece of American religious thought and experience.[10] Darwinian evolution so blatantly contradicted the familiar Genesis story that the ordinary churchgoer, unfamiliar with the sophisticated apologetics of Christian modernism, would think that either Darwinism or the Bible could be true, but not both. By railing against evolution, Bryan could position himself as a champion of the Bible. To many ordinary people, that was exactly what he remained, regardless of elite interpretations of the trial that was to come.

Meanwhile, survival-of-the-fittest social Darwinism and the new "science" of eugenics[11] both made the moral consequences of Darwinism look exceedingly nasty, as Bryan clearly recognized. Both could be made to reflect the dark underside of secularism's elitist character, since social Darwinism seemed to justify the accumulation of wealth by a favored few, and eugenics explicitly favored the breeding of a genetically superior master class. Whether Bryan knew it or not, the Darwinian theory of natural selection was still in flux in the years before 1920, from several decades of questioning within the scientific community.[12] Mendelian genetics had called into question whether natural selection was the true mechanism of evolution, and the synthetic realization that genetics actually provided the mechanism whereby natural selection occurred would not be solidified until the early 1930s.[13] Needless to say, neither the doubt about Darwinism nor its potential resolution had made its way into high school biology textbooks. They were more likely to reflect a crude Darwinian presentation of evolution as the survival of the fittest, intermingled with the social Darwinist baggage, commonplace in the period, applying the same eliminationist message to people, races, and ideas.

In any case, Bryan's crusade caught on quickly—perhaps even more in the lecture halls he filled than in the church pews where echoes of his message could be heard. He began lecturing against Darwinism in 1921, and by February of 1922 had already been invited to address the Kentucky legislature in support of a proposed law to ban the teaching of evolution in public schools. The fact that the Kentucky Baptists who had proposed the law were seeking to regulate the public secondary schools, not the university, must have seemed perfect to Bryan. Universities, in any case, were still refined environments to which the yeomen citizens of his traditional populist base had little or no access. Their children, however, all attended the public schools, which symbolized American values far better than did the goings-on in college classrooms. As Bryan knew from his years of political experience, the Bible and the schools made a potent combination. The public schools were therefore the ideal battleground for a fight about popular values, American symbols, and the Bible, still read daily in most schools.

The newly emerging fundamentalist movement wasted no time in jumping on Bryan's bandwagon, which offered them the opportunity to galvanize support around an issue of wide appeal. Fundamentalism was engaged and energized by politics, a pattern that would recur later in its history. William Riley guided the WCFA into support for the anti-evolution crusade, which grew from 1922 to 1924 and eventually succeeded in early 1925 in passing legislation prohibiting the teaching of evolution in Tennessee. Bryan had toured the state, advocating such a bill in town halls or any spaces big enough to hold his audiences; once the legislation was introduced, the state became a focal point for fundamentalist and evangelical attention, culminating in a weeklong revival meeting run by the nationally prominent preacher Billy Sunday and attended by one out of every ten Tennesseans.[14] When local boosters in the small but aspiring town of Dayton, Tennessee, conspired to create a test case for the constitutionality of the law that would put Dayton on the map, the Scopes monkey trial was born.

Pitting the biblical literalist Bryan head-to-head against Clarence Darrow, who had succeeded Ingersoll as the nation's most outspoken secularist, the trial became a sensation, reported on the front pages of newspapers everywhere. Suitably enough for a confrontation invented as drama, the trial was to be repeated for another fifty years on stage and screen. In Dayton, secularism and fundamentalism brought the warfare of science and religion into American living rooms. The results were mixed. Although secularists believed they had won a major victory when Darrow used the familiar array of secularist arguments to force Bryan into equally familiar apologetics, the court ultimately enforced the anti-evolution law by convicting the schoolteacher John Scopes. Aided by Darrow's own atheism, evangelicals, for their part, succeeded in associating science with radical religious denial. In retrospect, Darrow's "victory" would be the last gasp of strong secularism in America.

The facts of the trial are relatively well established. When the Tennessee law came into effect, the New York–based American Civil Liberties Union decided to challenge its constitutionality on the ground that it violated teachers' freedom of speech. From the ACLU perspective, which was religiously skeptical but not yet ardently secularist, the law infringed on academic liberty, which was becoming the norm in most prominent universities. The ACLU then embarked on a historic process of expanding constitutional free speech rights in the courts, challenging, with varying success, the restrictive laws that had come out of the World War I obsession with subversive antiwar speech at home.[15] The Tennessee anti-evolution law, the first and only one of its kind at the time, must have looked vulnerable to a constitutional challenge in an era when the courts were increasingly saying that free speech could be limited only when there was a clear and present danger to public security. The ACLU published an advertisement in the Tennessee newspapers offering to put up the money for prosecution and defense if anyone would come forward and be prosecuted for teaching evolution. The burghers of Dayton accepted the offer and convinced Scopes to agree to stand trial in a test case.

For its part, the WCFA saw the trial as an opportunity to continue the momentum it had begun to build by attaching itself to Bryan's anti-evolution crusade. It was the WCFA that got Bryan to agree to join the prosecution in the case as an adviser, a move that immediately raised the case's national profile. It remained only for Clarence Darrow to be drawn to the flame for the case to become a confrontation between religion and secularism.[16]

Darrow did not share the ACLU's plans to focus on free speech, which was not one of his pet issues. The sixty-eight-year-old Darrow was known nationally for his aggressive "agnostic" secularism, for his masterful defense of labor leaders and unions against prosecution by capitalist-dominated government, and, most recently, for convincing a Chicago jury to spare the lives of Leopold and Loeb, two young men of good family who murdered another man in a bizarre attempt to assert their will to power over him. Although the ACLU itself probably would not have consented to Darrow's very public offer to represent Scopes, the young teacher's local counsel (himself an eccentric Louisiana State University law professor) accepted Darrow's offer almost as soon as it was made.[17] Following advice of then Harvard law professor Felix Frankfurter, the ACLU tried to maneuver Darrow out of the job, but keeping Darrow out of a high publicity case like this one was hopeless.[18] To its own surprise, the ACLU found itself footing the bill for a case in which the free speech issue became distinctly secondary to a front-page battle between the new fundamentalism and radical, antireligious secularism.

THE CURIOUS FAILURE OF STRONG SECULARISM

The fight between Bryan and Darrow that followed was both old-fashioned and profoundly up to the moment. Both Bryan and Darrow were relics of the pre–World War I world, the former of populism infused by religious faith, the latter of the kind of strong secularism that declared flat-out that the Bible was bunk. Both had made their careers as much in the lecture hall as in the courtroom or the political convention. In the Scopes trial, the meeting of famous lecturers, public schools, and that perennial favorite, the Bible, made for a uniquely potent, self-publicizing brew. For Bryan and Darrow, this was a last hurrah. With the widespread availability of the radio just around the corner, they belonged to the last generation of famous public lecturers. Elite national religious leaders were as embarrassed by the old-fashioned tenor of Bryan's unstudied biblical literalism as the national progressive establishment was by Darrow's "Victorian" attacks on religion.[19]

Yet despite Bryan's age and outdated political sensibilities, he managed to strike a deeply resonant chord with his anti-evolution campaign. Not only had the crusade made gains in the South, but the new fundamentalist movement had hitched itself to Bryan precisely because it saw the popular appeal of the anti-evolution position. The source of this appeal did not lie in any well-developed theological position of the kind that the WCFA leaders possessed or that *The Fundamentals* had articulated in writing. The attraction of Bryan's stance, and perhaps ultimately of fundamentalism, lay in its rejection of top-down elitism and its embrace of plainspoken, ordinary belief. The public who rallied in support of Tennessee's anti-evolution law were resisting the idea that their most basic beliefs about how the world was ordered could be countermanded by scientific fiat. No one whom the ordinary Tennessean knew personally could explain exactly why it should now be accepted that man was descended from the apes. But the textbooks said so, and it was understood that an educated person should believe it.

The cognitive dissonance created by the tension between evolution and received religious opinion was awaiting resolution; with his national prestige and his ear for populist politics, Bryan was the man for the job. His anti-evolution crusade told ordinary people that they could stand up to the theory that the elites were pressing upon them and that they could use the power of laws, which they as a majority controlled, to reject the implausible new beliefs. Far from being out of date, this message could not have been more current to a population who sensed dimly that their society and even their religion were shifting under them as they modernized to accommodate skepticism and science.

Darrow's message was timely in a different way. The religiously skeptical point of view had gained currency among educated Americans, as the 1916 study of college campuses revealed. If in the 1870s Darwinism was still controversial, by 1925 educated Americans would have agreed that evolution was a scientific fact and that religion would just have to accommodate it or disappear. In 1865, when Cornell University was founded, it was still a major innovation for a university not to reflect, however liberally, some sectarian religious viewpoint; in 1925, every prominent American university assumed that its scholars in nearly all departments operated within an intellectual framework given by science and reason. Religion had not been rejected entirely by American elites; modernist Christianity remained the official creed of the better churches, and Protestant zeal of a new, forward-thinking sort could be found in the temperance movement[20] and even Midwestern progressive politics. But dogmatic religious faith was an embarrassing relic of the past, not a trend for the future. Educated Americans reading about the Scopes trial assumed that the people of Tennessee must be pretty backward if they thought they could reverse the course of evolution by legislating against it. The journalists who covered the Scopes trial for the national (and especially the Northern) press brought home the image of Tennessee hicks; apparently elitism extended to journalists, who at the time might not have been university-educated but who shared at least some of the social attitudes of their better-educated readers, and were eager to pass those attitudes along to the rest of their audience.[21]

By poking fun at Bryan, whom he lured onto the stand with the prospect of testifying to the Bible's truth in front of the entire nation, Darrow allied his radical secularism with the attitude of superiority that characterized educated American elites' view of traditional religion. Darrow's arguments were fifty years old—he relied on White and Draper, and challenged Bryan to explain how Joshua could have made Earth stand still without causing earthquakes or other terrestrial disasters—but his dismissive assumption that the Bible could not possibly be the literal truth was by now broadly shared by American elites. Darrow's contempt for religion in any form distinguished him from the educated norm, which was not prepared to jettison the social values of religion altogether. But Darrow's cross-examination of Bryan did stand, in the mind of the educated public, as a symbolic nail in the coffin of the popular dogmatic faith on whose behalf Bryan made his last public stand. The Great Commoner, on this reading, was also the Great Loser of his era in American history. First his rurally oriented political populism was defeated by urban capital; then his equally backwater, equally popular religious dogmatism was beaten by the triumphant science of the elites.

This interpretation of the Scopes trial as a victory for science—an interpretation suggested by at least some of the Northern press at the time, made standard by history books in the 1930s,[22] and implicitly adopted by the play and later the film *Inherit the Wind*—misses much of what the trial meant for the relationship between religion and government in the United States. The first crucial fact of the trial was that Darrow's client lost. The court upheld the constitutionality of the anti-evolution statute and convicted Scopes, who was assessed a $100 fine by a judge eager to avoid making a martyr out of him. The Supreme Court of Tennessee, after an eighteen-month delay, affirmed the constitutionality of the statute, explaining that the law did not restrict teachers' freedom of speech, since it applied to them only in their official capacities. Using a legal stratagem designed to keep the case out of the U.S. Supreme Court, the Tennessee court then vacated the conviction on the equally questionable theory that it had been a mistake for the judge to impose the fine himself rather than submitting the question of punishment to the jury, as Tennessee law required. The case ended there, and it singularly failed to become a legal precedent of any importance. Today, no casebook of church-state legal decisions bothers to give the text of the opinion, which is assumed to be irrelevant to students of the subject. In fact, notwithstanding the notoriety of the trial on stage and screen, a typical course on church and state in American constitutional law would never bother to mention Scopes at all.

Symbolically, fundamentalists gained ground from the enormous publicity associated with the trial. In evolution they had found a reliable enemy, one they would be able to exploit periodically until today, often with remarkable popular success. The anti-evolution movement has in recent years shifted its emphasis from opposing the teaching of evolution to demanding equal time for creationism, recast as "creation science." Yet the populist wellsprings remain the same: the intuitive implausibility of the scientific elites' claim of human descent from "lower species," coupled with evolution's obvious incompatibility with biblical literalism. Even the Southern geographical focus of creationist fundamentalism has not changed, although fundamentalism can now be found as much in suburbs and exurbs as in the rural South. While fundamentalism did not burgeon into the powerful national movement that it is today until the 1970s, neither did it disappear in the wake of the Scopes trial, as secularists imagined that it would. Instead, fundamentalism retreated from the national scene and began a slow process of building itself up until the time would come for its re-emergence.

For strong secularism of Darrow's triumphalist, antireligious variety, however, the Scopes trial arguably was a defining moment: it marked the movement's last gasp of national prominence before it disappeared into oblivion. In 1925, Darrow could still enjoy at least the implicit, snickering support of agnostic journalists. H. L. Mencken, Baltimore-based but nationally syndicated, came down clearly on Darrow's side, warning of the "Neanderthal man" who was "organizing in these forlorn backwaters of the land, led by fanatics, rid of sense and devoid of conscience."[23] But with the Second World War just ahead, secularism of the antireligious type was soon to disappear from mainstream American society, to be replaced by a new complex of ideas that focused on secularizing the state, not on secularizing society. Between 1926 and 1950, church membership nationwide grew 59.8 percent, while the population went up just 28.6 percent[24]—this despite a dip in mainline church membership during the Great Depression. The overall growth in membership corresponded to a decline in the public respectability of strong secularism.

To put it simply, Ingersoll and Darrow failed to convince many others that religion was a fraud. Eventually their view became profoundly unfashionable, as organized religion not only refused to disappear but became stronger and stronger. Writing in 1955, the sociologist Will Herberg marveled at Ingersoll's onetime political prominence: "Today that would be quite inconceivable; a professed 'unbeliever' would be anathema to either of the big parties and would have no chance whatever in political life."[25]

Why did strong secularism fail to achieve its professed twin goals of freeing the American mind from the baleful influence of religion and reordering the relationship between government and religion in America? Part of the answer is that mainline American religion rose to the challenge that science posed to traditional faith by offering a reconciliation of the two. By allowing for an allegorical reinterpretation of Scripture that was consistent with the pervasive influence of science and technology, liberal Christianity made it unnecessary for college students exposed to Darwinism or psychology to abandon their belief in God. For organized religion to survive in America, God-centered theology had to take a backseat to pragmatic, community-centered concerns—and it was prepared to do so, giving way to a social gospel that focused on human concerns and minimized the role of theology.

Strong secularism had always attacked religion for opposing scientific inquiry, so when mainstream organized religion stopped resisting, the most important weapon in the secularists' assault began to miss its mark. Moreover, as we shall see in the next chapter, the nonsectarian Christianity that remained in the schools through World War II and the early Cold War proved itself easily accommodating to the patriotic battles against Nazism and communism. To be antireligious could suddenly be depicted as Communist sympathy, since Marx had, after all, been a strong secularist who condemned religion as the opiate of the masses.

But perhaps more than these other factors, strong secularism failed both ideologically and politically in America because it could not overcome its self-imposed burden of elitism. Darrow's rhetorical victories over Bryan, if such they were, resonated with people who looked down on religion as uneducated, backward, and popular. The better universities remained environments in which agnostic or atheist professors trained new elites in a form of scientific skepticism, which, starting in the 1930s, moved beyond Darwinism to equally atheist Freudian psychology.[26] But as university education gradually expanded to include institutions that were, by sheer virtue of their numbers, less and less elite, the degree of indoctrination (or enlightenment, if you prefer) declined. Strong secularism could not get the Bible or public prayer out of the schools because it could not convince the majority of the people that this was worth doing.

From the birth of Progressivism through the 1930s, left-oriented elites believed that the way to spread their views and values was through popular politics. Progressives were the many; conservatives the beleaguered few. Legislatures, motivated by electoral pressures, passed progressive laws and eventually Congress enacted the New Deal; old judges, waving the Constitution, struck down laws governing wages, hours, working conditions, and labor organization as violating a right they called "the liberty of contract," which could not be found written anywhere in the constitutional text but which meant, in practice, that Republicans could stand in the way of economic reforms. Difficult as it may be to imagine today, judicial restraint was then the battle cry of the left rather than the right, and Progressives rarely looked to the federal courts for help in promoting their policies.

Gradually, though, Progressives who were also strong secularists came to realize that, while their ideas for economic redistribution were finding favor with a desperate public, their beliefs about religion were going nowhere fast. What secularists needed for their views on church and state to prevail was a solution to the problem of the unpopularity of secularism itself. As we shall see in the next chapter, they found one.

5

⁂

THE COURTS AND
THE RISE OF
LEGAL SECULARISM

On October 22, 1844, the world failed to end. What to other Americans was just another ordinary day, the sun setting and also rising, was life-transforming for the followers of William Miller, who had come to believe that the Advent was upon them. In the wake of what skeptics called their Great Disappointment, the Millerites split into various smaller millennialist groups emphasizing intense missionary work, biblical interpretation weighted toward the Old Testament, and—hope springs eternal—an imminent apocalypse. One of these groups was to become the Witnesses of Jehovah, formally founded in 1872, and numbering some three hundred thousand in the United States by the end of World War II.[1]

Despite the world's disdain, the Witnesses clung to their belief that the end was near and displayed a corresponding uncompromising commitment to keeping the essentials of their faith pure. Among their other principles, the Witnesses maintained a steady vigilance against the sin of idolatry. Their strictly defined position on the subject would eventually land them in the middle of a national outrage: World War II was looming, and the Witnesses would not salute the flag.

THE WITNESSES IN THE COURTS

In the patriotic atmosphere of the pre–World War II period, some new customs, like a daily flag salute, were introduced into the public schools. To the Witnesses the practice seemed idolatrous. In particular, the Witnesses believed that the outward extending of the right arm—a form of salute oddly reminiscent of the National Socialists' straight arm—was no better than bowing down to a false idol: it violated the commandment "Thou shalt have no other gods before me."[2]

This religious interpretation of the civic practice of flag saluting captured something significant about the emergence of ritualized patriotism in America. The public schools had always been devoted to the inculcation of republican ideals. Over the first half of the twentieth century, however, a self-conscious patriotism had entered the curriculum. America's involvement in the First World War had generated a degree of self-definition over and against the European world, and this American intervention on the world stage had corresponded neatly to the enormous—and enormously diversifying—emigration from Southern and Eastern Europe that took place between 1880 and 1920. The schools took as their task the Americanization of the new immigrants, and part of that process involved the development of a distinctive American patriotic ideology.

Unlike earlier Irish immigrants, who spoke English and could be mapped onto a familiar Anglo-American pattern of Protestant-Catholic relations, the Italian, Polish, and Jewish immigrants of this period represented a kind of foreignness even more exaggerated than that which had been attributed to Irish Catholics. The American racial strategy before World War II was to exclude Asians, keep African Americans subordinate, and deny Latinos citizenship while drawing on their labor when the economy needed it. The corresponding ethnic strategy was to Americanize European immigrants, who at the turn of the century were conceived as distinctive "races" but by the time of the war were universally considered white. Patriotism in the schools was part of the Americanization project, and after the United States entered the war, it became all the more important to marshal all of America's new ethnicities (though not, to be sure, its races) to the war effort.

By refusing to salute the flag, and by impugning the practice as idolatry, the Witnesses in effect denounced war patriotism as irreligious. The problem was not simply that the Witnesses were opposing the war; indeed, before Pearl Harbor, when the first of the flag salute cases arose, most of the mainstream American denominations, horrified by the carnage of World War I, had opposed U.S. involvement in the war already being fought in Britain and Europe. Once the United States was at war and the mainstream denominations had reversed their position, however, the Witnesses' implicit suggestion that it was wrong to put nation before God sounded threatening. The perceived need for national unity was especially acute because the country had been divided about entering the war just a short time before.

The popular response to the Witnesses' protest was immediate and vituperative. Children who would not salute the flag were expelled from school. Protests were held outside Witnesses' homes. Witness missionaries were attacked on the streets.[3] Faced with this sort of concerted harassment, and with no hope of aid from the local authorities who had started the ball rolling with the school suspensions, Witnesses turned to the federal courts. In defense of their refusal, they argued that being compelled to salute the flag violated their liberty of conscience and freedom of speech.

To win an exemption from the flag salute in the federal courts, the Witnesses needed to clear two different legal hurdles. The First Amendment said that "Congress shall make no law" prohibiting free exercise of religion. Before they could argue that their free exercise had been violated, the Witnesses first had to convince the courts that the Free Exercise Clause applied to a situation in which not Congress but a state government was requiring them to salute.

Traditionally, church-state debates had been state-level affairs since the framing of the First Amendment, with occasional exceptions for anomalous issues like Sunday mail service or the cynical Blaine amendment. The Supreme Court had gradually begun to hold in the previous decades that some of the restrictions the Bill of Rights imposed on Congress applied to the states, because the Fourteenth Amendment said that no state could abridge "the privileges and immunities" of U.S. citizens, but the Court had not yet applied the Free Exercise Clause to the states.

Even if the Court was ready to "incorporate" the First Amendment so as to apply it to a local school board's actions, though, the Witnesses would still have to convince the Court that saluting the flag actually violated their freedom of religious exercise. That would require the Supreme Court to intervene in the affairs of the school board that mandated the pledge and the salute and to take the side of the unpatriotic Witnesses at a time when the need for national unity seemed most pressing. In the spring of 1940, when the first of the flag salute cases reached the Supreme Court, the Justices were willing to meet the Witnesses partway. In the case of *Minersville School District v. Gobitis*, they agreed that the Constitution required the states, as much as Congress, to respect the freedom of religion, but they concluded that the state was not violating religious liberty by requiring students to participate in patriotic exercises designed to "secur[e] effective loyalty to the traditional ideals of democracy."[4]

The extension of the Free Exercise Clause to the states (which technically took place two weeks before the first flag salute case was decided, in a separate case also involving Jehovah's Witnesses[5]) fundamentally transformed the face of church-state relations in America. For the first time in its history, the Supreme Court assumed the responsibility—and the power—to draw the boundary between permitted government action and guaranteed religious liberty. With *Brown v. Board of Education* still fourteen years in the future, the popular image of the Supreme Court as the ultimate protector of basic liberties had not yet emerged. To the contrary, the Supreme

Court had historically intervened in state affairs primarily to strike down legislation that limited workers' hours and protected their health and safety. Progressives, therefore, still looked with concern on the idea that the Supreme Court would overrule state laws it considered unconstitutional. The legacy of constitutional review by conservative judges obscured the potentially revolutionary effects of the doctrine for those who sought to expand individual liberties.

Notwithstanding its willingness to consider the Witnesses' claims against their local school boards, the Court in 1940 was not prepared to reinstate the Witnesses' children and exempt them from the obligatory salute. The Court's decision in the *Gobitis* case was written by Justice Felix Frankfurter, who was completing his first full year as a Justice, having filled the Court's so-called Jewish seat in 1939 with the retirement of Justice Benjamin Cardozo. Frankfurter had been, and remained while on the Court, a close associate of President Franklin Delano Roosevelt, and he had been instrumental in crafting the policies and goals of the New Deal. He was also, like many American Jews of his age, an immigrant to the United States, fiercely loyal to his adopted country, and deeply concerned about the rise of Nazism and the threat it posed to European Jewry. The only naturalized citizen to have served on the Court before or since, Frankfurter had come from Austria with his parents at the age of twelve.

Frankfurter left no doubt either about the importance of the protection of religious liberty or about the competing concern of allowing schools to teach unifying American patriotic values. His own patriotism was a product of New York public schools, in which the Americanization process had reached its most developed form. For Frankfurter, saluting the flag was not an empty gesture but an object lesson in the creation of responsible citizenship. "The ultimate foundation of a free society is the binding tie of cohesive sentiment," he wrote, and symbols were an integral part of creating the social cohesion necessary to sustain freedom. More to the point, cohesion meant a common national identity that excluded no one: "the flag is the symbol of our national unity, transcending all internal differences, however large, within the framework of the Constitution."[6] The theme of nonexclusion would become crucial to Frankfurter's thinking about the role of religion in public schools, where, he fervently believed, young Americans must be taught what they had in common, not what made them different. In a time when Jews had just been segregated from formerly integrated schools in Germany and in Frankfurter's native Austria, Frankfurter preferred to allow American public schools to insist on treating everybody the same.

The difficulty, of course, was that unlike German Jews who were differentiated against their will by Nazi racial laws (modeled, ironically enough, on America's own Jim Crow regulations), the Witnesses wanted to preserve their distinctness to the extent it was necessary to defend their religious scruples. Only one member of the Supreme Court dissented from the decision, but in his dissent, Justice Harlan Fiske Stone, the New Hampshire–born Republican who was soon to become Chief Justice, explained bluntly that the mandatory salute "seeks to coerce these children to express a sentiment which, as they interpret it, they do not entertain, and which violates their deepest religious convictions." Reaching for historical precedent, Stone claimed that the law in question was "unique in the history of Anglo-American legislation."[7]

Here Stone overstated the case. The overt requirement of an expression of loyalty, even against conscience, was in fact all too common in Anglo-American legal history. Stone's strongest argument was forward-looking rather than tradition-based: "there are other ways to teach loyalty and patriotism which are the sources of national unity, than by compelling the pupil to affirm that which he does not believe."[8] Compelling expressions of loyalty could not properly be understood to promote national unity. The "religious freedom of small minorities"—the Witnesses, and by implication, Jews—must be preserved.[9]

Mentioning minorities had special significance for Stone, who just a couple of years earlier had proposed, in the most famous and consequential footnote in American constitutional history, that the Supreme Court should be especially vigilant in reviewing laws that seemed to disadvantage "discrete and insular minorities."[10] In the context of the flag salute case, Stone must have meant to refer obliquely to a possible parallel between oppressed European Jews and the marginalized Witnesses. Not coincidentally, Stone was breaking new ground in thinking about the rights of religious dissenters as a species of the rights of minorities more generally. Although the association seems natural today, earlier discussions of religious liberty in America typically imagined the religious dissenter as an isolated Protestant individual with idiosyncratic beliefs, not as a member of a community of persons deserving special protection. Now, with Jews evidently vulnerable as a religious minority in Europe, and a Jewish community present and increasingly visible in the United States, it was becoming natural to think of religious minorities as communally distinct and vulnerable.

In 1940, however, Stone lost, and the effect of the majority's decision allowing the compulsory salute in the *Gobitis* case was to send Americans the message that dissent from the rituals of patriotism was a threat to national unity. In the days after the decision was announced, attacks on Witnesses increased, and hundreds were assaulted, some brutally.[11] In less overtly violent jurisdictions across the country, local school boards adopted new rules mandating the teaching of patriotic subjects. With the entry of the United States into the war, rituals of patriotism increased, subjecting Witnesses in other places to the requirement of saluting. A month after Pearl Harbor, the West Virginia State Board of Education adopted a rule that required saluting the flag and ominously directed teachers to punish refusal as an "act of insubordination."[12] This time several other groups, including the PTA, the Scouts, and the Federation of Women's Clubs, objected that the "stiff-arm" salute accompanying the Pledge of Allegiance was "too much like Hitler's."[13] But only the Witnesses refused to perform it, and only their children were expelled from school.

In the two years since the first flag salute case, President Roosevelt had named three new members to the Supreme Court.[14] Now the Witnesses decided to try their luck in federal court again, in *West Virginia State Board of Education v. Barnette.* This time the Court went the other way, quoting now–Chief Justice Stone in his *Gobitis* dissent to show that there was no reason for the state to coerce anyone to make a public profession with which he disagreed. The Court also reframed the case as one about free speech rather than the free exercise of religion—although the Witnesses' motivation not to salute the flag was religious, the Court said, a nonreligious motivation would have been just as good a reason not to be compelled to speak out against one's will. "Public education," the Court said, must be "faithful to the ideal of secular instruction and political neutrality," and therefore "will not be partisan or enemy of any class, creed, party, or faction."[15]

This was the first time in the Court's history that it said anything about the "secular" character of instruction in public schools, but this passing reference mattered less for the opinion than did the insistence on "political neutrality," which can be understood only as a repudiation of Justice Frankfurter's argument that the schools were an appropriate place for teaching unity and patriotism. The Court went further: "to believe that patriotism will not flourish if patriotic ceremonies are voluntary and spontaneous instead of a compulsory routine is to make an unflattering estimate of the appeal of our institutions to free minds."[16] The unflattering estimate, it seemed, was the position the Court had taken in *Gobitis.* The Court built to a rousing rhetorical finish: "If there is any fixed star in our constitutional constellation, it is that no official, high or petty, can prescribe what shall be orthodox in politics, nationalism, religion, or other matters of opinion or force citizens to confess by word or act their faith therein. If there are any circumstances which permit an exception, they do not now occur to us."[17]

Intuitively obvious as this proposition now seems, it was actually an innovation in official rhetoric about what government could or could not do. Although in theory it had long been well established that no American would be compelled to speak or act against his religious principles, in practice, nonsectarian Christianity frequently required citizens to participate in a range of religiously inflected public practices whether they liked it or not. The Lord's Prayer and Bible reading were still staples of the school day. The curriculum in the schools did, to some degree, prescribe "what shall be orthodox" in matters ranging from science to civics, and continued to do so even after the ringing declaration of the Supreme Court in the *Barnette* case. With these words, however, the Court wrote the script for the movement that was to become legal secularism. The state must not "prescribe" in the area of religion. In context, that meant only that government could not force citizens to adopt a certain belief or form of words. In the future, however, it would be expanded to claim that the government must itself remain neutral on questions of religion.

In order to chart the way that legal secularism grew from the Court's protection of the rights of the Witnesses in the *Barnette* case, we must first consider Justice Frankfurter's response to the Court's reversal of the decision he had authored just two years before. Two other Justices who remained from the earlier Court, Justices Owen Roberts and Stanley Reed, stated without opinion that they adhered to their earlier decision. Frankfurter, however, wrote alone, in a dissent that surely numbers among the most remarkable documents anywhere in the four-hundred-plus volumes of the *United States Reports.* This dissent, and its explicit engagement with Frankfurter's Jewishness, begins to reveal the role of religious diversity in the growth of legal secularism. Frankfurter's constitutional views did not prevail, but his concern for the integration of religious minorities into the project of American national unity set the tone for an entire movement.

FRANKFURTER AND THE QUESTION OF
RELIGIOUS MINORITIES

Pained by the Court's reversal of his opinion from just two years before, and by the implication that his earlier decision had authorized religious oppression, Frankfurter began by calling attention to his Jewish immigrant heritage—a rhetorical move attempted neither before nor since in an opinion of the Supreme Court: "One who belongs to the most vilified and persecuted minority in history is not likely to be insensible to the freedoms guaranteed by our Constitution. Were my purely personal attitude relevant I should whole-heartedly associate myself with the general libertarian views in the Court's opinion, representing as they do the thought and action of a lifetime. But as judges we are neither Jew nor Gentile, neither Catholic nor agnostic. We owe equal attachment to the Constitution and are equally bound by our judicial obligations whether we derive our citizenship from the earliest or the latest immigrants to these shores."[18] The first sentence in particular upset some Justices who saw Frankfurter's draft.[19] Why would Frankfurter, writing in the midst of World War II and so concerned about the importance of national unity, draw attention to his Jewish minority status in this self-dramatizing manner? This was, after all, just another Supreme Court case, and while the Court does not overturn its recent decisions every day, such a thing was hardly unprecedented.

The Justices' notes reveal that Justice Frank Murphy—the Court's lone Catholic—urged Frankfurter to modify the highly personal remarks, but Frankfurter adamantly refused.[20] Frankfurter did not take tradition lightly. In fact, he worshipped the notion of what he liked to call "the Anglo-American legal tradition" with the profound love of an immigrant and adopted son, and his opinions are liberally sprinkled with references to the importance of continuing and extending that legal past into the future. The fact that he now insisted on departing from the well-established practice of keeping personal references out of judicial opinions suggests the depth of feeling that accompanied his dissent in *Barnette* and makes it all the more important to consider the substance of the argument about church and state that he presented in the opinion. For Frankfurter, clearly, this was not just another case, but the most important he would face in his nearly two decades on the Court.

Some writers have understood Frankfurter's insistence that he, of all people, would not lightly consent to the oppression of a religious minority as an essentially defensive posture. The legal ground had shifted under Frankfurter's feet with the appointment of the new Justices and the looming ascendancy of a jurisprudence that emphasized the Court's responsibility to ensure individual liberties. On this reading, Frankfurter did not want it thought that he lacked the human feeling or progressive attitudes that seemed to motivate the majority in protecting the Witnesses from the mandatory flag salute.[21] In response to Stone's focus on the protection of minorities, now taken up by the majority of the Court, Frankfurter wanted to emphasize that he, as a member of a traditionally oppressed religious minority, was not reaching his decision through any lack of solicitude for another one.

No doubt some measure of defensiveness did enter Frankfurter's calculus—it must have, for Frankfurter to be willing to expose himself to the criticism of hypersensitivity to which he was often subjected during his life. But something deeper and more intellectually coherent than mere sensitivity motivated Frankfurter to invoke Jewish persecution alongside the dictum that "as judges we are neither Jew nor Gentile, neither Catholic nor agnostic." For Frankfurter, the *Barnette* case was fundamentally about the relationship between religion and American national identity, and in his view, the key to that relationship was transcendence of religious difference or particularity at the constitutional level, just as a school might seek to inculcate universal patriotic values at the curricular level. No wonder, then, that Frankfurter, unconsciously or otherwise, echoed Paul's statement in Galatians that "there is neither Jew nor Greek, there is neither bond nor free, there is neither male nor female: for ye are all one in Christ Jesus."[22] In Frankfurter's conception, all were one in their American citizenship; courts and schools alike must therefore treat all Americans the same.

For Frankfurter, the Witnesses' claim could best be understood as an argument to be treated differently. The Witnesses, according to this interpretation, were urging that their religious scruples must, under the Constitution, guarantee them an exception or "immunity" from "civic measures of general applicability." The law from which they sought exemption, in other words, had nothing to do with religion but simply was aimed to promote "good citizenship and national allegiance."[23]

Frankfurter made it clear that the state could under no circumstances demand that anyone profess allegiance to a religion. Nor could the government support "any mode of worship," or compel others to provide such support. Yet constitutionalizing this separation, as the framers had done, did not mean giving the individual dissenter the right to refuse to follow the law whenever he asserted that doing so would infringe on his conscience. "It never would have occurred to them to write into the Constitution the subordination of the general civil authority of the state to sectarian scruples."[24] The consequence of allowing such an exemption would be to subordinate law to religion. Worst of all, it would treat citizens differently depending upon their faith and so undermine any hope of a common system of law applying to all citizens. "There are in the United States more than 250 distinctive established religious denominations,"[25] Frankfurter said, any or all of which could raise objections to different legal requirements. The law would become a piecemeal affair, applying differently to different persons depending upon their religious beliefs.

Frankfurter foresaw the danger of a constitutional approach that would treat members of various religious denominations differently rather than the same. *This* was the lesson that he, as a Jew living in the era of Nazi persecution, believed he could understand more clearly than the other members of the Court, and this was the reason for pointing to the fact of his own Jewishness, even as he insisted that his personal perspective was irrelevant to his constitutional judgment. Government must pay no mind to religious difference if loyalty was to be universal.

That the law under review aimed to inculcate patriotism made the problem of constitutional division of the denominations all the more directly relevant. Allowing exceptions that would arguably deny the state the capacity to teach unity highlighted, for Frankfurter, the mistaken approach of the majority. How best to teach common values did not rest with the courts. Frankfurter was quick to acknowledge, as indeed he had done in the *Gobitis* decision, that in his personal opinion, patriotic citizenship could be taught without mandatory flag salutes. Libertarianism, or at least a focus on civil liberties, had indeed been "the thought and action of a lifetime" for Frankfurter. But in Frankfurter's view, values instruction was a matter for state government and local school boards.

In preferring to leave complex decisions of church and state affairs to legislatures, rather than courts, Frankfurter followed consistently the Progressive position of his entire career, according to which the courts must allow majorities the laws they wanted unless, under very limited circumstances, they violated a core set of basic and fundamental rights. Frankfurter could not countenance the way the new Roosevelt-appointed majority on the Court seemed prepared to blithely abandon the position of judicial restraint he and other Progressives had advocated for the previous forty years, during which Republicans had controlled the Court and used judicial review to overturn laws passed by progressive majorities.[26] In his *Barnette* dissent, Frankfurter saw the writing on the wall. He realized that for most judges, the argument for judicial restraint would turn out to have been little more than a tactic adopted by whatever party did not control five votes on the Supreme Court. Yet he himself, bound by his own vision of the restraint he believed necessary for a federal judge, stuck with his prior view, derived from the writings of Justice Oliver Wendell Holmes: the people, not the courts, must ultimately defend liberal rights. "Of course patriotism cannot be enforced by the flag salute. But neither can the liberal spirit be enforced by judicial invalidation of illiberal legislation . . . Reliance for the most precious interests of civilization, therefore, must be found outside of their vindication in courts of law."[27]

Today almost no liberals and very few professed conservatives would agree with this formulation, which for Frankfurter amounted to a profession of faith in the liberal character of American society. Today the standard view on left and right is that the liberal spirit is precisely "enforced by judicial invalidation of illiberal legislation," and that constitutional courts, not merely in the United States but also elsewhere in the world, must serve as guardians of liberty and equality, protecting fragile rights against the tyranny of the majority. Frankfurter did not deny that basic rights or decisions of profound national importance were involved in questions of church and state; he denied only that courts ought to be the venue for deciding them.

In *Barnette*, however, the die was cast. Although the Court avoided saying so by holding that the mandatory flag salute violated free speech, not free exercise of religion, it had opened the door to protecting the rights of religious minorities in the courts. Aware that they now had the opportunity to win in the courts what they could not win from legislative majorities, secularists turned to litigation and invented legal secularism. Their tactics were to prove so successful that eventually, unable to beat them, evangelicals would join them in looking to the courts to vindicate their views on the proper relationship between religion and government. One of the great political struggles in American life was about to go legal.

THE INVENTION OF THE JUDEO-CHRISTIAN

A rich and unresolved debate still circles around the question of whether postwar American religion—especially of the Protestant variety—was in some sense "secular," focused more on worldly relations and affairs than on inward faith. Whatever the answer, mid-century polls showed that nearly all Americans professed to believe in God. Politicians publicly espoused the importance and value of religious affiliation, which they expressly associated with the "American way of life."

With war's end, Americans began to look to their churches for a range of activities and associations that had seemed lower priority during the economic hard times that began in 1929 and lasted almost twenty years. The baby boom period saw enormous growth in the organizational and bureaucratic structures of individual churches and of denominations organized at the national or regional level. Individual congregations came to have not only Sunday schools but bowling teams, women's leagues, and teen groups. National offices of denominations such as the Presbyterians and the Methodists employed hundreds of office professionals to coordinate activities on a broad scale. The National Council of Churches was founded in 1950 "to promote greater unity among its 29 constituent bodies" and to participate in a World Council of Churches that aspired to become a kind of Protestant United Nations.[28] The religion of this era also incorporated a significant social dimension. Church membership, which rose to unprecedented levels, provided the idealized nuclear family and its 2.5 children not only a degree of spiritual succor, but, perhaps to a greater extent, a network of associations. Denominational background and social class remained closely linked, making church membership an important marker in a country where class hierarchies are forever in search of acknowledgment and validation.

Most important for the question of religion and government,

Americans of the 1950s developed a public language for speaking about religion in which they emphasized the importance of belonging to a church without specifying the beliefs that membership might entail. Dwight Eisenhower, recruited to run for the presidency in 1952 by Republicans and Democrats alike, was surely speaking as the embodiment of middle-of-the-road American ideology when he said, "Our government makes no sense unless it is founded in a deeply felt religious faith—and I don't care what it is." At just about the same time, the Supreme Court proclaimed that "we are a religious people whose institutions presuppose a Supreme Being."[29] The Court's dictum, more highfalutin than Eisenhower's, nonetheless suggested the same basic idea: that religion related somehow to American government, but that the details of that relation were better left unstated.

Communism had something to do with Americans' formulaic insistence on the importance of religion or God to their form of government. As the Cold War began, it became commonplace to speak of "godless communism" as the ultimate enemy of the American way of life. By implication, the American way of life was the opposite of godless. Congress's addition of the words "under God" to the Pledge of Allegiance in 1954 came as the result of a conscious campaign by a Catholic national organization, the Knights of Columbus, to add religious content to a civic ritual that had become central to the expression of national patriotism. The point was not lost on observers at the time: the nation without God was an incomplete expression of American values, insufficiently differentiated from Communist ideals that claimed to be themselves democratic and egalitarian. In 1956, Congress officially declared "In God We Trust" to be the national motto.[30]

Alongside the reaction against communism, however, another social force helped shape the public invocation of religion and God into something new and subtly different from the nonsectarian Christianity that had long been America's unofficial state religion. In the postwar era, American Jews appeared in a new light in the

American public imagination. No longer perceived as a curiosity, and less often seen in anti-Semitic terms as an alien presence, American Jews presented themselves as citizens with an equal claim on the symbols of American identity. The existence, for the first time, of a sizable and publicly acknowledged non-Christian minority of Americans required modification in the rhetoric of America as a Christian nation.

The presence of Jews in America was nothing new. A handful of mostly Spanish and Portuguese Jews had lived in the United States since before the founding; German Jews who came as part of the broader German immigration of the 1840s and '50s had quietly prospered, building businesses in department store retail sales and banking, and producing cabinet secretaries under both Roosevelts. But the large wave of Eastern European Jewish immigration in the years 1880 to 1920 had taken longer to assimilate itself, both because the latest Jewish immigrants were less wealthy and well educated than their predecessors, and because their greater numbers made them a noticeable target for anti-Semitism, which remained socially acceptable in polite circles until the war. Nazi anti-Semitism, however, succeeded in making the less extreme social variety unfashionable, even as Jewish immigrants' economic success pushed them up the class ladder. By the 1950s, with Jews increasingly present in elite universities as students, and gradually as faculty, the time had arrived for remodeling the ideology and rhetoric of nonsectarian Christianity. Not long before, it had been confidently said that America was a Christian nation. Now, in the 1950s, our heritage was reinvented as inclusive: America had been built, it was now increasingly said, on Judeo-Christian roots.[31]

The Massachusetts congressman and wit Barney Frank once quipped that he would understand what was meant by "Judeo-Christian" when he met one. For without doubt, the idea of ascribing Judeo-Christian traditions to American institutions depended on no historical reality and essentially co-opted a vague idea of Jewishness into a familiar array of symbols and ideals that had in the past always been identified as unapologetically Christian. From a skeptical standpoint, it would be easy to dismiss the rhetoric of Judeo-Christian origins as an easy move for Christians, who after all had always acknowledged the Hebrew Scriptures as the Old Testament, while rather harder for Jews, whose theological position had traditionally included denial of the religious validity of Christian faith.

Yet in context, the invention of the term "Judeo-Christian" signaled a remarkable openness on the part of the long-established American Christian majority, an openness unparalleled, for example, in Western Europe, where Christian and national identities remain deeply intertwined despite the decline of religious faith. It took more than a century of prejudice before America's Protestant Christian identity came to fully include American Catholics under the rubric of the "Christian nation." Arguably, many Protestants did not accept Catholics as entirely American until the election of John F. Kennedy to the presidency. By contrast, the acceptance of Jews as full participants in American identity came a relatively short time after most Protestant Americans took on board the fact that a significant number of Jews lived in America. To speak of a Judeo-Christian heritage was to engage in a creative misreading of the American past with the aim of retrospectively including Jews in the American national project. The goal of inclusiveness more than justified any historical anachronism involved.

Forcing Jews who sought to associate themselves with mainstream American identity to decide whether to embrace the term "Judeo-Christian" involved them in a complicated rethinking of their own ethnoreligious status. One of the most ambitious efforts to conceptualize the relation between Jewish and other religious identity in America came in the form of a classic book in the sociology of American religion: Will Herberg's 1955 best seller, *Protestant—Catholic—Jew*. Although framed as a general theory of religion in American society, Herberg's book can also be read as a fascinating attempt to raise Jewishness to a level of national prominence and permanence that it had not to that point achieved in American life.[32]

Herberg argued that the multiethnic mix that immigration had cast into the American melting pot had yielded three "religious" identities corresponding to Protestantism, Catholicism, and Judaism. These identities, Herberg predicted, would be more durable than the ethnic identities—Italian, Polish, Swedish, etc.—they had largely replaced.[33] Herberg's book was short on systematic statistics but long on brilliant theorizing. Some of the most convincing evidence was taken from studies finding that while fewer and fewer Americans married within their own ethnic group, the overwhelming majority of Protestants, Catholics, and Jews did marry within their own religious group.[34] More important, though, Herberg pointed to public rhetoric about the importance of religion—of whatever kind—to argue that the distinctively American version of "common faith" required the citizen to belong to one of the three religious "communions" for which he named his book: "three diverse, but equally legitimate, equally American, expressions of an over-all American religion, standing for essentially the same 'moral ideals' and 'spiritual values.' "[35]

As early as Tocqueville, keen observers had noticed that Americans seemed to believe that their various religious denominations shared a common morality; indeed, that idea lay at the very core of nonsectarian Christianity. Although Catholics often sought to differentiate themselves from this coercively inclusive conception by rejecting the nonsectarianism of the schools as covertly Protestant, the Protestant refusal to acknowledge Catholic difference eventually helped create a willingness on the part of Catholics to acknowledge their own values as shared. What Herberg did was update this conception and identify the shared values as not merely Christian, but Christian and Jewish both. The extraordinary thing about this analysis was that, as Herberg noted only toward the end of his book, America in 1955 was 66 percent Protestant, 26 percent Catholic, and just 3.5 percent Jewish.[36] For America to define itself as Judeo-Christian to accommodate just three and a half out of one hundred Americans was remarkable, to say the least. What was more, as Herberg noted almost casually, American Jews were the only one of what he called the three American "communions" whose identity was simultaneously religious *and* ethnic.[37] Herberg could just as plausibly have compared Jews to Italians and Poles, whom he assimilated into American Catholicism, as to Catholicism writ large. By focusing on Jewish religious identity, however, Herberg could compare American Judaism to religious denominations eight and twenty times bigger. The very title of his book achieved the effect of putting Judaism on a par with the Christian confessions that by his own account together comprised 92 percent of the American population.

Although Herberg did not use the term "Judeo-Christian" in the book, and he took pains to offer a historically accurate account of America's Christian origins, his work had the effect of making it seem natural to assume that the America of the 1950s was a country of Christians and Jews. The notion of Judeo-Christian origins responded to and further underscored the same imaginative conception. Much like the rhetoric of nonsectarian Christianity that it gradually displaced, the imagined ideal of a Judeo-Christian nation could be used to justify a series of familiar customs that had already taken root in schools and elsewhere in public life. In 1955, three-quarters of American Jews were concentrated in five big cities, and two out of five lived in greater New York. That meant that most of the country, most of the time, did not have to give much thought to adding Hanukkah songs to their Christmas carols. In big cities where there happened to be Jews, and especially New York, the new conception of Judeo-Christian identity justified the preservation of prayer in schools alongside some recognition of Jewish distinctiveness there.

Yet the recognition that America was not solely Christian, and the accompanying self-confidence of American Jews, came to play a more significant role in the development of legal secularism. Although American Jews had long played a quiet role in encouraging separation of church and state (Rabbi Isaac Wise, the man responsible more than anyone else for the transplantation of Reform Judaism to America, had been a founding member of the National Liberal League), they now increasingly were prepared to speak out publicly in favor of separation. The best strategy for American Jews was not, however, strong secularism, with its open hostility toward organized religion; such a stance would have been perceived as anti-Christian and would have been risky for American Jews eager to avoid open confrontation with the majority. Legal secularism offered the more attractive option of saying that religion was just fine, but that the law must draw a sharp line between religion and government. One of the purposes of the wall of separation between church and state, legal secularists argued, was to protect religious minorities—and to the extent that American Jews were full participants in American identity, there could be nothing inappropriate or unpatriotic in their calling for such separation in the interests of their own protection. Thus American Jews gradually began to play an important part in the development of the strategies of legal secularism beginning in the postwar era.

LEGAL SECULARISM IN THE COURTS

The earliest postwar sorties aimed at advancing legal secularism involved an intriguing coalition of anti-Catholic evangelicals, mainstream liberal Protestants, and fringe Christian groups such as the Seventh-Day Adventists and Christian Scientists. The original members of Protestants and Other Americans United for Separation of Church and State, founded in 1947 and still going strong, included members of all of these denominations.[38] The organization would grow to be one of the most important drivers of legal secularist litigation. It came into being in the course of one of the first important lawsuits in which legal secularists won from the

Supreme Court new declarations about the importance of separating church and state, even as they lost the particular case that they asked the Supreme Court to decide in their favor. The case was *Everson v. Board of Education of Ewing Township*, and the target of the litigation was a program that reimbursed parents for their children's bus fare to school, not only for public school transportation but also for children who attended Catholic parochial school.[39]

The background for the program was economic necessity. When the Depression hit, many clergy initially expected that the national crisis would turn Americans to religion. But no awakening took place; indeed, the best evidence suggests that organized religion, measured by church attendance and membership, declined during the Depression years, whether because of population displacement or other reasons.[40] Revival meetings, an important element in rural and small-town Protestant religion, often filled the social function of a mini-vacation for churchgoing folk, which may be one reason that such revivals faded as discretionary income shrank.

For Catholics, the crunch meant even greater hardship for those who wanted to send their children to the parochial schools that had proliferated in the previous decades. Even before the Depression, the Catholic church had had trouble sustaining its vast network of schools. Unable to attract government funding, Catholic leaders had, in the 1920s, hit on several strategies, all of which were tried independently in New York and elsewhere. One was to seek indirect government assistance: if the state would bus Catholic children to their schools, that would defray some of the costs of parochial education and enable children from a larger catchment area to attend. Failing that, the state could be asked to provide the Catholic schools with secular schoolbooks, the same ones that would otherwise be provided for students in the public schools. This suggestion had the added benefit of creating no extra direct costs for the taxpayer while relieving Catholics of the burden of paying doubly for their children's education, once in taxes and a second time in tuition.[41]

If there was no choice but to send children to the public schools, the state could alternatively be asked to release children from classes during school hours so that they might receive religious education, either in the school itself or nearby. "Released time," as it was called, arose in an economic environment in which Catholic leaders had to acknowledge that many of their flock could get religious education in no other way than in spare moments taken from the ordinary curriculum. Carving particular times out of the public school week for religious instruction was an imperfect substitute for a parochial school education, but it was better than nothing, and hard times made for compromise. Tried sporadically before the Depression, released time became the subject of statewide discussion in New York in the 1930s and was officially sanctioned by state law in 1940.[42]

Everson, which raised the busing issue only, was an unusual case in several respects, beginning with who brought it before the federal courts: an ordinary New Jersey taxpayer who objected to the idea that state funds were being used to support transportation to Catholic schools.[43] The plaintiff, in other words, could claim no injury to himself other than that some small-to-vanishing bit of his taxes was arguably being expended in support of religion. As a general matter, the door to the federal courts is closely guarded by the requirement that anyone presenting a claim have standing to sue, that is, be able to show direct personal injury of the kind sufficient to give him a stake in pursuing the case diligently. It was therefore remarkable for the Supreme Court to entertain a suit by an ordinary taxpayer alleging misuse of his funds in paying for school bus transportation. (Indeed, in subsequent cases, the Court has made it clear that only in the context of a potential violation of the Establishment Clause is the mere fact of taxpayer status enough to get a plaintiff into court.) A taxpayer suit is not only easy to bring, it also has a special symbolic significance, because it suggests that any person should be able to vindicate a public wrong that the government is committing. Allowing taxpayer standing in Establishment Clause cases practically invited legal secularists to turn to the courts to advance their claims.

Once the Supreme Court had decided to allow taxpayer standing to sue for a violation of the Establishment Clause, it also broke new ground by officially recognizing that the separation of church and state at the level of state government was now a requirement of the federal Constitution. The first step in this direction had already been taken six years earlier when the Court had ruled that the Free Exercise Clause applied to the states,[44] but because the incorporation of provisions of the Bill of Rights into the Fourteenth Amendment's state-regulating ambit was occurring piecemeal, each extension had its own historical significance. In order to justify its entrance into the realm of regulating the relationship between government and religion in the states, which had long been the province of state legislatures following majoritarian political forces, the Court had to say something about why separation of church and state was important, a topic it had previously addressed just once in more than 150 years of Supreme Court opinions—in the Mormon polygamy decision.[45]

The *Everson* opinion was written by Justice Hugo Black, the sole Southern Baptist on the Court and, on the face of it, not the most likely man to become the judicial godfather of legal secularism. Black's populist Alabama roots had led him from a youthful Klan membership to the ranks of the New Deal loyalists in the Senate, and Roosevelt had put him on the Court despite a dearth of judging experience.[46] Faced with the challenge of explaining in a nutshell the American practice of separating church and state, Black argued that the overarching purpose of the Establishment Clause was to protect religious minorities from persecution. The events of World War II and what had not yet come to be called the Holocaust cannot have been far from Black's mind, because he set out to describe religious persecution as a peculiarly European disease. In Europe, he explained, "[w]ith the power of government supporting them, at various times and places, Catholics had persecuted Protestants, Protestants had persecuted Catholics, Protestant sects had persecuted other Protestant sects, Catholics of one shade of belief had persecuted Catholics of another shade of belief, and all of these had from time to time persecuted Jews. In efforts to force loyalty to whatever religious group happened to be on top and in league with the government of a particular time and place, men and women had been fined, cast in jail, cruelly tortured, and killed."[47] Early in American history, Black continued, this European plague of religious persecution was "transplanted to and began to thrive in the soil of the new America" through religious establishments that required everyone "to support and attend" and that were "accompanied by a repetition of many of the old world practices and persecutions." Dissenters, according to Black's narrative, were "persecuted because they steadfastly persisted in worshipping God only as their own consciences dictated"; they were also "compelled to pay tithes and taxes to support government-sponsored churches whose ministers preached inflammatory sermons designed to strengthen and consolidate the established faith by generating a burning hatred against dissenters."[48]

The cure for the persecution disease, said Justice Black, was the separation of church and state, which came into being because persecution "became so commonplace as to shock the freedom-loving colonials into a feeling of abhorrence. The imposition of taxes to pay ministers' salaries and to build and maintain churches and church property aroused their indignation. It was these feelings which found expression in the First Amendment."[49] Black was right to emphasize the role that coercive taxation had played in the minds of those who supported nonestablishment at the state and later the federal level. But describing the nonestablishment movement as a result of a historical "shock" in response to widespread persecution said much more about Black's own motives and those of his colleagues on the postwar Supreme Court than it did about eighteenth-century America.

As we have seen, the period of the framing was not characterized by general religious persecution so much as by increased confidence on the part of religious dissenters who did not want to pay taxes to support worship with which they disagreed; neither they nor their more enlightened supporters like Madison and Jefferson experienced any moment of shock surrounding what was, after all, a long-established practice. By contrast, recognition of the extent of Nazi persecution in Europe had indeed produced a shock to reasonable American minds by 1947 and was playing a real part in pushing Black and his colleagues to believe that the federal Constitution should be interpreted to protect religious minorities. When Justice Black quoted Madison and Jefferson on the importance of the liberty of conscience, as he went on to do in the opinion, he read them through the lens of the Holocaust and concluded that the reason to protect conscience was to protect minorities from violent persecution. For the framers, however, the motivation had run in the opposite direction: the reason to prohibit government coercion in the realm of religion was to protect individual conscience from self-contradiction and sin.

Having grounded the separation of church and state on a foundation of avoiding religious persecution, Black went on to announce, in the absolutist terms that he favored in constitutional interpretation, what was to become the credo of legal secularism:

> Neither a state nor the Federal Government can set up a church. Neither can pass laws which aid one religion, aid all religions, or prefer one religion over another. Neither can force nor influence a person to go to or to remain away from church against his will or force him to profess a belief or disbelief in any religion. No person can be punished for entertaining or professing religious beliefs or disbeliefs, for church attendance or non-attendance. No tax in any amount, large or small, can be levied to support any religious activities or institutions, whatever they may be called, or whatever form they may adopt to teach or practice religion. Neither a state nor the Federal Government can, openly or

secretly, participate in the affairs of any religious organizations or groups and vice versa. In the words of Jefferson, the clause against establishment of religion by law was intended to erect "a wall of separation between Church and State."[50]

Then, surprisingly enough, Black concluded that reimbursing parents for transportation to Catholic schools did not violate the wall of separation between church and state at all.

Four Justices dissented, astonished that after declaring that no tax could be levied to support religious activities of any kind, the majority could then conclude that the reimbursement plan was constitutional. For Black, however, and for the Court, the fact that the reimbursement reached every parent made it similar to the protection afforded by the police or fire department—public goods available to all citizens regardless of whether they were engaged in the exercise of their religious freedom. Indeed, Black intimated, it was possible that denying equal transportation benefits to parents whose children attended religious schools might conceivably limit their free exercise.[51] It was to take forty years, however, for Black's dictum about withholding benefits to become a potent constitutional weapon. Before that, legal secularism would win numerous victories that would begin to transform the schools and some other public arenas from sites where Christian nonsectarianism still prevailed without question to contested places in which American secularism would struggle to emerge.

Just a year later, in 1948, the secularists won their first Supreme Court case applying the new principles *Everson* had announced.[52] A self-described "humanist" in Champaign, Illinois, the biblically named Vashti McCollum,[53] challenged a program in which Protestant, Catholic, and Jewish teachers were given access to public school students for half an hour per week during school hours. The students were released from regular classes if they wanted to attend the religious instruction, a model that typified the released time programs that had begun to develop where Catholics had confronted the reality that many of their children were attending public schools and not getting organized religious instruction. Justice Black this time held for the Court that the use of public school facilities violated the "no support" principle announced in *Everson*; the decision was eight to one, with only Justice Reed dissenting to make the point that any aid to religion provided by the released time was at most incidental.[54]

In a subsequent case, the Supreme Court would hold that a released time program in which students left school grounds did not violate the Establishment Clause; so in practice, released time was able to continue nationwide. In that case, the Court would hold that the Constitution is not violated when the state "encourages religious instruction or cooperates with religious authorities by adjusting the schedule of public events to sectarian needs."[55] The holding, therefore, is not the important thing about the *McCollum* decision. More important than Justice Black's opinion was a concurrence by Justice Frankfurter, joined by two other Justices, in which he returned to concerns, first voiced in his writings in the two flag salute cases, about the public schools as educational engines of national unity.[56]

Frankfurter began with a review of the history of public education in America. But instead of acknowledging the Christian character of the nonsectarian common schools, Frankfurter maintained that the "nonsectarian" schools had in fact been "secular," and to support this proposition he went so far as to quote President Grant's speech to the Army of the Tennessee, in which Grant had first sketched the outlines of the proposed Blaine amendment.[57] For Frankfurter, the purpose of the secular public schools was to promote unity among all Americans: "The public school is at once the symbol of our democracy and the most pervasive means for promoting our common destiny. In no activity of the State is it more vital to keep out divisive forces than in its schools."[58] The Champaign released time program, to the contrary, reminded students that they were different each time the moment of release occurred: "The law of imitation operates, and nonconformity is not an outstanding characteristic of children. The result is an obvious pressure upon children to attend . . . The children belonging to these non-participating sects will thus have inculcated in them a feeling of separatism when the school should be the training ground for habits of community, or they will have religious instruction in a faith which is not that of their parents."[59] The presence of religious instruction in the schools, Frankfurter believed, subjected the religious minority to a cruel dilemma: dissent and be reminded of your religious difference, or conform and compromise on your principles because of the coercive effects of peer pressure. What distinguished the children subjected to released time from the Witnesses' children required to salute the flag was simply that the purposes of released time were purely religious, not secular. Frankfurter did not object to coercion in the schools per se; he objected to any arrangement in which the state chose to make religion into a defining feature of students' experience.

What Frankfurter evidently found most disturbing was the psychological observation that the program "sharpens the consciousness of religious differences at least among some of the children committed to its care."[60] Once again, it is possible to see glimpses of Frankfurter's conception of the schools as places where Jewish children ought not to experience difference on the basis of religion so much as commonality on the basis of American citizenship. If Herberg sought to naturalize American Jews by putting their faith on a par with Protestantism and Catholicism, Frankfurter adopted the alternative strategy of legal secularism: suggesting that religion ought to be disentangled from the public sphere altogether.

SCHOOL PRAYER AND THE MINORITY EXPERIENCE

The view that schoolchildren must not be subjected to circumstances in which their religious difference is emphasized did not go unnoticed by the other Justices in the *McCollum* case. Justice Jackson wrote separately to disagree with Frankfurter and to insist that the Constitution protected the individual from coercion, not "from the embarrassment that always attends nonconformity, whether in religion, politics, behavior or dress."[61] But it was a version of Frankfurter's view that prevailed when, more than a decade later, in 1962, the Supreme Court took up the enormously controversial issue of school prayer in *Engel v. Vitale*. This time, Justice Black, still on the Court (Frankfurter, who retired that same year, did not participate in the hearing of the case), held that prayer in the public school classroom violated the Constitution even if individual children were given the option not to participate. By writing an official prayer and having it recited in schools, the Board of Regents of New York State had crossed the line into prohibited union of church and state.

The coercive effects of peer pressure in the school environment were part of the constitutional problem. "When the power, prestige and financial support of government is placed behind a particular religious belief," Black wrote, "the indirect coercive pressure upon religious minorities to conform to the prevailing officially approved religion is plain."[62] Black emphasized that the presence of coercion was not a necessary feature for the Constitution to be violated, because "[t]he Establishment Clause, unlike the Free Exercise Clause, does not depend upon any showing of direct governmental compulsion and is violated by the enactment of laws which establish an official religion whether those laws operate directly to coerce nonobserving individuals or not."[63] But the concern for the subjective experience of religious minorities in the schools, a concern almost entirely absent from the long history of American public education, had now, through the influence of Justice Frankfurter, become a standard element of the Supreme Court's treatment of the Establishment Clause.

The stage was set, then, by the early 1960s, for the Supreme Court to effect a fundamental change in the way religion was handled in the public schools. A year after the Court struck down the official prayer composed by the New York Regents, it confronted for the first time the oldest and most contentious problem in the history of church-state relations in the schools: the practice of Bible reading, still a mainstay of many classrooms in the nation, as it had been since the birth of the common school. In *School District of Abington Township, Pennsylvania v. Schempp*, students in Maryland and Pennsylvania challenged the practice of reading Bible verses at the beginning of the school day. The record included, and the court cited, testimony from experts such as the noted Jewish historian Solomon Grayzel (a colleague of Will Herberg's) to the effect that Jewish children might experience psychological harm by hearing New Testament verses that "were not only sectarian in nature but tended to bring the Jews into ridicule or scorn."[64] The question of divisiveness and the subjective experience of the religious minority were therefore squarely in view. Needless to say, Catholics had been arguing for well over a century that reading of the King James Version in schools harmed their children in a religious sense. But the "psychological" argument that Grayzel advanced fit more neatly with the beliefs of the 1960s, in which concern for the mental well-being of children was coming into vogue. Indeed, a famous aside in *Brown v. Board of Education* had pointed to the psychological effects of segregation on African-American children.[65] By emphasizing the Jewish children's minority status, Grayzel was suggesting the implicit parallel to *Brown*.

The argument for protecting religious minorities had, as never before, a chance of success. In response to it, the Supreme Court formulated the first two parts of a constitutional test that would make legal secularism the law of the land. To withstand a challenge under the Establishment Clause, the Court said, the law must have "a secular legislative purpose and a primary effect that neither advances nor inhibits religion." The Court then concluded that the Bible must surely be "an instrument of religion," not used "either as an instrument for nonreligious moral inspiration or as a reference for the teaching of secular subjects."[66] It followed that reading of the Bible in school, long considered a bulwark of American education, violated the federal Constitution and must be prohibited.

For the better part of the nineteenth century, during which disputes about the reading of the Bible in the common schools raged, the strongest argument in favor of continuing the practice turned on the necessity of moral education and the centrality of the Bible in teaching morality. Yet in the Court's opinion in *Abington*, this concern was nowhere to be seen. It was enough for the court to point to the obviously religious significance of the Bible to conclude that reading it in the public schools did not have a "secular" purpose or primary effect. A decade later, in the case of *Lemon v. Kurtzman*, the Court would add a further element to the test, a prohibition on the entanglement of government with religion, thus giving the name "Lemon test" to the classic formulation of legal secularism.[67] But already in *Abington*, legal secularism had reached its logical apotheosis: according to the Supreme Court, secular purpose was actually a requirement of constitutionality under the Establishment Clause.

How did secularism emerge as the official test of constitutionality under the Establishment Clause, only fifteen years after the Court even began considering the possibility that state laws or arrangements violated the federal Constitution? Until the 1870s, the word "secular" did not even figure in American discussions of church and state. "Secularism" in the contemporary sense was a term unknown to the framers and unmentioned by the Reconstruction Congress that drafted the Fourteenth Amendment. As late as the Scopes trial of 1925, "secularism" was still a term of opprobrium to most Americans, associated as it was with radical atheism and contempt for religion. By almost every account, the immediate postwar period was among the most religiously committed in American history, at least at the organizational level. Yet in 1963, in an opinion stating respectfully that "the place of religion in our society is an exalted one," the Supreme Court was prepared to hold,

with precious little historical precedent, that the Constitution required government to act with a "secular" purpose, and that civic
practices deeply ingrained in American life would have to be eliminated.[68]

WHY LEGAL SECULARISM SUCCEEDED

The change depended on the growth to respectability of a strategy
that changed secularism from a general antireligious stance to a particular position within constitutional law. Legal secularism went to
great lengths to insist that it had nothing against religion, so long
as religion remained disconnected from government. Instead of
impugning religion, legal secularism offered a vision of how an
America composed of Christians and Jews could extend inclusive
citizenship to both. Religious diversity could be reconciled with national unity by keeping the state secular.

The very dominance of religious membership and denominational identity in 1950s America was one of the reasons this strategy succeeded. With church membership at an all-time peak, and
godless communism named as the enemy of American values,
strong antireligious secularism had no chance of becoming the
dominant view in American public life. Unlike the years in which
Darwinism and science were rising, and religion was apparently fal-
tering, secularism by the 1950s did not seem like a meaningful
threat to religion. Because they did not feel the threat, religious organizations in the postwar years did not organize against the new,
legal secularism in any serious way. For their part, secularists turned
to a version of secularism that made no great claims about religion
or its lack of value, focusing instead on its relationship to the law.

Alongside its decoupling of antireligious sentiment from separation of church and state, legal secularism succeeded because it addressed itself to the courts. In the postwar period, the federal
courts, and the Supreme Court in particular, found themselves, for

the first time in American history, redefining their role to include the protection of the rights of vulnerable minorities. That meant that the courts not only were prepared to take certain governmental decisions out of the hands of state legislatures, but that the Justices actually *expected* cases involving fundamental rights to pose the interests of minorities against those of the states. These were the years that produced the legal part of the civil rights revolution: *Brown v. Board of Education*, which condemned segregation from a constitutional perspective, formed a kind of archetypal model of what the Court could do when it was faced with deep and traditional injustice. Bible reading in the schools might be an ancient practice in American terms, but no more ancient than segregation and the slavery that preceded it.

By directing its arguments to the Court, not to the general public, legal secularism was able to turn the limited popular appeal of secularism into a virtue. If secularism, like integrationism, could never have won at the polls, it could become the consensus among educated elites who looked on their opponents as regressive and insufficiently attuned to the rights of minorities. To embrace legal secularism was, for the Court, continuous with a set of liberal values characteristic of enlightened citizens and educated jurists. Just as the Constitution was being transformed at the hands of the Justices to protect the rights of the accused, racial minorities, and other downtrodden persons, the Constitution could be seen to police a separation between government and religion that protected vulnerable religious minorities.

Further enhancing the elite appeal of legal secularism was the implicit suggestion that the religious minorities most in need of protection were Jews. Cases might be brought by Jehovah's Witnesses or by isolated atheist curmudgeons, but as the testimony in the lower courts in the *Abington* case suggested, the religious minority most excluded by Bible reading or the Lord's Prayer was the only statistically important non-Christian one. It helped enormously that these were also the years in which anti-Semitic prejudice became socially taboo among the same elites who were deciding constitutional cases. The book and then 1947 Best Picture winner *Gentleman's Agreement* encapsulated this change in social attitudes. In it, a well-meaning Protestant, skeptical of the suggestion that anti-Semitism persists in the modern era, consciously chooses to tell friends and acquaintances that he is of Jewish origin and is astonished and horrified by the subtle and not-so-subtle discrimination that results. Rather doubtfully identifying anti-Semitism as a distinctively upper-class prejudice (the agreement to exclude Jews is, as the title suggests, one made among gentlemen), the film seeks to shame those who control access to elite institutions and simultaneously to build an alliance between Jews and other members of the working class, who apparently are also victims of the enmity and disdain of rich Protestant capitalists.

Although not a classic of the same magnitude, *Gentleman's Agreement* belongs in a sense to the same genre as *Protestant—Catholic—Jew*: a widely disseminated work aimed to establish Jews alongside other Americans as fully coequal citizens. The film purports to unmask prejudice, while the book insists that the American Jewish experience may be taken as an ideal type of what it means to be American; thus they approach the same problem from two different sides. Each participated in the project of transforming the public rhetoric of American identity from being distinctively "Christian" to being more inclusive. This project stood only to gain from Eisenhower's insistence that American character rested on religion but not on any religion in particular. Legal secularism represented itself as only one further development of this same inclusive, universalizing tendency that found its expression in the new theory of America's Judeo-Christian character. Americans could remain a religious people, but the American government would be secular and, consequently, inclusive.

This may be the reason why, even as the courts went on to strike down a moment of silence "for meditation or voluntary prayer" in Alabama schools, a nondenominational prayer offered by a rabbi at a high school graduation, and a series of creatively imagined programs that funded the teaching of secular subjects in parochial schools,[69] legal secularism never successfully took the motto "In God We Trust" off coins or courtroom walls, and never changed the oaths taken by public servants or witnesses in court. It was as if the Supreme Court did not want to undercut too drastically those symbols of the divine in American public life that were incontrovertibly inclusive. Although a lone agnostic might complain about the coinage as a matter of principle, no one really believed that very many Americans found the symbol alienating. In contrast, by the 1970s it came to be widely recognized that, no matter how superficially nondenominational, prayer in the schools excluded Jews precisely because the default background religion in the American mind was certainly Christian and ordinarily Protestant. In the public schools, the state was presiding over the rituals of that religion and so, it seemed, participating in the exclusion of those whose religion was not being practiced there.

Yet notwithstanding the normalization of inclusiveness, legal secularism did generate a dissenting response. Beginning in the 1970s, the apex of legal secularist dominance, opposition to the transformation of the symbols of American public life began slowly to coalesce. When this impulse to restore religion to its traditional role encountered a resurgence of fundamentalism, and a historical shift in which, for the first time in American history, conservative Catholics and evangelical Protestants began to identify common values, it gave birth to a new ideology with the capacity to meet legal secularism on a level playing field. The new position was values evangelicalism.

6

———— ◈ ————

THE VALUES EVANGELICALS

In the tumultuous year 1968, Martin Luther King Jr. was slain, cities burned, protests against the Vietnam War rose to a crescendo—and the Supreme Court revisited Scopes and his monkeys. An Arkansas law, enacted in 1928 under the direct influence of the Tennessee anti-evolution statute, prohibited public schools from teaching "the theory or doctrine that mankind ascended or descended from a lower order of animals." Notwithstanding the astonishing differences between the worlds of Bryan and the Beatles, the statute was still on the books forty years later when Susan Epperson, a Little Rock high school biology teacher with a master's degree in zoology, decided to challenge its constitutionality. Although the law was unenforced, Epperson would be breaking it by assigning chapters on evolution from the standard biology book.[1]

When in 1925 the substitute teacher John Scopes had agreed to be prosecuted for teaching evolution, his lawyers had argued that the law limited his free speech, not that it violated the separation of church and state. In 1968, with legal secularism in the ascendant, the Supreme Court put aside the question of free speech and decided that the Arkansas law violated the constitutional requirement of state neutrality toward religion because it had been enacted to prohibit a theory that contradicted the biblical account of creation "literally read." In short, the anti-evolution law was unconstitutional because it had a religious purpose, not a secular one. Scopes had ended up convicted by a jury of his peers; Epperson emerged triumphant, vindicated by the highest court in the land. It would be hard to imagine a more telling example of how legal secularism had replaced strong secularism, and succeeded where its predecessor had failed.

On the brink of the new world that the 1960s promised, legal secularism appeared as permanent a feature of the new liberal constitutional order as equal rights or expanded free speech. A handful of religious leaders initially attacked the school prayer and Bible-reading decisions as victories for antireligious secularism and called desultorily for a constitutional amendment to reverse them. But the power of legal secularism became clear when numerous religious leaders from the mainstream denominations came out in support of the school prayer decisions on the grounds that religion would be more successful in the churches than in a watered-down form in the schools.[2]

Reacting to the rise of legal secularism, the sociologist Robert Bellah proposed, in a widely discussed 1967 essay, that American public life had long been suffused by a set of beliefs and public rituals amounting to a distinctly American "civil religion" that was "still very much alive" even though it seemed to be fading.[3] In the public debate that ensued, legal secularists condemned the idea that an official religious vision was necessary for American citizenship or identity, while some religious figures criticized Bellah for suggesting a set of religious beliefs that were not those of traditional Christianity. Both sorts of criticism overread Bellah's loosely sociological claim that civil religion constituted, in fact, a *religion*; nonetheless, the debate marked a moment in which the eventual triumph of legal secularism seemed all but assured.

But beginning in the early 1970s, there came into being a new national religious movement that was to change the face of American religion and politics alike. The new American evangelical fundamentalism drastically expanded the diversity among religious worldviews in the United States, and its political arms, from the Moral Majority to the Christian Coalition and beyond, drove the development of yet another new theory of how church and state should interact. According to this approach, religion was to be the source of something called "values" that alone could hold together the diverse participants in the common American enterprise.

Owing much to traditional nonsectarianism, with its belief in a common morality, the new values evangelicalism was also distinctly contemporary. Although at first the movement presented itself as majoritarian, over time, it cleverly drew on the secularists' insight that religious groups should be conceived as minorities that needed to be protected against discrimination and encouraged to flourish in the public sphere. Values evangelicalism then argued that the principle of nondiscrimination should be extended to guarantee religious groups both a fair chance to influence politics and a fair share of the resources distributed by government. So conceived, values evangelicalism was more than just a conservative reaction against legal secularism. It became a full-fledged approach to church and state, without which our present arrangements and ideas cannot be understood.

ENTER THE EVANGELICALS

Opponents of contemporary American evangelicalism like to dismiss it as a return to the backward fundamentalism of the early part of the twentieth century: the same old religion but with cable stations, makeup, and toupees. Yet while contemporary American fundamentalists may share their predecessors' beliefs in a personal savior and the literal truth of the Bible, this continuity is far outshadowed by differences in intellectual approach, sophistication, and organization—differences without which the evangelicalism we know today could not have achieved its extraordinary success. Where early popular fundamentalism depended on sporadic local outpourings of the spirit inspired by camp revivals or the visits of itinerant inspirational preachers, modern evangelicals can boast a highly developed network of organized churches that deliver a wide range of religious and social services. Early fundamentalism lacked its own homegrown ministerial leadership, relying on writings by a diverse range of thinkers to begin to form an identifiable ideology. But beginning in the 1920s, and continuing during the period before the 1970s in which fundamentalism kept a low national profile, fundamentalists founded institutions of higher learning devoted to crystallizing evangelical faith. As these Bible colleges came to confront not just the Holy Scripture but the world to which it must be applied, they helped open the way for a national mobilization of evangelicalism that looked beyond the individual spiritual sphere to seek changes in the broader society. The colleges—from Pepperdine University and Lynchburg College to Bob Jones University and beyond—produced leaders who could provide a strong intellectual foundation for what had originally been a popular religious movement without an official ideology.

The idealized image of Eisenhower-era mainstream, main-line religion, in which everyone went to church or synagogue but nobody took religion too seriously, left no room for fundamentalism. If the popular media ever acknowledged fundamentalism—it rarely did—the assumption was that it had gone the way of the dodo. The 1955 play *Inherit the Wind,* and the 1960 film based on it, actually killed off the fictionalized Bryan character by the end; he was the last of his kind, the audience was told, and good riddance besides. In fact, the play was not so much an attack on fundamentalism as an allegory of McCarthyism. Like the Salem witch hunt in *The Crucible,* religious fundamentalism functioned in *Inherit the Wind* as a convenient metaphor for contemporary intolerance, drawn from America's distant past.

The perceived crisis in religion and religious affiliation in the late 1960s and early '70s made fundamentalism seem more obsolete still. As it turned out, however, the sexual revolution and the rise of the counterculture helped fuel an oppositional revival of evangelical faith and fundamentalist belief. Outside of the cities, where change was in the air, and the *Ice Storm* suburbs where a fashion for change briefly fluttered, middle- and lower-middle-class Americans in the expanding exurbs—especially in the South—reacted to reports of loose morals with a renewed commitment to biblical faith and personal salvation. By the middle of the 1970s, Southern Baptist Jimmy Carter became the first modern president to speak openly about being born again in Christ. America's Third Great Awakening was in full swing.[4]

The evangelical religion of this awakening turned out to have staying power, institutionalizing itself locally and nationally. Many of the private schools that had sprung up in Southern states after the Civil Rights Act of 1964 as bastions for whites facing desegregation transformed themselves into Christian academies, in which the refuge from public schools was not only racial but religious. Because the timing also corresponded to a process of court-ordered secularization in public schools, advocates of the academies had the option of explaining their advantages in the more appealing terms of faith.[5]

Evangelicals also deployed the new media, especially television, in innovative and durable ways. Pat Robertson's *700 Club* (a name chosen to raise seven thousand dollars for the nascent Christian Broadcast Network at ten dollars a head) began broadcasting in 1966 and shows no signs of declining. Moving beyond sermonizing of the kind that could already be heard on local radio throughout the South, the show developed from a religious-themed program featuring charismatic worship to a newsmagazine format, featuring interviews, reportage, and on-air banter, thus engaging with current events and offering an evangelical angle on the world.[6] Other preachers, like Oral Roberts and Jim and Tammy Faye Bakker, established national reputations primarily through TV appearances despite being less polished and more regionally specific than the slicker Robertson (son of a senator and a graduate of the Yale Law School). Even Billy Graham, who came of age earlier than the others and in a sense prefigured their advent, enormously widened his recognition and appeal by the judicious use of television. Graham's strategy depended on large revival meetings in places like Madison Square Garden, attended mostly by people who already belonged to some church or other. But by drawing on anticommunist politics and forging close relationships with politicians like Richard Nixon, Graham entered public consciousness as something like a fixture of popular religion, cementing his unique stature with regular appearances at every presidential inauguration from Nixon through Clinton.[7]

The fund-raising telethon, originally invented to raise money for cancer research in 1949 (a sixteen-hour broadcast hosted by Milton Berle, which raised $1.1 million), also turned out to be an extraordinary mechanism for including a homebound audience in a collective religious endeavor. It had its roots in passing the plate after church, but by virtue of its potentially national reach, the religious telethon created a new kind of virtual participatory community—and with the right inspirational speakers, it could raise money like nobody's business. Notwithstanding the received wisdom that television viewers sit alone on their couches and lose contact with others, television, even before cable, helped form and maintain a sense of national evangelical community. No other religious movement in America has so successfully used similar communications strategies. These techniques are a major reason for the reach and political influence of evangelicals in the age of television; the rise of cable has made the approach all the more nationally effective.[8]

Although Jimmy Carter's evangelical faith has kept him building houses for the poor into his ninth decade, Carter was no fundamentalist, and he willingly aligned himself with the Democratic Party's liberal establishment in order to win the presidency in 1976.

His brand of religion led him to speak in contrite, classical evangelical terms of having committed adultery in his heart—but to do so
in an interview with *Playboy* magazine, hardly the venue of choice
for the conservative faithful, and one presumably chosen to establish his manly bona fides. Fundamentalists helped win the South
for Carter, but they felt spurned by the liberal bent of his policies.
In 1979, with the next presidential election looming, this disillu-
sionment led a previously minor televangelist, Jerry Falwell, to join
prominent New Right strategists in founding an organization they
called the Moral Majority.[9]

The name echoed the "silent majority" of whom Nixon had spoken in a famous Vietnam-era speech, an echo that made it all the
more clear that this majority would be shouting from the rooftops.
The name also assumed, brilliantly and presumptuously, that the
members of the Moral Majority were not a minority representing
special interests, but the people themselves. Perhaps most interestingly, the name Moral Majority avoided the word "Christian" despite the fact that the organization made no attempt to hide its
Christian fundamentalist roots and program. (A decade later, when
Pat Robertson founded the Christian Coalition after the Moral Majority collapsed in scandal, he would feel no need to downplay
Christianity in the name of a national political organization.) The
Moral Majority came into being, in any case, with the stated goal of
promoting morality in American life. Evangelical and fundamentalist values would be promoted not on the grounds of their religious
truth but of their moral worth and majoritarian appeal.

The idea of the Moral Majority was catchy: by the time of the
1980 election, the year-old organization boasted of having two
million members. Placing itself squarely behind the campaign of
Ronald Reagan and his moralized "generic Christianity," the Majority managed to influence the election significantly, mobilizing
members and others to vote for Reagan and against several liberal
senators, who were unseated.[10] The new evangelical movement had

found its political expression, and a bold force of new religious diversity had entered the lists of American public life.

The Moral Majority's national political program reflected its distinctive approach to questions of church and state. School prayer loomed high on the list, as evangelicals reclaimed an issue that had lain dormant since the Supreme Court's decisions in 1962–63 and reformulated it as necessary for encouraging a shared morality. Their argument resembled the old claim that schools must teach morals, but where the nineteenth-century argument had emphasized the Bible as a source of moral education, the new advocates of school prayer described collective daily prayer as crucial to the formation of the student's individual moral personality and the reinforcement of values taught at home. Evangelicals who belonged to the Moral Majority might have believed personally in the direct efficacy of individual prayer, but they did not frame the political argument in such expressly religious terms. Instead, drawing on the idea that public rituals of civic religion bound Americans together as a cohesive moral unit, they mourned the loss of school prayer as a severing of Americans' collective national engagement with values derived from religion. A school day that began without prayer remained unconsecrated to the collective goals of learning and good values.[11]

The transmutation of religion into values reflected a tendency, also present in nonsectarianism, for public religion to serve the interests of government more than those of faith. Under Falwell's leadership, the Moral Majority effectively put religious commitment in the service of politics, not the other way around. Some members may have believed that by supporting the candidates identified by the organization they were advancing true religion, but a vote for a divorced former B-movie actor was not (yet) in itself a way of spreading the faith. Voting en masse for Reagan was, rather, a way of signaling to the broader American public that evangelical politics must now be taken seriously as a social force. The purpose of injecting morality into politics was to make government better, not to bring individuals around to the faith necessary for true salvation.

Evangelical politics, in other words, did not promote religion per se but rather a set of moral values that were derived from faith and relevant to practical politics. This fact bore enormous significance for the development of values evangelicalism. Rather than arguing openly, as had the National Reform Association, that Christianity must necessarily play a greater role in American public life, the evangelicals of the Moral Majority, and their successors to varying degrees, argued that America needed more in the way of moral values of the kind that only religion could provide. They presented religion not as a good in itself but as a much-needed ingredient in a recipe to restore America's greatness by uniting diverse faiths in a common national enterprise. This impulse to unite meant that political claims potentially grounded in theology instead got expressed in terms of values. Opponents might denounce the evangelicals' views as relevant only to people who shared a particular religious faith, but evangelicals were sure to respond by insisting on the universality of the values they espoused. As a result, the complex of ideas about government and religion that emerged from American evangelical politics came to be *values* evangelicalism—not just evangelicalism itself.

BROADENING THE ALLIANCE: CATHOLICS AND EVANGELICALS UNITE

The issue of abortion is almost as prominent today as it was thirty years ago when it first entered national consciousness with the *Roe v. Wade* decision[12]—and the main reason the controversy has not faded in the way it did, for example, in Europe, is that evangelicals and Catholics raised it to the level of a central American moral-political question. Evangelicals were taken by surprise when the

Supreme Court ruled that there was a constitutional right to abortion; no national pro-life organizations yet existed.[13] Nor, for that matter, did dedicated national pro-choice organizations[14]—the attorneys who represented "Jane Roe" to the Court were not seasoned advocates paid by NARAL or NOW, but Sarah Weddington and Linda Coffee, aged twenty-six and twenty-seven, recent graduates of the Texas Law School who had taken on the project of trying to convince the federal courts to create a constitutional right to abortion.[15] Once the Court announced the new right, however, the Moral Majority became the first organization to make reversal of *Roe* into an effective national rallying cry.

Evangelical Protestants opposed a constitutional right to abortion because they opposed abortion itself as a violation of God's law and as a symbol of the triumph of materialistic humanism.[16] But they did not choose to frame the national debate in terms of faith. Rather, in a sophisticated co-optation of the 1960s rights language that Roe's lawyers had used to win in the Supreme Court, abortion opponents described themselves as defending a "right to life." To make the argument that abortion violated the right to life, the self-described pro-lifers still had to show that a fetus was, in fact, a life. Again, religious belief could have provided the public rationale, as it certainly provided the private reason for evangelicals who could have argued that life begins at conception because that is when the soul enters the physical substance of the fertilized egg. But the nascent pro-life movement instead generally relied on the nontheological logic that, from the moment of conception, the fetus has the chance to grow to a fully formed human. As technology improved, the pro-life movement came to depend increasingly on ultrasound and other images of the fetus to argue that it is, in fact, a living being. Wrapped in scientific or at least technological swaddling, the visual argument for the personhood of the fetus was self-consciously nonreligious, grounded instead in moral values.

The choice to define public arguments in terms of general morality, rather than particular religious doctrine, had the all-

important consequence of opening the doors of values evangelicalism to people other than evangelical Protestants. The abortion
question became the first topic of national importance on which a
significant number of Catholics (especially the church hierarchy,
but also many laypeople) systematically agreed with evangelical
Protestants. The roots of Catholic opposition to abortion lay not in
biblical literalism but in a rich canon-law tradition; official Catholicism, unlike most Protestantism, opposed not only abortion but
also contraception, focusing on the sacredness of potential conception as well as on the actually viable fetus. So Catholics' sense of the
wrongness of abortion differed markedly from evangelicals'. Yet the
two could agree that abortion was morally wrong and that its con-
stitutionalization as a fundamental right ought to be reversed.[17]
When many Rust Belt working-class Catholics defected from traditional Democratic loyalties to vote for Ronald Reagan, a broader
Catholic-evangelical alliance on social issues suddenly seemed possible for the first time. Although the Reagan administration refused
to prioritize the pro-life fight to the extent desired by abortion abolitionists, Reagan did in his first term put his name to an article
committing his full support to proposed legislation and a constitutional amendment seeking to illegalize abortion.[18] As the pro-
life movement grew, drawing on parallel tracks of evangelical and
Catholic activism, anti-abortion politics became a bridge between
Protestants and Catholics who had been on opposite sides of practically every church-state issue since Catholics began to immigrate
to America in numbers.[19]

Ironically, the changed conditions created by the successes of legal secularism made possible this tentative new alliance, one that
was eventually to effect a seismic shift in the fault lines of America's
religious diversity. Catholics had once opposed Bible reading or
other manifestations of religion in the public schools as sectarian Protestantism; now that these were gone, some conservative
Catholics began to bemoan the decline of religious discourse and
symbolism in public life. For their part, hard-line Protestants had

long sought to prevent the Catholic church from using government resources to fund education that the Protestants considered theologically mistaken. Now that Catholics and Protestants could form an alliance over questions of morality and public religion, however, the threat associated with the existence of Catholic schools looked much less dangerous. Along with much of their traditional anti-Catholic rhetoric, evangelical Protestants began to abandon their political opposition to government measures that might benefit the Catholic church. Although pockets of anti-Catholic theology remained—the website of Bob Jones University until recently posted a 1980 article that condemns the Moral Majority for its ecumenism and its alliance with "the church of Antichrist"[20]—the sense that evangelicals and conservative Catholics were on the same side of a culture war pitting traditional values against secularism changed the Catholic church from Protestant evangelicalism's enemy number one to its most valuable and influential ally.[21]

The emergence of a cautious alliance between conservative Catholics and evangelical Protestants, formed initially around hot-button topics such as abortion and public displays of religion, fundamentally transformed the public conversation about religion and government in America.[22] Ironically, the thinker who made the greatest intellectual contribution to this alliance was (at least to begin with) neither a Catholic nor a self-described evangelical but a Canadian-born Lutheran neoconservative, Father Richard John Neuhaus, who had idiosyncratic ties ranging from liberal theologians to the New Right and the Moral Majority. In what is probably still the most influential dissection and condemnation of legal secularism, *The Naked Public Square*, Neuhaus argued that the secularists' goal of excluding religion from public consciousness was deeply misguided. American values, he claimed, were not secular but deeply religious. The "public piety" of civil exercises of religion therefore remained crucial to American identity and should not be abandoned: removing the crèches from the public square would create a literal nakedness corresponding to the metaphorical nakedness of a public discourse stripped of faith. It followed that Americans should develop a public philosophy that expressly acknowledged the importance of religious faith in shaping common values.[23]

As a religious intellectual, Neuhaus carefully avoided the Moral Majority's unconscious tendency to put religion in the service of politics. For Neuhaus, the reason to preserve and develop the religious component of American public life was to move us closer to the ideal of the Augustinian City of God.[24] Yet despite his greater sophistication, Neuhaus, like the evangelicals, adopted the strategy of making no claims for any particular religious denomination. Instead he married Bellah's insights about the cultural importance of civil religion to the newly powerful language of American values and morality.

Though by his own account skeptical of the goals of the Moral Majority, Neuhaus did much to develop the ideology of values evangelicalism. Above all, he offered values evangelicals a respectable intellectual pedigree for their claim that government should be actively involved in the promotion of moral values that were inseparable from religious commitment. When Neuhaus juxtaposed Jerry Falwell and Martin Luther King Jr. as "profoundly patriotic figures" who sought to "disrupt the business of secular America by an appeal to religiously based public values," he was marshaling the considerable moral authority of King to show values evangelicalism to be necessary to the American political future.[25] Of course it was true that the Moral Majority was following a well-trodden path of building political support out of the churches. Not only had King done the same, but abolitionists had pressed their political case from Northern pulpits, and the temperance movement that succeeded in passing Prohibition had drawn on church organizations to build grassroots support for a ban on alcohol.[26] But the Moral Majority, unlike these predecessor movements, had failed to capture the sympathies of America's educated elites. Neuhaus hoped to remedy that defect.

In the course of his argument, Neuhaus left no doubt that the enemy of values evangelicalism was secularism—not strong secularism of the old-fashioned, overtly antireligious variety (which he called secular humanism, and dismissed as dead), but secularism that used the courts to remove religion from the public sphere.[27] Although he did not call it legal secularism, nor describe its evolution out of strong secularism, it was certainly legal secularism with which Neuhaus was grappling. Mainstream Protestant churches had contributed to the evacuation of religion from public discourse by joining the fight for separation of religion from government and giving up their claim to provide unique moral truths. The result, Neuhaus argued, inevitably gave secular liberal ideas primacy over religion. To regain its distinctive role in the moral life of the community, religion must make good on its claim to offer a comprehensive, faith-based vision of the universe, from broad precepts to particular stands on public policy matters. That vision would in turn inform America's role as a force for good in the world. Religion must be unafraid to engage and affect government and the public sphere, in order to save both democracy and itself.[28] Eventually, convinced that the Roman Catholic church offered the richest public and theological expression of these ideas, and that they were vividly personalized in the pontificate of Pope John Paul II, Neuhaus became a Roman Catholic, from which vantage point he has been able to deepen Catholic-evangelical ties.[29]

VALUES EVANGELICALISM IN POLITICS

The 1984 presidential election saw values evangelicalism flexing its newfound muscles. The Democrats warned their pro-choice constituency that, with the impending retirements of several aging Justices, including moderate Chief Justice Warren Burger, Ronald Reagan was on the verge of appointing enough Justices to overturn *Roe v. Wade*. Energized by the possibility of such a reversal, Christian evangelicals embraced as hope what Democrats feared and re-doubled their efforts on behalf of Reagan. Conservative Catholic Democrats who had begun to swing toward Reagan in the 1980 election voted for him again, and with the economy in an upswing, Reagan took an extraordinary 59 percent of the vote and managed to lose just a single state, Walter Mondale's Minnesota.

Reagan quickly signaled his embrace of values evangelicalism with the appointment of an important figure in the movement, William Bennett, as secretary of education. Bennett, a Catholic, had headed the National Endowment for the Humanities in Reagan's first term and had spoken widely about the need for moral values in public life; the much more prominent education position gave him a bully pulpit from which he could press the argument that an America without commonly shared virtues and values could not succeed. (After leaving office, Bennett wrote a series of best-selling books touting virtues and values.[30])

But more important, Reagan kept up a steady stream of conservative judicial nominees, most of whom believed that legal secularism had gone too far and that the Supreme Court had erred in creating a constitutional right to abortion. On Burger's retirement in 1986, Reagan appointed arch conservative William Rehnquist as Chief Justice of the Supreme Court and filled his empty seat with the brilliant conservative Catholic Antonin Scalia, whom he had put on the D.C. Circuit Court of Appeals just four years earlier. In the mid-1980s, values evangelicalism was an identifiable and increasingly popular political position, but it had not yet made any meaningful inroads into the constitutional jurisprudence of legal secularism, because the federal judiciary had not budged. New judges, nominated by a president who enjoyed a national mandate, were the values evangelicals' best hope for combating legal secularism in its preferred arena.

What the values evangelicals sought in the courts was nothing less than a reversal of the revolution of legal secularism: they set out to overturn decisions like *Lemon*—which required every law to have a secular purpose—almost as avidly as they sought to overturn *Roe*. As it turned out, complete victory remained elusive in both quarters. Matters might have been different if in 1987 Judge Robert Bork had been confirmed for the Supreme Court seat vacated by the moderate Virginia gentleman Justice Lewis Powell. Bork, a former law school professor, judge of the D.C. Circuit, and onetime solicitor general of the United States, had a prodigious intellect, force of personality, and values-evangelical views that put him to the right of Justice Scalia; he would have been a clear fifth vote for a bloc that appeared poised to reverse *Roe*. But the Democratic Senate rejected Bork after a contentious political battle led by legal liberals like Professor Laurence Tribe of Harvard. Instead the job went to the moderate Justice Anthony Kennedy, who within just a few years would join Justice Sandra Day O'Connor (another Reagan appointee, the first woman on the Court) and Justice David Souter in crafting a compromise position that preserved *Roe* on the basis of precedent, without embracing its reasoning.[31]

But if *Lemon*, like *Roe*, was not to be overturned with a sure swift stroke, it nonetheless suffered the death of a thousand cuts. The key figure in draining the life force from this monument of legal secularism was to be Justice O'Connor, whose opinions in her nearly quarter century on the Court have defied easy classification and have enraged conservatives and liberals by turns. More than those of any other Justice, O'Connor's opinions tend to become the law of the land through her penchant for casting the deciding fifth vote in close cases.[32] Often the other Justices do not share her perspective when it is first expressed, but over time, once her distinctive position has become the law, it begins to seem inevitable, and the Justices eventually find themselves signing on to it.

Justice O'Connor's views on the meaning of the Establishment Clause perfectly fit this paradigm: first introduced in a lonely concurring opinion that provided a necessary fifth vote, they have since come to embody constitutional orthodoxy. The original case in which O'Connor began to chip away at legal secularism involved a

challenge to a Christmas display in a public park in the shopping
district of downtown Pawtucket, Rhode Island. The display, which
was owned and erected by the city, boasted a Christmas tree; a sign
reading "Season's Greetings"; a house for Santa Claus; reindeer
pulling Santa's sleigh; assorted candy-striped poles, carolers, lights,
and clowns; a cutout elephant; and a "talking wishing well." In
keeping with the Catholic cultural tenor of urban Rhode Island,
the display included a crèche depicting the Nativity scene: kings
bearing gifts for the baby Jesus, in a manger crowded with not only
Mary and Joseph but also angels and shepherds borrowed from the
Annunciation. The crèche had been included in the display for at
least forty years without attracting any special comment or notice,
but in 1981, with the logic and precedential weight of legal secularism on its side, the Rhode Island ACLU chapter led a legal challenge to the crèche.[33]

By the time the case reached the Supreme Court in 1984 under
the name *Lynch v. Donnelly*, it nicely symbolized Neuhaus's worry
(expressed in the book published the same year) that the courts
would literally render the public square naked of religious content.
The Justices found themselves split on the question. Four of them,
with Justice William Brennan in the lead, applied the *Lemon* test
and concluded, just as the District Court and Court of Appeals had
done, that because the crèche was so fundamentally a religious symbol—a "re-creation of an event that lies at the heart of Christian
faith"[34]—erecting it could not possibly have a secular purpose, had
the effect of advancing religion, and entangled government with religion. But a bare majority of five concluded to the contrary that
the display was constitutionally permissible. Chief Justice Burger,
then still on the Court, wrote an opinion arguing that the inclusion
of the crèche was secular, no different from the display of old master paintings with religious themes in government-funded muse-
ums.[35]

Justice O'Connor was one of the five, but, apparently dissatisfied
with comparing the Christmas display to a Rembrandt in the Na-

tional Gallery, she wrote a separate concurrence in which she set out a new understanding of the *Lemon* test. In order to determine whether a law had a secular purpose, she wrote, the Court must ask "whether the government intends to convey a message of endorsement or disapproval of religion." The way to discover whether the law had a secular purpose, by extension, was to ask "whether, irrespective of government's actual purpose, the practice under review in fact conveys a message of endorsement or disapproval." In short, the test of constitutionality under the Establishment Clause was to be whether government was endorsing or disapproving of religion: "Endorsement sends a message to nonadherents that they are outsiders, not full members of the political community, and an accompanying message to adherents that they are insiders, favored members of the political community. Disapproval sends the opposite message."[36]

The concurrence did not look to precedent, to the framers, or to the history of church and state in America to explain why the Establishment Clause should be understood as a ban on government endorsement of religion. Instead, Justice O'Connor summed up her reasoning in a simple aphorism: "The Establishment Clause prohibits government from making adherence to a religion relevant in any way to a person's standing in the political community."[37] This enormously attractive idea certainly had a basis in earlier thinking about religious liberty. The Constitution, even before the Bill of Rights, prohibited religious tests for office, and no one today would dispute that the Constitution would be violated by laws like the nineteenth-century enactment in the Idaho Territory that banned Mormons from voting. It did not necessarily follow, however, that any government endorsement of religion must automatically amount to making religion relevant to the political standing of individuals.

The appeal of Justice O'Connor's approach lay in its reformulation of legal secularism's doctrine of government neutrality toward religion in terms of individual equality. The reason that government should not get involved in the endorsement or disapproval of religion was that doing so would make some people less equal than others. The goal of government in its engagement with religion should not be secularism; it should be equality. The crèche did not violate the Constitution, O'Connor concluded, because, in the context of the display, it did not make anyone feel like an outsider to the political community. By invoking egalitarianism, O'Connor could avoid the Court's strained suggestion that the crèche was secular while still allowing it to remain on display.

Within five years of its invention in a concurrence that no other Justice joined, Justice O'Connor's endorsement test became the law in *County of Allegheny v. ACLU Greater Pittsburgh Chapter*.[38] The facts of that case looked very similar to those of the earlier one: a crèche was displayed in a public place, this time the main staircase of the courthouse in Allegheny County, Pennsylvania. The majority opinion for the Court, written by Justice Blackmun, who had dissented in *Lynch*, explained that the right test was essentially the one O'Connor had invented. Joined by the other *Lynch* dissenters— Justices Brennan, Marshall, and Stevens—with O'Connor providing the crucial fifth vote, the Court's opinion held that the display endorsed Christianity and was unconstitutional.

This conclusion put the Court in the awkward position of explaining why the crèche in the courthouse in Pennsylvania was different from the crèche in the public park in Rhode Island. In fact, only Justice O'Connor thought the two were different; the rest of the new majority thought the cases were exactly the same and had voted that the crèche was unconstitutional in both cases. But to keep O'Connor on board, some solution was needed. Justice Blackmun wrote that the Pawtucket crèche had been embedded in a broader Christmas display, complete with the reindeer and the talking wishing well, whereas the Pennsylvania crèche was alone in a frame of flowers on the courthouse steps and therefore more directly endorsed religion.[39] This attempt at reconciliation, which has gone down in legal history ignominiously as the "three plastic rein-deer rule," revealed something important about the endorsement test: because it depended on intuiting the "message" of state action, it was more than ordinarily indeterminate. What one reasonable person sees as the government expressing its approval of religion, another, equally reasonable person may see simply as the continua-tion of an old custom, communicating nothing of the kind.

The endorsement test was not inherently advantageous to the position of the values evangelicals. Applied literally, it has in fact led to a series of restrictions on public manifestations of religion, as the courts have been forced to ask whether various public rituals en-dorse religion. In another way, however, the endorsement test did represent a great victory for values evangelicalism. Under the test's influence, the word "secular," which under *Lemon* was the touch-stone of analysis, began to disappear from the Court's discussions of the Establishment Clause. Instead of asking whether government's actions were secular, the Court began to ask whether the govern-ment action was "neutral" with respect to religion. The concept of neutrality had appeared alongside the word "secular" in the cases that had originally inaugurated legal secularism, but in the different sense that the government had to have a secular motivation in order to show that the laws it was passing were neutral with respect to re-ligion. Now neutrality came gradually to mean that the govern-ment must treat religion and nonreligion equally. Equal treatment was, in fact, the very core of endorsement analysis: the government must treat religion and nonreligion equally in order to make certain that all citizens feel like equal participants in civic life.

Needless to say, legal secularism had not rested on the idea that government should treat religion and nonreligion equally. To the contrary, the secularists believed that government should *not* treat religious motivations the same way it treated secular ones: in effect, it should disfavor them. Secular reasons for the laws and secular ef-fects were the preferred norm, while religious reasons and effects were banned by the Constitution. Indeed, even before the advent of legal secularism, the Establishment Clause had been understood to say that religious entities would be treated differently from those organized around other beliefs and values. Nothing in the Constitution prohibited Congress from establishing and supporting nonreligious institutions—only religion must not be established. Similarly, the Free Exercise Clause gave special protection to religious activity, greater than the protection available to nonreligious conduct, which the government was free to ban unless doing so would violate some other basic right.

By making equality into the core Establishment Clause value, the endorsement test opened the door to a creative and original legal strategy for values evangelicals. Legal secularism had depicted itself as protecting vulnerable minorities, like Jews and Jehovah's Witnesses, from the imposition of religious values by a dominant majority. In response, the Moral Majority had protested that legal secularism's emphasis on minorities slighted the interests of the majority of Americans who in fact wanted religion in public life. But beginning in the early 1990s, Christian evangelicals started describing *themselves* as minorities, discriminated against by powerful government institutions that were refusing to treat them equally when it came to government support. In legal terms, the claim was that where government made certain funds available for a variety of civic speech activities, it was discriminating against religious organizations if it failed to make the same funds available to them. In cultural terms, the evangelicals' suggestion was that, in an era of legal secularism, religion was subject to discrimination at the hands of secularist elites who controlled public institutions. Their proposed solution was for the state to treat religious groups as part of America's broader cultural diversity, entitled to the same respect and access to government resources.

THE RELIGIOUS AS VULNERABLE MINORITIES

The brilliance of the twofold legal and cultural strategy of depicting religion as subject to discrimination revealed itself in a 1995 case, *Rosenberger v. University of Virginia*.[40] The defendant could not have been better chosen. The University of Virginia, founded by the arch-separationist Jefferson himself, stood as a symbol of secularism in a region where evangelical religion was now a powerful force, with Jerry Falwell's base in Lynchburg just a few miles away from Charlottesville. The university had a student activities fund, collected from mandatory student contributions that were then disbursed for worthy extracurricular activities, including student publications. Because it was a state university, however, it followed a guideline under which it would not give the funds to organizations or publications that primarily promoted belief in God or in an "ultimate reality."[41] According to the university, this policy enabled it to avoid violating the Establishment Clause by providing government money for religious purposes.[42] A group of students sought $5,800 for an evangelical publication called *Wide Awake*; the university denied the funding. The stage was set for a challenge to the policy in what would become the first case in which evangelicals successfully presented themselves as minorities, discriminated against and in need of judicial protection.

Enter Professor Michael McConnell, law professor and would-be Thurgood Marshall of values evangelicalism. A prominent constitutional theorist and expert on the law of church and state, McConnell was perfectly placed to identify the advantages of claiming minority status. He had served as a law clerk to the liberal icon Justice William Brennan and, unlike most values evangelicals, had spent his academic career in a prestigious law school, the University of Chicago, where he had been in daily contact with the academic currents of legal secularism. The key to McConnell's insight lay in noticing that when the government seemed to be infringing on the free-exercise rights of religious minorities, even legal secularists became sympathetic, and the courts tended to find in their favor. The trick was to take that sympathy, so prevalent in free-exercise cases, and transpose it into the Establishment Clause context.

To bring about this shift, McConnell turned to the "viewpoint discrimination" doctrine of free-speech law, under which the government may not pick and choose what kinds of speech to regulate by looking at the viewpoint of the speaker.[43] A city council could not, for example, pass a zoning law banning Republican campaign announcements from sound trucks while permitting Democratic ones. McConnell argued that the same principle applied to the University of Virginia's student activities fund, maintaining that by funding some student magazines, but not those that advocated belief in God, the university was discriminating on the basis of religious viewpoint.

The university responded that the Establishment Clause allowed and even required exactly such discrimination, because it banned support of religious speech while permitting support of secular speech. But the Supreme Court adopted McConnell's argument and held by a five-to-four vote that the university had indeed engaged in viewpoint discrimination, and that funding *Wide Awake* would not violate the Establishment Clause. Justice Kennedy, writing for the majority, mentioned his own view that the Establishment Clause was not violated because nobody was being coerced; but to gain Justice O'Connor's all-important fifth vote, he added that funding the magazine would not violate the Establishment Clause because the generally available student activities fund could not be understood to endorse religion.[44] In later cases, this endorsement-driven proposition was to become the law. Where the state made funds generally available for a range of civic purposes, the Establishment Clause would not be violated by allowing those funds to go to religious organizations, among others. The reason was that according to the Court, a general-purpose fund could not be understood as an endorsement of religion.[45]

McConnell had brilliantly turned the Establishment Clause on its head. Although himself an originalist who claimed to rely on the framers' intention as the sole legitimate guide to constitutional interpretation,[46] McConnell had convinced the Supreme Court to adopt a position almost squarely the opposite of the original intent of the Establishment Clause. The framers meant the Establishment Clause primarily to guard against the possibility that a citizen's tax dollars would be used to support religious teachings with which he might possibly disagree. Now the Supreme Court held that the Establishment Clause was not violated by using state funds to support religious publications, so long as state funds were also being made available to other diverse forms of speech.

From this decision it also followed that there would be nothing constitutionally wrong with state funds going to support vouchers that would be provided to children attending religious schools, since generally available voucher payments for religious or nonreligious schools would not appear to endorse religion. Seven years after *Rosenberger*, the Supreme Court, by the same five-to-four margin, reached exactly that conclusion, permitting a nominally neutral school voucher program, even though 96 percent of the money in the program under review ultimately ended up paying for religious schooling.[47] Not long after, in 2002, President George W. Bush made Michael McConnell a federal judge.

McConnell had certainly earned the honor; his qualifications were of the first order. But remarkably enough, the liberal law professors who had led the charge against Robert Bork did little to oppose McConnell's nomination to the Court of Appeals, even though it seemed possible that McConnell's next stop might be the Supreme Court. In fact, more than three hundred professors, among them many prominent liberals, signed a letter supporting McConnell.[48] Part of this had to do with McConnell's personal ties in the legal academy, but then Robert Bork had been a law professor, too. The real reason for this outpouring lay in the fact that McConnell had actually convinced many erstwhile legal secularists that he was standing up for the rights of the evangelical minority against majoritarian discrimination. It also helped that the secularists typically sided with McConnell in the fight for the free-exercise rights of obvious religious minorities whose practices were affected by an otherwise neutral government law. Legal secularists and Mc-Connell could agree that Indians who used peyote as a religious ritual should be exempted from antidrug laws, even though the Supreme Court had held otherwise in a 1990 decision.[49] But Mc-Connell had done more than just identify points of common sympathy with secularists in the legal academy. He had made stunning progress in convincing liberal law professors that the value of equality made discrimination against religious viewpoints indefensible.

Through the combination of Justice O'Connor's endorsement test and the pro-equality advocacy of McConnell and others, values evangelicals in the 1990s won a series of major victories in the area of government funding of religion, which had been the framers' main concern when they enacted the Establishment Clause. That string of victories is not yet complete. Its final step would be for the Court to hold that state laws banning direct support of religious organizations discriminate against religion. One version of this argument, which values evangelicals pressed unsuccessfully on the Supreme Court in a recent case involving the use of state scholarship money by a theology student in Washington State, is that state constitutional amendments that prohibit the funding of religion themselves violate the Free Exercise Clause of the federal Constitution.[50] On this view, the state Blaine amendments, enacted in a wave of anti-Catholic fervor, discriminate against religion and must be found unconstitutional,[51] just as a state constitutional amendment prohibiting local governments from protecting gay people against discrimination has been held unconstitutional as a violation of the principle of equal respect.[52]

The Supreme Court has not yet addressed the constitutionality of the state Blaine amendments, nor has it held that states must fund religious programs whenever they fund secular ones. But the fact that the Court upheld a voucher program even where almost all the funds went to support religious schooling shows that it would be easy for a state to provide token funding for nonreligious purposes when its actual intent is to support religion. Under the endorsement test and the present state of the law, the Court could hold that there would be nothing wrong with government giving citizens "culture vouchers" that could be used to fund a ballet subscription, library membership—or church dues. In short, the old Establishment Clause tradition devoted to separating religious institutions from government by denying funding to them is now in retreat. Sound scholarship emphasizing the anti-Catholic history of the Blaine amendment has contributed to the trend.

Yet ironically, at the same time that values evangelicalism has changed the law of government funding of religion, it has made almost no ground at all on the "values" issues that first gave the movement political impetus. In the realm of religion in the public schools and the public square more generally, the endorsement test has not only failed to bring about a retrenchment in the doctrines originally crafted in the heyday of legal secularism, but has actually extended the legal secularists' aspiration to remove religion from state-sponsored environments. In areas ranging from a nondenominational prayer offered by a rabbi at a high school graduation[53] to the recitation of the Lord's Prayer by an officially designated student before Friday-night high school football games,[54] the Supreme Court has found that invoking God in school-related contexts violates the Establishment Clause by endorsing religion.

On one level, this divergence can be laid at the doorstep of Justice O'Connor. In cases about government funding—like the vouchers decision, often decided five-to-four—O'Connor has voted with the conservative wing of the Court and concluded that funding religion alongside other civic activities does not convey a message that the government is endorsing religion.[55] In cases about public manifestation of religion, however, O'Connor has often joined the Court's liberal wing to hold, also by five-to-four majorities, that public rituals involving prayer or the explicit invocation of God impermissibly endorse religion.[56] O'Connor is the only member of the current Supreme Court who believes both in extending permission for the government to fund religious teaching and also in restricting public displays of religion in the public sphere.

But because constitutional law as practiced by the Supreme Court operates by the setting of precedents that are then basically followed until altered or overturned, O'Connor's endorsement approach has been solidified into law through decisions on both sides of the issue. No longer merely O'Connor's view, the endorsement test, with its strange fruits, is the law of the land shaping the relationship between government and religion. It affects nearly every decision in which religious issues are raised, whether the case is squarely about the definition of establishment—in which case endorsement is the touchstone—or about the scope of free exercise, in which case the state's ability to accommodate religious preferences is limited by the constraint that the accommodation not amount to an endorsement of religion. As a result, a new generation of constitutional lawyers and advocates has increasingly come to accept both the expansion of government funding of religious institutions and restrictions on public religion as normal and constitutionally appropriate. Values evangelicals have continued to fight, and lose, battles over public prayer. Legal secularists have continued to fight against extended government funding of religion, even though they have lost almost every major case on the subject in the last decade. We are witnessing the way constitutional ideas pile up, instead of arranging themselves neatly. Values evangelicalism has not totally replaced legal secularism as the only theory about church and state. It has, rather, pushed secularism to the side, squeezing it against the edge of the tectonic plate and creating pressure for the future to address.

THE CONTRADICTIONS

Today, the battle being fought over church and state in the United States is political, ideological, and, in a sense, religious—implicating not only specific questions of symbolism and government funding but American identity itself. Both sides have brought about fundamental changes in the way religion and government interact compared to half a century ago. Yet despite fifty years of fighting, neither side is winning the war.

Consider first the changes wrought by legal secularism. In 1954, religion was seen by an overwhelming majority of Americans as a bulwark against godless communism. An act of Congress supported and signed by President Eisenhower inserted the words "under God" into the Pledge of Allegiance, which was recited in schools across the country. In a carryover of nineteenth-century nonsectarianism, most schools started the day with a short prayer, often the Lord's Prayer. Public schools were not unique in assuming that every American family celebrated Christmas and Easter in more or less the same way. They reflected the same background assumption of American culture on show in *It's a Wonderful Life* (1946) and *Miracle on 34th St.* (1947). "White Christmas" (1942) may have been written by Irving Berlin, a Russian-born American Jew, but it was no less a nationally unifying song than "God Bless America" (1938), by the same composer.

By the year 2004, the place of religion in the schools had changed drastically. School prayer was deemed unconstitutional in 1962,[57] and a moment of silence for private prayer was banned in 1985.[58] As noted, in 1992, the Supreme Court held that nondenominational prayer opening a school graduation violated the Constitution,[59] and in 2000 it added public prayer before high school football games to the list.[60] Required teaching of biblically inspired "creation science" has been rejected as an attempt to teach religion in the schools.[61] Meanwhile, the background cultural assumption that everyone is Christian has been undermined in much of the country by the rise of multiculturalism. In urban areas, the nominally secular Kwanzaa is more likely to be celebrated in schools than Easter. Christmas pageants have disappeared from most public schools, Halloween has begun to be replaced by Fall Festival,[62] and principals have to think long and hard about which holiday songs they can teach without being sued.

Legal secularism has had, in short, a major effect in some areas of public life in America. By contrast, although 2004 was the fiftieth anniversary of legal desegregation, many American schools remain single race. As its name suggests, legal secularism has been powered primarily by court decisions, but those decisions belong to a broader cultural change. In polite company on East and West coasts, and in ever-cautious corporate America, it is becoming rarer for people to wish one another a Merry Christmas. One is more likely to hear the Wal-Mart checkout specialist say "Happy Holidays," more likely to be invited to the company holiday party than to the Christmas bash. When, every year, the Justices of the Supreme Court hold their Christmas party for employees, there are inevitably grumblings among Jewish law clerks and lawyers: to some, the Court's party seems anachronistic, out of step with the secularized sensitivities of the elites who work at the Court or appear before it, and maybe even with the Court's own jurisprudence on endorsement.

Yet these secularizing changes in American life tell only part of the story of developments in religion and government since the 1950s. Those on the other side of the national argument have themselves drastically changed the shape of church-state relations both culturally and legally. Eisenhower and his vice president, Nixon, spoke of their belief in God only in the most general terms. Out of necessity and inclination, John F. Kennedy, our first Catholic president, tried to minimize the role of his religion in the public eye. But from Carter to Reagan to Clinton to the younger Bush, it has become the norm for our leaders to speak in detail of their religious faith and of being born again in Christ. This evangelical bipartisanship even appeals across religions, as evidenced by Joe Lieberman's religiously infused, Jewishly inflected campaign rhetoric in 2000 and 2004, which expressly adopted biblical values in the political sphere.[63] This open embrace of a particular religion in politics would have seemed very strange at midcentury, when religion was understood to be something that one perhaps believed privately but did not trumpet.

Institutionally, values evangelicals have successfully pursued some changes almost unimaginable fifty years ago. In 1954, the century-old consensus that the government would not pay for tuition at private religious schools seemed impregnable. If anything, the legal trend was toward greater separation between Catholic schools and the government, as the Supreme Court prohibited the provision of school buses and secular maps and magazines to them.[64] In 2002, however, the Supreme Court held that the government could support religious schools so long as it did so by providing tuition vouchers to parents who would then direct the government funding to schools of their choice.[65] Even though relatively few school districts have so far chosen to adopt voucher programs, this remarkable holding shattered an old taboo against state support of religious education. Through charitable choice, billions of dollars flow to religious charities for programs that may include religious elements. Public school facilities or student activities funds, previously closed to religious organizations, must now be opened to them. The values evangelicals can point to these changes as evidence of their influence on the relationship between government and religion in America. Like the legal secularists, they have changed the landscape of our national identity in the courts and in the realm of political culture.

What we have, then, is a contradiction, or rather a series of contradictions. Victories by the legal secularists have removed religion from formal public spaces such as schools, at least during school hours.[66] Successful efforts by values evangelicals have broken down once-strong institutional barriers between the state and organized religion, and have actually increased the degree of religious discourse in politics. Instead of pulling America either in the direction of greater public secularism or toward a greater role for religion in its relation with government, we have gotten some of each. As a result, no single, unified theory or logical reason can explain the arrangements that we now have. They are the product of an ongoing battle. The field has changed, some objectives have been captured and others lost, and disorder reigns.

Even though its arena today is often the courts, the continuing struggle between the values evangelicals and the legal secularists should not be understood in isolation from other political conflicts of the present and recent past. During the twenty-five years since Reagan was first elected president, the right and left in American politics have been locked in a set of pitched and increasingly polarizing battles over cultural and economic issues. To simplify slightly, liberals have mostly been winning the culture war. The courts have validated gay rights, and even some of those who voted preemptively to bar same-sex marriage seem open to same-sex civil unions. The liberal push to establish racial, ethnic, and sex diversity has taken hold in the culture so deeply that even Republicans who staunchly oppose affirmative action understand the need for diversity in political appointments.

Meanwhile, conservatives have been winning the war over institutions and economics. Redistributive economic and social policies have moved sharply to the right. Richard Nixon's health-care reforms and earned-income tax credit were more progressive than anything Bill Clinton proposed in office. Incarceration rates are at an extraordinary all-time high, and almost no money is spent on rehabilitation programs, which are broadly assumed to be failed relics of the progressive 1960s. The gap between rich and poor has grown as fast as the economy, and yet redistributive taxation is nowhere on the agenda. Even to raise the issue opens liberals to the charge of "class warfare," universally assumed to constitute political suicide even though middle-income earners outnumber the wealthy by an enormous margin.

A useful comparison emerges between church-state affairs and the broader political realm. Public displays of religion belong, in a sense, to the culture wars—and legal secularists, who tend to be liberals, have been winning in this sphere. The funding of religion through government grants, however, belongs properly to the sphere of economic and social policy, because it involves redistribution of wealth by the government after collection of taxes. Here, the values evangelicals have met with success, as have their conservative counterparts in social welfare policy more generally.

Why this result? Why has American policy become increasingly liberal in the symbolic realm while conservatism has grown in the context of fiscal policy? One might have expected the opposite result in the light of the reaction to 1960s liberalism that helped give rise to the Third Great Awakening and values evangelicalism. That movement belonged primarily to the universe of culture. The Moral Majority identified school prayer and abortion as the issues it cared about, and Richard Neuhaus's powerful argument against legal secularism focused on the detrimental effects of symbolic exclusion of religion, not on an argument in favor of government funding of religious institutions.

Part of the answer lies in the courts, where Reagan and Bush appointees made inroads into legal secularism's territory without defeating it altogether. The fact that secularism had won the major legal victory of transforming church-state relations into a federal constitutional issue constantly before the courts meant that the people who decided cases would be elites who were relatively unlikely to be moral majoritarians. For swing members of those elites who, like Justice O'Connor, seek compromise, it may be easier to adopt the liberal view on cultural questions and the conservative view on economic ones, for the simple reason that their social contacts are primarily with other culturally secular elites. But this is only part of the answer, because it depends on the prior assumption that liberal elites care more about symbolic cultural issues than underlying economic ones. The reason for this phenomenon, in turn, is surely complicated. A cynic (or a Marxist) might say that well-off liberal elites actually benefit from nonredistributive economic policies and so have less motivation to promote redistribution than to promote cultural reforms that serve their interests more directly. A more generous observer might guess that liberals do what they can and suffer where they must. The disproportionate influence of liberalism among educated elites gives liberals the opportunity to affect social mores through the media, the arts, and the courts, all of which can influence culture much more easily than they can economic relations. Conservatives, on the other hand, have done better with legislatures and so have won the important economic policy issues of the last quarter century.

The fascinating irony of the church-state debates is that, in the era of the endorsement test, legal secularists have failed to hold the line on the ban of government funding for religion, the cornerstone of early legal secularism and indeed of the American tradition of the separation of government institutions from the institutional church. Values evangelicals have simultaneously found themselves frustrated in the symbolic sphere about which they care most, and the loss of which inspired them to action in the first place. To make matters worse, values evangelicals have had trouble consolidating their victories in the sphere of government funding. Suburban Protestants (and Catholics) have declined to push hard for the funding of faith-based programs, most of which turn out to benefit inner-city poor. Where public schools are strong, there is reduced pressure for school vouchers, and such programs, while held constitutional, have not yet spread widely. Both sides, legal secularist and values evangelical, are losing the fights they care most about.

Plenty of important constitutional debates in American public life, from affirmative action to capital punishment, get resolved by a political-judicial-popular compromise that is hard to defend logically on its own terms. In the case of church and state, however, we have less a compromise than an unresolved, continuing argument over basic questions of national identity. It is therefore worth looking closely at the most sophisticated arguments on each side, in order to tease out their problems and implications, and ask whether either one can plausibly guide us into the future.

7

OUT OF MANY, ONE

Legal secularism and values evangelicalism are both attempts to deal with the challenge of achieving national unity in the face of religious diversity. Their solutions, however, differ fundamentally, with the former maintaining that religion must be removed from the public realm so that all can participate on equal terms, and the latter insisting that only shared values, derived from religion, can sustain a national community. Having shown how each emerged as a response to a new form of religious diversity, I now want to consider their adequacy to deal with the present and future realities of American life, especially the coming wave of new religious diversity, by evaluating both the practical effects of these two approaches and the extent to which each satisfies the demands of logic and ethical judgment. After all, this book's historical analysis is intended to help us clarify not only where we have been but also where we ought to go.

LEGAL SECULARISM AND ITS DISCONTENTS

Earlier, I described strong secularism as the view that religion should not play any role at all in how we organize and arrange our public or private lives, and showed how this somewhat extreme approach failed to transform church-state relations in its first incarnation. Yet secularism met with real success when it morphed into legal secularism, the more restrictive view that religion should not play a significant role in how we organize, arrange, and discuss politics and government. Although the two forms of secularism have close historical connections, the legal secularist does not have to believe that religion should play no role in our individual, private lives. Focusing on the political sphere, the legal secularist can simply say that neither organized religion nor religious belief should play a role in the arena of government. Our collective, democratic decisions should be made on the basis of nonreligious reasoning, and the actions that our government takes should not reflect religious values or preferences. Two elements make legal secularism "legal." It is restricted to the public, political sphere where law governs and where laws are made, and it proposes strict legal rules to keep religion out of government. Legal secularists think that the Constitution should be used to manage the relationship between church and state.

Strong secularism may still be the motivation of some legal secularists: if religion in general is of little value or actively does more harm than good in the world, it follows that its influence should be excluded from important decisions of politics and government. But outside the seminar room, this bleak view is rarely voiced in American public life. Moreover, reticence about dismissing others' most deeply held beliefs as flatly useless would today deter many thoughtful people from strong secularism in its purest form.

The more usual justifications for legal secularism today derive from the inescapable fact of religious diversity and the demands of

inclusiveness associated with liberal democracy. The historical experience of religious persecution helped form the background for the
writings of early liberals like Locke who advocated religious liberty,
and modern legal secularism continues to reflect concern that vulnerable religious minorities will be pushed to the margins.[1] Although it is implicit in democratic governance that the majority
may use the state to promote programs, institutions, and ideas that
a minority may not value, legal secularism seeks to carve out religion from the ends that the state may rightfully advance or the
means it may use to do so. The reasonable concern is that, even in
the face of diversity, allowing citizens to use the government to express or give effect to religious belief enables some to exclude or disadvantage those who believe differently. Christians might organize
against non-Christians, or religious people might marginalize the
nonreligious. Either way, if a majority deployed the resources of the
state to enhance beliefs and attitudes not shared by minorities, it
might make it hard for those excluded to participate fully.[2] If the
state is functionally Christian, how can Jews or Muslims be equal to
Christians as citizens?

Moreover, with so many different, competing faiths and traditions in our society, it seems hopeless to find consensus once we allow religion to be invoked in public discourse. It is notoriously
difficult to carry on reasoned debate between people who invoke
different religious presuppositions to support their views, yet
democracy requires collective deliberation and the exchange of reasons, not just voting on outcomes. If I assert in public debate that
God, speaking through the Bible, has instructed me to oppose
abortion or capital punishment, then perhaps there will be nothing
the other side can say to me to change my mind. Correspondingly,
there will be no reason for my interlocutors to listen to what I am
saying unless they share my initial faith-based assumption about
what God commands. The discussion may break down if we are
not speaking in common terms.

One influential strand of legal secularism suggests that we solve this problem of stalemated debate by agreeing to propose only arguments in the political realm that other reasonable people could logically accept, regardless of their religious beliefs. If we agree to this precondition of politics, then our political conversations will be secular, in the sense that no one will invoke religious beliefs or attitudes to justify policies or laws. Given the fact of religious diversity, and the existence of many different potentially contradictory beliefs, this solution, associated in its formal aspect with the philosopher John Rawls, seems like the best mechanism for keeping the conversation going.[3] The Supreme Court's now all-but-moribund *Lemon* test, which represented the high point of legal secularism, embodied a constitutional rule of thumb to keep religion out of the political conversation: if a law or government action has a secular purpose, it passes the test, but if the purpose is not secular, then we have gone off course, and the law or government action should be deemed unconstitutional.

Legal secularists accept religious liberty and free speech as basic rights and would not favor a rule formally prohibiting religious arguments in public discussion or in Congress. But legal secularists *are* in favor of a constitutional rule under which the fact that supporters have invoked religion in support of a bill in Congress could disqualify that bill from taking effect as a law. If enough supporters of the bill explained their reasons for passing it in religious terms, then the bill would surely no longer have a secular purpose but a religious one, making it unconstitutional under the *Lemon* test. As a result, even without a ban on religious arguments about how we should act as a nation, such arguments would be systematically marginalized or eliminated from public discourse, because making them could actually render one's preferred course of action unconstitutional.

Both the appeal and the serious problems with legal secularism emerge from this proposed solution, which the *Lemon* approach tried to constitutionalize. Creating a disincentive for religious speech in the political context would seem to balance religious liberty against the desire for a secular public sphere.[4] Yet consider the consequences to religious believers of restricting or disadvantaging religious ideas and arguments in politics. Suppose the reason I want abortion banned really is simply that I believe life begins at conception because my religious tradition tells me so. In order to support a law limiting abortion, though, I will not be able to rely on my religious faith in my efforts to convince others, lest a court invalidate the law as religious in purpose. I will have to come up with some other kind of argument, based on some set of values that could be shared by people who do not belong to my faith. Perhaps, then, I will say that life begins at conception because once conception has occurred, a baby will be produced in the normal course of events. As we saw, values evangelicals have often adopted just this strategy, emphasizing nominally secular reasoning for positions held on religious grounds. The problem is that such arguments are stand-ins, not at all the same as the religious assertion for which they substitute. If legal secularism bars the way to advancing religious arguments, then it is actively blocking me in the realm of politics from expressing my most deeply held values about human life. I am, in theory, allowed to say whatever I want, but my words will be prevented from having practical effects by the requirement that every law have a secular purpose.

In a society in which some citizens base their political choices on deeply held religious beliefs, requiring political discourse to be secular systematically excludes them from the political conversation.[5] This exclusion effect is an unintended consequence for most legal secularists, who sincerely believe that making politics secular is meant to include everybody equally in political debate and keep the conversation going even where there is deep disagreement. But here the legal secularists, and the liberal philosophers on whose views they rely, devalue something basic about how a large number of Americans experience political participation. When it comes to the most important subjects, like freedom and equality, many people do not want to exclude their foundational values from the discussion. They want to be able to explain why they think abortion is wrong or why they oppose same-sex marriage. Asking them to leave out the religious basis for their most fundamental beliefs means cutting them off at the knees, crippling their ability to participate fully. Faced with such strictures, many religious believers will either opt out of the debate altogether or else demand a change to the rules of the game.

So despite secularism's aspiration to generate inclusive discourse through neutral ground rules, keeping public debate secular fails to involve everyone in the conversation. Why would anyone wish to debate crucially important subjects without the benefit of his foundational commitments? Because their own bedrock beliefs tend to be based on nonreligious propositions, legal secularists are in practice suspiciously unaffected by a rule that political argument must not be religious. Asked why he thinks that all people are equal, a legal secularist is likely to respond that it is just a basic commitment that he holds. His answer, then, may not differ greatly from that of the believer who holds that God created all people equal. Both the secular and the religious arguments depend upon the foundations of particular belief systems. Why, then, should religious beliefs be excluded from the debate while secular beliefs are allowed to remain?

The usual answer made by legal secularists is that religious perspectives are not subject to reasonable disagreement, whereas secular beliefs, even when they are foundational, can always be questioned, challenged, and investigated. I might change my secular foundational beliefs as a result of the conversation, but my religious beliefs will be unshakable. Legal secularists who argue in this vein like to say that religion is a "conversation stopper."[6] In a political system that relies on debate, not force, to resolve controversial questions, stopping conversation is imagined to be just about the worst thing one can do.

The problem is that imagining religion to be the end of the political conversation represents a serious misunderstanding of the nature of religious belief, its capacity to change, and its relation to democratic politics.[7] Ask a religious person why he has faith, and he may give reasons for his belief—for indeed many religious traditions see faith as fully compatible with reason—or he may respond that he just believes and cannot explain why. To end the conversation after this one question might produce the impression that there is nothing to talk about when it comes to religious belief, or that there is no room for flexibility in discussing important moral topics unless beliefs are shared. But what if one follows up by asking the believer how his faith directs him to make moral judgments about the world and how we ought to act in it? Almost no believer will simply repeat that he just knows morality as an automatic matter, or that God has directly told him the right way to live. Prophets hear directly from God; most religious believers will point to religious texts and traditions that they consider authoritative guides for living. They will mention the Bible or the Qur'an, the teachings of a church or of rabbis or other sages. Even denominations that believe in direct inspiration, such as Quakers or some evangelicals, rarely think there is no room for interpretation. If one asks the believer *how* he knows what his Scripture or his tradition teaches about the good life, he will likely answer that he, alone or with others, must interpret the teachings of his faith to make sense of how they apply to the real world.

Once the believer acknowledges, as he almost surely will, that religion calls for human interpretation, the possibilities for holding a conversation about important moral topics open up dramatically. For one thing, anybody can engage a believer on the question of how his or her religious tradition should be translated into the political sphere. If a Catholic tells me she believes life begins at conception, I can still ask her whether she thinks this religious belief should be expressed in a legal-political judgment about the legality of abortion. If she says it seems obvious to her that abortion should be illegal on account of her belief, I can reply that perhaps the state should not protect life per se, but rather fully born humans. We now have a basis for debate, neither more nor less tractable than would be a debate with someone who argued, for secular reasons, that early-term fetuses should not be considered "life."

So religious belief can jump-start conversations as well as stop them. No religious tradition is without internal discussion, debate, and disagreement about hard questions, and even an outsider can take on these subjects if he bothers to learn the basic beliefs from which the believers are arguing. If believers do not want to engage outsiders' interpretations of their tradition, the outsiders can still argue about how the religious beliefs should be applied in the context of lawmaking. If the religious believer asserts that the answers to these second-order questions, too, are dictated by religious belief, the outsider can still ask why it should be so and find a subject for discussion in the answer to that question.

In short, the notion that political debate must be secular in order to keep democratic deliberation going is misplaced. Aspiring to inclusiveness, legal secularism instead generates exclusion of citizens who draw heavily on their religion for political guidance. It fails, therefore, to offer a satisfactory solution to the problem of religious diversity and national cohesion.

VALUES EVANGELICALISM: THE TENSIONS WITHIN

Unlike legal secularists, who think we need inclusive procedural ground rules to facilitate political argument, values evangelicals maintain that national unity requires Americans to reach some basic substantive agreement on the values we share. Apart from a connection to Christian evangelicalism itself, what makes this commitment to shared values "evangelical" is that it presumes it possible and desirable to convince all Americans to share those values that are embraced by the majority. But values evangelicals have in common with legal secularists a love for freedom of conscience and religious liberty; they rely on persuasion, not coercion, to spread the values they consider fundamental.

Values evangelicals have learned that, in order to make their aspiration of shared values plausible, they need to identify these values at a relatively high level of generality, making them accessible to people who come from diverse religious traditions or even (perhaps) those who reject religion altogether. Learning this lesson took a long time, and its embrace distinguishes values evangelicalism from the nonsectarianism that preceded it. As we have seen, American Protestants sometimes denied that they shared morals with Catholic immigrants; in turn, Catholics reacted with skepticism and hostility to Protestant efforts at sometimes coercive inclusion. It took more than 150 years from the first major Catholic immigration to the United States for Catholics and evangelical Protestants to make common cause and develop contemporary values evangelicalism as a movement that would represent their collective interests. Now, however, values evangelicals understand that they cannot get bogged down in doctrinal disagreement when identifying shared values. Today they are less likely to point to the old rhetoric calling America a Christian nation and more likely to focus on Supreme Court language from the 1950s—the product of the inclusive rhetoric of that decade—declaring that "we are a religious people whose institutions presuppose a Supreme Being."

Values evangelicals see the schools, correctly, as instruments for inculcating values and therefore believe that schools must be vigilant in teaching those that are true and can be broadly shared. They fear that schools tuned to the legal secularists' frequency will be so busy avoiding religious topics that they will either teach the value of strong secularism, with its attendant hostility to religion, or no values at all. Values evangelicals hope to inject into the schools enough religion to help produce good moral judgment in the students.

Just as important, many values evangelicals want the public

schools to help produce national unity by teaching common narratives that imagine Americans unified rather than fragmented. They do not necessarily reject the idea of teaching about America's diversity, so long as different cultures and religions are depicted as sharing common commitments to faith, family, and virtue. The overwhelming theme in values evangelicalism is that we need to find ways to identify and express shared values to avoid falling into the trap of isolation, deracination, and collapse. Like legal secularism, values evangelicalism seeks to make unity out of diversity—but it seeks to do so by directly promoting some general religious values, not by excluding religion.

In its most sophisticated and attractive form, values evangelicalism is actually a type of multiculturalist pluralism, professing respect for faith as faith and for cultural tradition as tradition. This inclusive vision of a society in which one can partake in the common American project by the very act of worshipping as one chooses is more than broad enough to accommodate new religious diversity that has come about as a result of Muslim, Hindu, and Buddhist immigration. Values evangelicalism therefore appears as though it might provide a good solution to our increasing religious diversity, allowing us to maintain national unity without telling new immigrants today that they ought to exclude their faith when they go about forming their political judgments.

Unfortunately, the inclusive promise of values evangelicalism founders on the rock of shared values. The problem is not that it is hopeless for believers of various faiths, or of none, to feel their way toward values that most of them would be able to share. The problem is that the values evangelicals, in practice, cannot be satisfied with the abstraction of the shared values on which diversity forces them to compromise. The actual disagreement between adherents of various religious traditions is so great that a preference for religion generally turns out to be self-contradictory.

Most values evangelicals believe, for example, that if the schools celebrate Christmas, it should also be all right for them to acknowledge Hanukkah. But what if it turns out that some Jews think the spirit of Hanukkah lies precisely in rejecting the majority's Christianity in the same way the Maccabees resisted Hellenistic paganism? The Ten Commandments may appear at first to represent common ground. But what about Hindus and Buddhists, who are excluded by the commandments' theological assertion that the God who took the Israelites out of Egypt is the one true God who permits no other gods to be taken before him? What of Muslims, for whom the Bible is a preliminary, imperfect revelation, unlike God's definitive teaching, found only in the Qur'an? Even the text as rendered into English poses problems. The commandment usually translated "Thou shalt not kill" is more accurately translated from Hebrew as "Thou shalt not murder," a distinction that makes a big interdenominational difference.[8]

Religiously inspired disagreements on values do not end there. Today, most evangelical Protestants support capital punishment on a biblical basis, while many Catholics rely on the late Pope John Paul II's teaching about the sanctity of life to oppose the death penalty. Protestants and Catholics still differ over the permissibility of divorce—one of the issues that fueled the Reformation in England—even though many American Catholics are prepared to disobey their church's teaching on the question. Churches differ about whether to embrace same-sex marriage or reject it. When it comes to holidays, some Jews, especially the outward-looking Hasidim of the Chabad Lubavitch movement, welcome the chance to erect menorahs near public Christmas trees, but many other Jews oppose the celebration of Christmas in public venues on the theory that they do not want to be exposed to the religious symbols associated with the holiday. Their reason to reject Christmas celebrations is not that they have some problem with peace on earth and goodwill to men, but that, like Muslims, they do not accept the divinity of Christ and the virgin birth.

So values evangelicalism labors under a strange and troubling paradox often unnoticed by its advocates. Values evangelicals consider relativism the enemy. They are constantly asserting that the values they stand for *mean* something—that these values are true and good and worth fighting for, unlike the weak platitudes favored by legal secularists. But like other multiculturalists, values evangelicals often have to water down the traditions to which they belong in order to find common ground with one another. Values evangelicalism assumes an acceptance of others' beliefs that many religious believers cannot accept without sliding into relativism.[9]

Values evangelicals, ironically enough, can cling to the hope of creating common, shared religious values only because they are willing to paper over real theological differences. Some sincerely believe that different religions espouse similar morality, but many just assume—incorrectly—that other religious people must see tough moral issues the same way they do. A broadly shared reaction against 1960s-style secularism helped fuel the perception that believers of all stripes agree on social values, but the more religious diversity we have in the United States, the clearer the falsehood of that assumption becomes.

When confronted by the degree of disagreement on fundamental moral questions that exists among different religious groups, some values evangelicals respond by suggesting that the government should get out of the education business altogether and provide all parents with vouchers that they can use to educate their children in the religious tradition of their choosing. If there cannot be agreement on a common set of values in schools, why not let people vote with their feet, rather than putting government in the undesirable position of having to design schools where the values taught are so vague that they exclude no one? The vouchers option therefore has some real appeal, and values evangelicals have largely embraced it in theory, even though it has received relatively little on-the-ground political support in suburbs, where the public schools seem adequate to many residents, evangelicals included.

But from the perspective of values evangelicalism, a vouchers-based approach—which could be extended beyond the schools to

other contexts where the state supports scholarly or cultural proj-
ects—is ultimately unsatisfying. The trouble is that offering government support, in the form of vouchers, to advocates of *every* set
of values implies that every set of beliefs equally deserves the government's support. Whatever else they may be prepared to concede
in the interests of unity, values evangelicals cannot be prepared to
admit that. Values evangelicalism is committed to distinguishing
good values from bad. Vouchers schemes may superficially appeal
to values evangelicals because they create the option of state-
supported unabashedly religious education. On closer analysis,
though, vouchers also allow support of teachings that values evangelicals would certainly reject as immoral and unacceptable.

Some other values evangelicals take a more direct tack in defending their position, acknowledging openly that they like values evangelicalism precisely because it gives the Christian majority the
opportunity to promote its own particular religious values in the
guise of being inclusive. These values evangelicals will not be especially disturbed to discover that some Americans might disagree
with the prayers they offer in the workplace or the inspirational
Christian messages that some teachers in the South hang in their
classrooms. In a way, these values evangelicals are in a better position, logically speaking, than their more enlightened counterparts
who profess to favor values generally rather than evangelical Christian values in particular: they may even argue that they are going to
promote their beliefs because those beliefs are God's truth, worth
fighting for even if the Constitution limits their public promotion.
This tone of civil disobedience was heard among the supporters of
Alabama Chief Justice Roy Moore, who were prepared to be ar-
rested rather than to allow the removal of the two-and-a-half-ton
granite Ten Commandments monument he had erected in the state
courthouse in Montgomery. It did not matter, they said, that the
federal courts had officially declared the monument unconstitutional; they were standing up for the law of God, not the law of the
Constitution. Moore himself lost his judicial post over the issue—

some evidence that he was prepared to pay the price of disobedience.

This view is relatively uncommon among values evangelicals, however, who are out not to subvert the Constitution in favor of religion but rather to defend the Constitution in what they consider its truest form. They explain that, when a local majority wants to promote religious values in its schools or public buildings, there is no harm done. Outsiders like the ACLU or a few dissenters might raise a fuss, they say, but most locals are happy. By implication, these values evangelicals maintain that legal secularists are acting undemocratically, opposing the majority's preference for certain values and trying to impose their own secular value structure where it is neither wanted nor needed.

In practice, this could be true in some relatively homogeneous parts of America, where almost everybody is happy to open the school day with prayers and to acknowledge religion in public celebrations and the like. Insisting on a strong separation between government and religious displays in these contexts might well seem awkward and undemocratic, pitting outsiders and a local minority or two against the great majority. The values evangelicals are on to something when they protest that a few people are spoiling things for the majority.

Yet those values evangelicals who openly admit that their goal is to proselytize for their own particular religious values cannot really explain why they think there should be any distinction between religion and government at all. Surely there are some towns where no one would object even if the government started paying the ministers' salaries. A local majority might, in other words, favor the establishment of religion, complete with the public proclamation that the town is a Christian town. Locals would probably object if church attendance became mandatory, but it might make little difference if it did, because, presumably, most people in town already attend church on Sundays. After all, the Constitution must mean *something* when it says that there shall be no established religion.

The proud admission by some values evangelicals that they are out to use the government to convince people to believe as they do is therefore a classic example of an argument that proves too much. That is the reason so few values evangelicals are willing to admit that they think it is acceptable for government to promote one particular religion. They understand that the Constitution must have in mind at least *some* sort of inclusion, and that, more to the point, we are unlikely to develop national unity if one particular religious denomination tries to capture the apparatus of government for its own ends.

In sum, the inclusiveness of values evangelicalism is what makes it attractive, but it also contains the seeds of its downfall. It is appealing to think that, deep down, we all agree on what really matters. Only we don't—and we have to come to terms with that fact of disagreement while still engaging in a common national project.

8

RECONCILIATION AND THE
AMERICAN EXPERIMENT

We are, increasingly, a nation divided by God. Although we all believe in religious liberty and almost no one wants an officially established religion, we cannot agree on what the relation between religion and government should be. The distinctive church-state problem that our framers created when they declared the people sovereign is still with us. Our religious diversity, now fueled by immigration of Muslims, Hindus, and Buddhists, is greater than ever. Yet neither legal secularism nor values evangelicalism, our two most recent attempts at forging national unity in the face of this religious diversity, has lived up to its own aspirations. Both promise inclusion, but neither has delivered. To make matters worse, the conflict between these two approaches is becoming a political and constitutional crisis all its own.

Instead of trying to adopt once and for all either the apparently elegant solution of legal secularism or the moral appeal of values evangelicalism, we need to look ahead and try to find a fresh alternative: a solution that draws on our past practices, our highest aspirations, and our best sense of what is achievable. Most important, a workable solution to our church-state problem must reconcile secu-

larists and evangelicals by making both sides feel included in the experiment of American government and nationhood. So long as the
fight between the two sides continues as it has, it will be a zero-sum
game, winner-take-all at the ballot box or in the courts. Talk of blue
states seceding from red in the aftermath of the 2004 election is
meant ironically, but this kind of dark musing, with its explicit reference to the Civil War, is also not coincidental. It bespeaks a division deeper than any other in our public life, a division that cannot
be healed by the victory of either side.

The answer, I want to suggest, lies in preserving the value of religious liberty that has been a consistent feature of all the eras in
American church-state relations, while simultaneously respecting
the institutional separation of church and state that has been with
us since the beginning. This combination is not simple. Religious
liberty assumes that religion is profoundly meaningful, and it guarantees that citizens may draw on their own beliefs when they form
opinions and make political choices. Meanwhile, institutional separation requires a delineation between government and religion, severing one sort of connection between governance and a key source
of social organization for many citizens. They have it much easier
in France, for example, where the principle of *laïcité*—in effect,
constitutionalized strong secularism—simply rejects the notion that
religion is an inherently meaningful source of values, and so can
easily conclude that religion can be excluded from the public sphere
altogether. It is also simpler in the many Muslim countries where
constitutions declare Islam to be a principal source of legislation
and, correspondingly, do not institutionally separate religion from
government. Our experiment will have to avoid both extremes. We
want to acknowledge the centrality of religion to many citizens'
values while keeping religion and government in some important
sense distinct.

Despite the gravity of the problem, I believe that the history of
church and state in America that I have offered in these pages does

point toward an answer. Put simply, it is this: offer greater latitude for public religious discourse and religious symbolism, and at the same time insist on a stricter ban on state funding of religious institutions and activities. Such a solution would both recognize religious values *and* respect the institutional separation of religion and government as an American value in its own right. This would mean abandoning the argument that religion has no place in the public sphere while simultaneously insisting that government must go to great lengths to dissociate itself from any affiliation with or support for religious institutions.

In the courts, this would mean abandoning the *Lemon* requirement that state action must have a secular purpose, as well as Justice O'Connor's idea that the state must not "endorse" religion. For these failed tests, the courts should substitute the two guiding rules that historically lay at the core of our church-state experiment before either legal secularism or values evangelicalism came on the scene: the state may neither coerce anyone in matters of religion, nor expend its resources so as to support religious institutions and practices. These constitutional principles, reduced to their core, can be captured in a simple slogan: no coercion and no money. If no one is being coerced by the government, and if the government is not spending its money or other resources on religious institutions and practices, the courts should hold that the Constitution is not violated.

Both consequences of this approach—allowing greater space for public manifestations of religion, and cracking down on state support for institutional religion—go against the trends of the last several decades, which are for stricter regulation of public religious symbolism and more permissive authorization of government funding and support for religion. At first blush, then, the proposal may strike both sides of the current debate as mistaken, since it requires each to give up some of its victories in exchange for an alternative solution. Nonetheless, this approach is not only faithful to our constitutional traditions. It also stands a chance of winning over secularists and evangelicals alike and beginning to close the rift between them.

My reason for proposing that we loosen up on religious talk and symbols while cracking down on institutional affiliation of church and state is not just historical. We are under no absolute duty to return to the solutions of the past, and indeed those solutions must be tweaked and adjusted to update them to our present beliefs and practical situation, both very different from what came before. The fact that the church-state solution I am proposing resembles, in its general outlines, the approach adopted by the framers and inherited in later eras is not on its own a definitive reason for adopting it.

Rather, the justification for the approach I want to propose—no coercion and no money—is basically forward-looking: we need, as badly as any generation in the American past, to find a way toward greater national unity in the face of our religious diversity. In the past we can find a partial model for how we might meet that challenge. On one hand, if we begin by acknowledging that we share the objective of inclusion, then we may be able to begin the process of reinterpreting the meaning of public religious discourse and symbols. On the other hand, history should help us see that the expenditure of state resources to sponsor institutional religion will lead inevitably to discord.

The core insight is that citizens speak as individuals or as groups, and so long as all citizens have the same right to do so, no one group or person should be threatened or excluded by the symbolic or political speech of others, much as they may disagree. By contrast, when the state funds programs and institutions, it acts—after deliberation—as a unified actor controlling limited resources. In redirecting the collective resources of the state to particular ends, it cannot escape political competition over what counts as a worthy purpose and what does not. Speech and symbols, in other words, are not the same as funding. Talk can always be reinterpreted, and more talk can always be added, so religious speech and symbols need not exclude. Cold cash, by contrast, is concrete and finite, and thus subject to divisive competition of a different order.

Begin with political arguments that depend on religious premises. Legal secularists may fear that when such arguments are made, they will be unable to meet them and may lose. But in fact, as I argued earlier, secularists can make arguments of their own, which may be convincing. When the debate is over, the people (or, most of the time, their representatives) will vote, and that will decide the matter. Legal secularists cannot realistically expect that they will win more democratic fights by banning the evangelicals' arguments, which can usually be recast, however disingenuously, as secular. Once in a while they may, if the composition of the Supreme Court is just right, thwart the values evangelicals' numerical superiority with a judicial override, but in the long run, all they will accomplish is to alienate the values evangelicals in a way that undercuts the meaningfulness of participatory democracy.

When it comes to religious symbolism, typically some group of citizens will ask the state for an opportunity to acknowledge their holiday or tradition. Following a popularized version of Justice O'Connor's endorsement test, legal secularists typically object on the ground that if the state acquiesces, then the state is embracing the religious symbol and communicating exclusion to adherents of other religions. But this interpretation may not be the best or most natural one. The fact that others have asked for and gotten recognition implies nothing about the exclusion of any religious minority except for the brute fact that it *is* a religious minority. There is no reason whatever for religious minorities to be shielded from that fact, since there is nothing shameful or inherently disadvantageous in being a religious minority, so long as that minority is not subject to coercion or discrimination.

Take the fact that the government treats Christmas as a national holiday. It would be very strange if Jews or Muslims or Hindus or Buddhists felt fundamentally excluded from citizenship by this fact—and I would venture to suggest that very few do. Most Americans are still Christians who celebrate Christmas, and the state acknowledges it, just as the culture does through the songs on the radio and the merchandise in the stores. The celebration may not always be deeply religious, but the atmosphere corresponds to the realities of the Christian majority. Just what is threatening to religious minorities about Christians celebrating the holiday and the state acknowledging that fact? The state has not made Christianity relevant to citizenship—it has just acknowledged the preferences of a majority. Perhaps some members of religious minorities may choose to spend December feeling bad that they are not part of the majority culture, but they would have this same problem even if Christmas were not a national holiday, since Christmas would still be all around them. The answer is for them to strengthen their own identities and be proud of who they are, not to insist that the majority give up its own celebration to accommodate them.

The extreme version of the legal secularists' aspiration appears in the title of one academic's manifesto: *Please Don't Wish Me a Merry Christmas*.[1] But what, exactly, is the harm in being wished Merry Christmas when one is not celebrating? There need be no mistaken assumption that everyone is a Christian; it may just be a reasonable probability, provided one is not wearing a yarmulke or a turban. More to the point, how can it possibly make sense for *everyone* to have to stop saying Merry Christmas to strangers because of the outside chance that an unfamiliar addressee might not be celebrating?

In the last fifty years, legal secularists have feared that public manifestations of religion marginalize religious minorities and hence reduce the capacity of those minorities to participate in a common national public life. When Jews were almost the only non-Christians in the United States, apart from a handful of scattered atheists, the concern arguably made some sense. The cultural practices of old-fashioned nonsectarianism, from school prayer to crèches and beyond, could certainly be understood as underscoring the idea of a Christian nation. Some of these, especially involving mandatory exercises in school, were downright coercive. Minimizing public religious symbols—in effect, minimizing public Christianity—seemed on the surface like a plausible method for facilitating Jewish inclusion, since the only obvious options were a symbolically Christian nation or one without religious symbols.

But today, the increasing presence of other non-Christian religious minorities, and an attendant atmosphere of religious multiculturalism, means that public manifestations of religion—at least at the national level—are becoming increasingly pluralistic and inclusive. Consider the televised memorial service led by President Bush on September 14, 2001, a day he designated as a National Day of Prayer and Remembrance for the victims of the 9/11 attacks. With cabinet, Congress, Supreme Court Justices, and the foreign diplomatic corps in attendance, the president assured the congregation that God created a world "of moral design," and that "the Lord of life holds all who die and all who mourn." Urging that nothing, "neither death nor life nor angels nor principalities," could come between the American people and God's love, he closed with a threefold wish: "May He bless the souls of the departed. May He comfort our own. And may He always guide our country."[2] Suffused with as much theology as any presidential address since Lincoln's second inaugural, the speech directly addressed the problem of evil while commending the future of the republic to God's grace. Yet despite the high-Protestant venue—the Episcopalian Washington National Cathedral—the president was followed in the pulpit not only by the dean of the cathedral but also by the Roman Catholic archbishop of Washington, D.C., an African-American Methodist minister, Billy Graham, a rabbi, and an imam who recited verses from the Qur'an. The display of inclusiveness was driven not only by political imperative but also by the recognition that this extraordinary national-religious moment must reach out to America's religious diversity. In the future, if current immigration patterns continue, we can expect Hindu and Buddhist participation in comparable settings.

In this latest demographic version of a religiously diverse environment, where Protestants will soon no longer be a majority in the United States, the danger that public religious symbolism will marginalize non-Christians is substantially decreased. Some parts of the country are still dominated by particular denominations or trends, but even in the heart of the Bible Belt, diversity is growing as a result of immigration and patterns of shifting population. Although historically, nonsectarian public religion was experienced as exclusionary by Catholics and, later, Jews, and although a large majority of Americans are still Christian, it does not follow that public manifestations of religion must inevitably be exclusionary. They can include a wide range of symbols and practices without watering all of them down into a single nondenominational soup. Atheists—like Michael Newdow, who went all the way to the Supreme Court to argue against the words "under God" in the Pledge of Allegiance—will doubtless maintain that any public religion at all excludes them by endorsing the idea of religion generally. But this misses the point: it is largely an interpretive choice to feel excluded by the fact of other people's faith, and the atheist can just as easily adhere to his own views while insisting on his citizenship. So long as Newdow's daughter is not coerced into invoking God while reciting the Pledge in school, it makes little sense to accommodate his beliefs by barring everyone else from saying the words that one person finds exclusionary. The Jehovah's Witnesses never claimed that their conscientious scruples required that the pledge and salute be abolished for everyone—they just wanted their children to be exempt.

In some instances, pluralistic public religion even holds out the possibility of enabling new religious minorities to participate fully in the American public sphere. Muslims, Hindus, and Buddhists, for whom religion and immigrant status may be closely connected, might well seek opportunities for the symbolic recognition of *their* citizenship that can be gained in schools, legislatures, and elsewhere. Acknowledging holidays like the Muslim Eid or the Hindu Divali in what has traditionally been a Christian country may validate a sense of belonging like no secular civic symbol can. Fundamental values and beliefs derived from faith may undergird new citizens' political beliefs and choices as much as they do for those who have long been in the United States. Ultimately, the nation may have more success generating loyalty from religiously diverse citizens by allowing inclusive governmental manifestations of religion than by banning them.

There are good reasons, in other words, for secularists to reconsider whether their goal of inclusion will be best served by keeping religion out of the public realm—especially given that so many values evangelicals feel excluded from full citizenship by what they perceive as the removal of traditional religious symbols from public space. Secularists have a principled interest in allaying the evangelicals' sense of exclusion—they want everyone to feel included in citizenship. But a further motive is pragmatic politics. Evangelicals' perceived exclusion fuels resentment and a reactionary attempt to impose brand-new symbols, like the Ten Commandments in courthouses, where none existed before. In the attempt to make public discourse inclusive, legal secularists overshot the mark, unintentionally generating resentment that has motivated a strand of militant values evangelicalism.

Observing the political clout of the evangelicals, many secularists cannot imagine how the former could possibly feel marginalized from American society. They must realize, however, that the evangelicals' political strength has not often extended to the cultural realm, about which values evangelicals care the most. Evangelicals feel defensive not only because they believe they are losing the culture war and have trouble enacting religious values into public policy—in fact, they have made some strides on issues like abortion and same-sex marriage—but because they have difficulty making the religious sources of their ideas explicit in the cultural-political *conversation*.[3] When they try to make religious values the touchstone for debate, legal secularists tend to respond not by disagreeing with their values but by dismissively telling them that those values have no place in the public conversation—in other words, by telling them they are breaking the rules of good citizenship. The evangelicals' response is to try to appropriate the secularists' rhetoric and to claim that *they* are being excluded. Restricting public manifestations of religion then comes to be seen, for values evangelicals, as the symbolic counterpart of suppressing religious arguments in politics.[4]

A better approach for secularists is to confront the evangelicals' arguments on their own terms, refusing to end the conversation and instead arguing for the rightness of their beliefs about their *own* values. This will not produce easy agreement on abortion or same-sex marriage or anything else. To the contrary, hard moral questions will remain controversial. But acknowledging a moral debate *as* a moral debate in which all sides deserve a say will have the effect of communicating to evangelicals that their voices count. In the long run, this approach is more likely to focus our national debates on substance rather than on procedure—on what God or reason or whatever source of values teaches about human life and intimate choices, not about whether God belongs in the conversation at all. Secularists who are confident in their views should expect to prevail on the basis of reason, and evangelicals who wish to win the argument will discover that their arguments must extend beyond simple invocation of faith.

But if we are to progress toward reconciliation of our church-state problem, it will not be enough for secularists to reevaluate their attitude toward religious symbols and religious discourse. Values evangelicals must also change their ways and give something up. They ought to reconsider their position in favor of state support for religious institutions and re-embrace the American tradition of institutionally separated church and state. The reason they should be prepared to do so is that such state funding actually undercuts, rather than promotes, the cohesive national identity that evangelicals have wanted to restore or re-create. Even when filtered through vouchers distributed by the government and directed by individual choice, state financial aid for religious institutions like schools or charities does not encourage common values; it creates conflict and division.

Imagine a system where many or most citizens used voucher programs to send their children to private, mostly religious schools. Because we value religious liberty so highly, most Americans would surely agree that it would be wrong to regulate and supervise religious schools closely enough to ensure that they teach some version of prescribed American values. That is precisely why the Constitution has been interpreted to protect the right to educate one's children in private religious schools.[5] But given this right to educate according to one's own values, what is to ensure that the curriculum in state-supported religious schools will promote *common* values? It is at least as likely that balkanized schools will generate balkanized values as that they will promote a common national project.

While the great majority of schools run by most religious groups do encourage loyal citizenship by their lights, we cannot simply assume that any school of any religious denomination will teach shared American national identity or values. Some schools will teach that the best form of life is to prefer one's fellows—whether Protestants or Jews or Muslims or Catholics—to other Americans. No religious tradition is without at least a hint of such particularism, which is just one mechanism by which common citizenship may be undermined by some forms of religion. The disparate values of different religious traditions will also be taught in the religious schools, guaranteeing increased disparity when it comes to controversial issues. There is nothing inherently wrong with that type of values diversity, of course. Private schools unsupported by vouchers can in any case teach whatever they want about citizenship and loyalty. But while values evangelicalism claims to advocate national unity and inclusion through shared values, school voucher programs cut exactly the other way, promoting difference and nonengagement. Permitting schools supported by private funds to teach that there is no common American undertaking is not the same as encouraging that teaching through state subsidy.

Now consider what will happen when some delegate in the state legislature rises to argue that voucher payments should not be extended to schools that teach racism, or anti-Americanism, or sexism. Under the law as it has developed, the state cannot pick and choose but must fund all schools or none. Cutting funding for the offending school would require cutting it for every school. A debate will then inevitably ensue about whether the outrage of funding this one school outweighs the benefits of funding all the others. In essence, this will be a debate about how bad are the teachings of the religion under attack and how good the others. This scenario, reminiscent of the old legislative debates about the purported ills of the Catholic church, captures precisely the sort of divisiveness in politics that institutional separation aims to avoid. Only this time, it may not be Catholicism in the dock but something else—Islam, say, or polytheistic Hinduism. The sovereign people should not spend their legislative sessions debating the relative merits of different faiths and their compatibility with American values. That is a recipe for real and deep division.

Values evangelicals can fairly point to the anti-Catholic flavor of historical nonsectarianism to support the argument for funding religious schools through vouchers. It is certainly true that the American practice of not funding religious schools came about in large part through a discriminatory impulse against Catholic difference. But the taint of that history must not make us forget the older, blameless principle of institutional separation that came before the ugly bias. The framers who prohibited establishment at the federal level, and the Constitution drafters who did likewise in the states both before and after the framing, were not yet in the grips of bigoted anti-Catholic politics. Motivated by the principle that taxes distributed to religious institutions violate liberty of conscience, and the practical reality of denominational diversity, they came up with the solution of keeping separate the institution of the church and the apparatus of the state. When Catholics sought state funding for their schools, the rejection was consistent with maintaining the practice of institutional separation. What was illiberal and anti-Catholic was the refusal to accommodate Catholic schoolchildren, either by exempting them from practices they saw as Protestant, or by taking those rituals out of the schools altogether. Nor is this judgment anachronistic: there were Catholics and a few Protestants in the nineteenth century who saw the solution clearly.

The tradition of institutional separation that must be reasserted goes beyond funding for religious schools. All attempts to use government resources to institutionalize religious practices countermand the American tradition of nonestablishment, grounded historically in the belief that government has no authority over religious matters. When government funds social programs under the rubric of charitable choice, the programs must not be ones that rely on faith to accomplish their goals, or else the government is institutionally sponsoring the religious mission of the church in question. This is also why the state itself must not compose or mandate public prayers, which then take on the shape of state-sanctioned religious exercises. Madison himself understood that paying the chaplains of the House and Senate out of public funds was a constitutional anomaly, and he wisely suggested that the Congress ought to pay for their services from their own pockets.[6]

Surprising as it may at first sound, these changes from existing laws and practices have a realistic chance of being adopted and even embraced by values evangelicals. It may be possible to glimpse already a growing recognition among values evangelicals that voucher programs do not necessarily promote common values but may do just the opposite. The ballooning of school voucher programs that some expected in the wake of the Supreme Court decision holding them constitutional has not come to pass. Faith-based charities have not yet managed to crowd out secular service providers, although more extensive government funding for faith-based social services remains a possibility. Given that voucher programs are widely underused and have not spread widely, it should be relatively easy for values evangelicals to abandon them, especially since they will be getting something in return, in the form of greater recognition and acceptance for their values-based arguments and the corresponding symbols of public religion.

Government funding of religion is, after all, a relative latecomer to the ideology of values evangelicalism.[7] The movement from the start drew its energy from symbolic questions of culture and morality, not from any desire to see a merger of church and state. Catholics may have pressed hard from within the movement to make vouchers an important issue, but even they turn out to be relying little on those voucher programs for educating their own children; the voucher students in Catholic schools in Milwaukee or Cleveland are mostly African-American Protestants. Evangelicals should also be prepared to acknowledge the historical fact that our constitutional tradition, flawed though it assuredly is, has always made institutional separation the touchstone of nonestablishment. Keeping noncoercive, privately expressed symbolic religion from the public sphere was never part of the separationist tradition, however; that is an innovation of modern legal secularism.

If we could be more tolerant of sincere religious people drawing on their beliefs and practices to inform their choices in the public realm, and at the same time be more vigilant about preserving our legacy of institutional separation between government and organized religion, the shift would redirect us to the uniqueness of the American experiment with church and state. Until the rise of legal secularism, we tended to be accepting of public symbolic manifestations of faith. Until values evangelicalism came on the scene, we were, on the whole, extremely insistent about maintaining institutional separation. These two modern movements respectively reversed both those trends.

The novelty of these new developments does not mean they are wrong, of course. It can be said that the traditional manifestations of public symbolic religion marginalized minorities like Jews and Catholics, while our refusal to fund religious schools discriminated against those same minorities. Yet ultimately, seeing the history of the relationship between church and state in the United States primarily through the lens of inequality imposed by mainstream Protestants on religious minorities misses what is most remarkable and important about our experiment. It matters more that the experiment has at its best sought—mostly in good conscience—to protect religious liberty without sacrificing the aspiration of living together as a single nation.

CONCLUSION:
UNITING A NATION
DIVIDED BY GOD

The first time America was divided, it came, Lincoln believed, as punishment for the sin of African slavery. Though Lincoln attributed the dissolution of the Union to God, who "gives to both North and South this terrible war as the woe due to those by whom the offense came," his formulation left room for the possibility that the efficient cause was not special providence but human means. North and South were at war precisely because the founding generation had failed morally and practically by leaving the question of slavery unresolved.

The framers did much better with respect to America's church-state problem than they did with slavery, but they did not definitively resolve that, either. Their experiment enshrined both liberty of conscience and institutional separation at the federal level, but these innovations did not suffice to guarantee national unity in the face of the sovereign people's religious diversity. That task was left to their successors, whose experiments with nonsectarianism, strong secularism, legal secularism, and values evangelicalism still have not fully resolved the tensions that must inevitably exist when citizens with different beliefs must cooperate in the project of collective self-government.

We ourselves are divided by God in that we cannot agree on the role religion should take in regard to government, and vice versa. For this the responsibility lies with us and with the structure of our man-made Constitution. Perhaps, too, it might be said that God has divided us, by virtue of the profound religious diversity that we have long had and that is daily expanding. Since Madison, this diversity has often been called a blessing and a source of strength or balance, yet it also remains, as it has always been, a fundamental challenge to the project of popular self-government.

We can, I believe, do better than we have in recent years if we can recognize that secularists and evangelicals alike are animated by a common desire to reconcile unity and diversity. The latest division can be eased even if it cannot be wholly erased. Secularists must accept the fact that religious values form an important source of political beliefs and identities for the majority of Americans, while evangelicals need to acknowledge that separating the institutions of government from those of religion is essential for avoiding outright political-religious conflict. Taking these steps asks much of both sides, but it does not ask *too* much. In each case, I have suggested, the proposed shift follows a consistent internal logic. In each case, the shift aims to build on the common ground we already have, ground well trodden by our constitutional traditions, though not hallowed by them.

Out of the many strands of religious faith that have only increased in America since our founding, we have been trying to construct a single nation. That task is not yet complete—nor can it ever be. The persistence of America's church-state problem should not deter us from confronting it anew. The secret to success in the building of nations is to know that the work must always go on, and to welcome it as it comes.

NOTES

1. *Glassroth v. Moore*, 242 F. Supp.2d 1067 (M.D. Ala. 2002), *aff'd*, 335 F.3d 1282 (11th Cir. July 1, 2003), *cert den.*, 124 S. Ct. 497 (Nov. 3, 2003).

INTRODUCTION

1. For these and other exit polling statistics, see CNN's exit polls, available at www.cnn.com/ELECTION/2004/pages/results/states/US/P/00/epolls.0. html. The question that produced the answer regarding moral values has been criticized on the ground that the limited number of options produced a skew in favor of "moral values" for Bush voters. Without entering the debate, one may note that all such limited-option questions are liable to distortion, and that the important fact is that 18 percent of Kerry voters chose moral values as opposed to 80 percent of Bush voters.
2. Debate transcript at www.debates.org/pages/trans2004c.html.
3. I am therefore not taking issue with sociologist Alan Wolfe, who has argued that Americans' religious faith is not in itself a source of deep division. See Alan Wolfe, *The Transformation of American Religion: How We Actually Live Our Faith* (New York: Free Press, 2003); Alan Wolfe, *One Nation, After All* (New York: Penguin, 1998). My claim is that the division is over the role religious values should play in political choices.
4. *Zorach v. Clauson*, 343 U.S. 306, 313 (1952). The Court cited the statement approvingly as recently as 1984. See *Lynch v. Donnelly*, 465 U.S. 668, 675 (1984).
5. On the recurrent tension between religious diversity and national unity, see William R. Hutchison, *Religious Pluralism in America: The Contentious History of a Founding Ideal* (New Haven, CT: Yale University Press, 2003), 8, 10; Martin Marty, *The One and the Many: America's Struggle for the*

Common Good (Cambridge, MA: Harvard University Press, 1997). An important work on the broader question of unity and values diversity is Stephen Macedo, *Diversity and Distrust* (Cambridge, MA: Harvard University Press, 2000). The most thoughtful recent work on the relation between different religious and liberal conceptions of politics and the good is Jeffrey Stout, *Democracy & Tradition* (Princeton, NJ: Princeton University Press, 2004).

6. On the history of state religion, see Harold Berman, *Law and Revolution: The Formation of the Western Legal Tradition* (Cambridge, MA: Harvard University Press, 1983).

7. The principle of *cuius regio, eius religio* originated in the Peace of Augsburg (1555), but it was reaffirmed at Westphalia in 1648 with limited provisions for subjects to worship as they had in 1624.

8. Edward Gibbon, *The Decline and Fall of the Roman Empire* (New York: Knopf, 1993), 1:34 ("The various modes of worship, which prevailed in the Roman world, were all considered by the people, as equally true; by the philosopher, as equally false; and by the magistrate, as equally useful"). Gibbon was also taking note here of the religious diversity of polytheistic pagan antiquity, regarding which he cited Hume's *Natural History of Religion* (34 n. 3), which also influenced James Madison. For an extraordinary treatment of Gibbon on religion, see J.G.A. Pocock, *Barbarism and Religion*, 2 vols. (Cambridge: Cambridge University Press, 1999).

CHAPTER 1. THE ORIGINS

1. *Documentary History of the Ratification of the Constitution*, 13 vols. (Madison: State Historical Society of Wisconsin, 1976–), 10:1223–24. See also Jonathan Elliot, *The Debates in the Several State Conventions on the Adoption of the Federal Constitution, as Recommended by the General Convention at Philadelphia, in 1787*, 5 vols. (Philadelphia: Lippincott, 1861), 3:330. Of course, what was at issue was not yet the "First Amendment," since all the possible amendments were still but ideas being proposed in the state ratifying conventions. Nor was what became the First Amendment first on the list of proposed amendments submitted to the states—it was third, but the first two were not ratified. See William Lee Miller, *The First Liberty: Religion and the American Republic* (New York: Knopf, 1986); Thomas J. Curry, *The First Freedoms: Church and State in America to the Passage of the First Amendment* (New York: Oxford University Press, 1986). Nonetheless, the absence of a religious liberty guarantee was a major concern for many critics of the new Constitution, as I show below.

2. See Charles O. Paullin, *Atlas of the Historical Geography of the United States*

(Washington, D.C.: Carnegie Institution, 1932), 49–50 and plate 82. According to the eminent historian of American religion William Hutchison, Paullin is still the best source for these demographic numbers, despite some methodological flaws. The baseline is thirty-two hundred congregations as of 1780. See Hutchison, *Religious Pluralism*, 242 n. 19; see also Edwin S. Gaustad and Philip L. Barlow, *New Historical Atlas of Religion in America* (New York: Oxford University Press, 2001), 8–9, 37. For the figure 95 percent Protestant, see Hutchison, 20; of these, 90 percent came from the Calvinist side of the Protestant divide, not the Lutheran. There were also many unchurched Americans.

3. For a polemic popular book written by two scholars, see Isaac Kramnick and R. Laurence Moore, *The Godless Constitution: The Case Against Religious Correctness* (New York: Norton, 1996).

4. See Richard Hooker, *Of the Laws of Ecclesiastical Polity* (1597), in W. Speed Hill, ed., 7 vols., *The Folger Library Edition of the Works of Richard Hooker* (Cambridge, MA: Harvard University Press, 1977–98), 2:15. The first subheading in Chapter I reads: "True Religion is the roote of all true virtues and the stay of all well ordered common-wealthes" (16). A work that was known in the colonies and made the argument for support of religion was that of the Bishop of Gloucester, William Warburton, *The Alliance Between Church and State, or The Necessity and Equity of an Established Religion and a Test-Law Demonstrated, from the Essence and End of Civil Society, upon the Fundamental Principles of the Law of Nature and Nations* (1736). For further arguments on the necessity of religion to support obedience to royal government, see J.C.D. Clark, *English Society, 1688–1832: Religion, Ideology, and Politics During the Ancien Regime* (Cambridge: Cambridge University Press, 2000), 226–27.

5. Montesquieu, *The Spirit of the Laws* (1748) (New York: Cambridge University Press, 1989), bk. 11, chap. 6, 159–60.

6. Thus Anson Phelps Stokes, author of what was for many years the leading comprehensive work on church and state, says that only Roger Williams could "dispute [Jefferson's] claim to primacy in this field of influence." Anson Phelps Stokes, *Church and State in the United States* (New York: Harper, 1950), 333. On Jefferson's controversial character, see Bernard Bailyn, *To Begin the World Anew: The Genius and Ambiguities of the American Founders* (New York: Vintage, 2003), 37–59.

7. No other milestones were added. See Stokes, *Church and State*, 336 (noting omission of the presidency, secretary of state, etc.). One wonders if the other two were also chosen in part to assert ownership, given the recurrent issue of Benjamin Franklin's role in the writing of the Declaration and the legislature's necessary acquiescence in funding the university, for which Jefferson did not foot the bill. Yale and Harvard had both been renamed after

donations, a fact surely not unknown to Jefferson, who might have subsequently faded from the picture had the University of Virginia made a similar (mis)calculation.

8. For a detailed discussion of this letter and its context, see Daniel L. Dreisbach, *Thomas Jefferson and the Wall of Separation Between Church and State* (New York: New York University Press, 2002).

9. In a letter of 1801, he speaks of "the dominion of the clergy, who had got a smell of union between Church and State." Thomas Jefferson to Moses Robinson, quoted in Robert A. Ferguson, *The American Enlightenment: 1750–1820* (Cambridge, MA: Harvard University Press, 1997), 73.

10. A good representative work in this genre is Leonard W. Levy, *The Establishment Clause: Religion and the First Amendment* (Chapel Hill: University of North Carolina Press, 1994). Adherents of this position have been able to offer various pieces of evidence in support of it, including, for example, language from the Treaty of Tripoli, signed during Washington's presidency, which assured the Muslim leaders of what is today Libya that the United States "was in no way founded upon the Christian religion."

11. Mark DeWolfe Howe, *The Garden and the Wilderness: Religion and Government in American Constitutional History* (Chicago: University of Chicago Press, 1965).

12. Philip A. Hamburger, *Separation of Church and State* (Cambridge, MA: Harvard University Press, 2002).

13. For Williams's original use, see Roger Williams, "Mr. Cottons Letter Lately Printed, Examined and Answered," in Samuel L. Caldwell, ed., *The Complete Writings of Roger Williams* (New York: Russell & Russell, 1963), 392; see also Williams's "The Bloudy Tenent, of Persecution, for Cause of Conscience" (1644), ibid., 233. The "candlestick" that is taken when the wall around the garden is destroyed is certainly a reference to the candelabrum or menorah of the Temple, taken when the Temple was sacked (the Hebrew menorah is always rendered "candlestick" in the King James Version of the Bible); Hamburger's lengthy discussion of Williams's metaphor, *Separation of Church and State*, 45–50, misses this point.

14. Isaac Backus quoted Williams just once in all his pamphlets on liberty of conscience. See Isaac Backus, *An Appeal to the Public for Religious Liberty* (1773), reprinted in William G. McLoughlin, ed., *Isaac Backus on Church, State, and Calvinism: Pamphlets, 1754–1789* (Cambridge, MA: Harvard University Press, 1968), 322.

15. Some historians suggest that this alliance defeated an alternative "civic republican" view, according to which the state could not survive without the sanction of religion behind it. See, e.g., Michael W. McConnell, "The Origins and Historical Understanding of Free Exercise of Religion," *Harvard Law Review* 103 (1990): 1409, 1438–43 (arguing for distinct rationalist, evangelical, and civic republican positions on church-state relations); John

Witte Jr., "The Essential Rights and Liberties of Religion in the American Constitutional Experiment," *Notre Dame Law Review* 371 (1996): 371, 377–88. See also Colin Kidd, "Civil Theology and Church Establishments in Revolutionary America," *Historical Journal* 42 (1999): 1007, 1021–25. In general, notice of civic republicanism grew after publication of J.G.A. Pocock, *The Machiavellian Moment: Florentine Political Thought and the Atlantic Republican Tradition* (Princeton, NJ: Princeton University Press, 1975). Yet it is very difficult to show a distinct civic republican view on church and state, both because it was conventional to say that religion promoted obedience, and because civic republicanism was typically skeptical of religious faith. Indeed, for civic republicans, the engines of virtue were ordinarily identified as education; see Gordon S. Wood, *The Creation of the American Republic: 1776–1787* (Chapel Hill: University of North Carolina Press, 1969), 426, and, for good governmental arrangements designed to minimize the effects of corruption, 430–67. For the clergy, Wood points out, religion, not virtue, was the source of "salvation for a corrupted people" (427). In fact, as an example of precisely the wrong sort of relationship between church and state, Noah Webster invoked classical Rome, where, he reported, religion was used to support the authority of the legislature. Happily, he noted, "in North America, by a singular concurrence of circumstances, the possibility of establishing this influence [i.e., religion], as a pillar of government, is totally precluded." Noah Webster, "Debate, A Citizen of America" (Philadelphia, October 17, 1787), reprinted in Bernard Bailyn, ed., *The Debate on the Constitution* (New York: Library of America, 1993), 1:154–55.

16. For a statement of this view, see, e.g., Michael McConnell, "Establishment and Disestablishment at the Founding, Part I: Establishment of Religion," *William and Mary Law Review* 44 (2003): 2105, 2131 (listing six features of establishment).

17. Justice Rehnquist's dissent in *Wallace v. Jaffree*, 472 U.S. 38, 112 (1985) (Rehnquist, J., dissenting), is the clearest and most famous exposition of this view ("The Clause was . . . designed to stop the Federal Government from asserting a preference for one religious denomination or sect over others").

18. See, for the latest and most explicit example, Justice Thomas's concurring opinion in *Elk Grove v. Newdow*, 542 U.S. 104, 133 (2004) ("The text and history of the Establishment Clause strongly suggest that it is a federalism provision intended to prevent Congress from interfering with state establishments. Thus, unlike the Free Exercise Clause, which does protect an individual right, it makes little sense to incorporate the Establishment Clause"). Thomas cites, among other sources, Hamburger, *Separation of Church and State*, 106 n. 40, and Akhil Reed Amar, *The Bill of Rights: Creation and Reconstruction* (New Haven, CT: Yale University Press, 1998),

36–39. The federalism interpretation of the religion clauses is also sometimes called the "jurisdictional" interpretation, since it holds that the
clauses ensured that the federal government would have no jurisdiction
over religion. Not every advocate of this view is necessarily committed, as
is Justice Thomas, to the so-called nonpreferentialist view that the Establishment Clause only prevents preference of one religion over others. In
theory, one could believe that the Establishment Clause under the jurisdictional interpretation barred the federal government from *any* support for
religion, even nonpreferential support. One could also believe that even
if the original meaning of the Establishment Clause protected state establishments, the Fourteenth Amendment trumped this earlier restrictive
meaning.

19. This claim is substantiated—and many other ideas in this chapter prefigured—in Noah Feldman, "The Intellectual Origins of the Establishment
Clause," *NYU Law Review* 77 (2002): 346.

20. For a more detailed treatment of the history of the idea of liberty of conscience, see ibid.; Perez Zagorin, *How the Idea of Religious Toleration Came
to the West* (Princeton, NJ: Princeton University Press, 2003).

21. Michael G. Baylor, *Action and Person: Conscience in Late Scholasticism and
the Young Luther* (Leiden: Brill, 1977), 20:1, 24 (describing Jerome's use of
the Latin term *conscientia*, already found in earlier Latin authors, to translate the Greek word *syneidesis*); for Jerome's use, see S. Eusebius Hierony-
mus, "Commentarium in Ezechielem Prophetam," 22b, in 25 *Patrologiae
Cursus Completus*, Series Latina, ed. J. P. Migne (Leiden: Brill, 1844–64).
Aquinas's account of the intellect may be found in St. Thomas Aquinas,
Summa Theologica, trans. Father Laurence Shapcote, 2d ed. (Chicago: En-
cyclopaedia Britannica, 1990), Ia, questions 75–83.

22. Aquinas, *Summa Theologica*, Ia, IIae, question 19, art. 5.

23. Baylor, *Action and Person*, 251–62.

24. John Calvin, *Institutes of the Christian Religion* (1536), trans. Ford Lewis
Battles (Grand Rapids, MI: W. B. Eerdmans, 1986), 209 [4.20.3].

25. William Perkins, "A Discourse of Conscience" (1608), in Thomas F. Merrill, ed., *William Perkins: 1558–1602: English Puritanist* (Nieuwkoop,
Netherlands: B. De Graaf, 1966), 1, 31. Thomas More had earlier made
the argument that he could not obey the king when conscience stood in
the way. See his letter to his daughter Margaret, April 17, 1534, in Elizabeth Frances Rogers, ed., *The Correspondence of Thomas More* (Princeton,
NJ: Princeton University Press, 1947).

26. See, e.g., "Persecution'd for Religion Judg'd and Condemn'd" (1615),
reprinted in Edward Bean Underhill, ed., *Tracts on Liberty of Conscience
and Persecution: 1614–1661* (London: Hadley Press, 1846), 105 ("If
the intent of the law were to make me come to church to worship God,

and not of faith, [then] the intent of the law were to compel me to sin").

27. For an outright condemnation of liberty of conscience, see Nathaniel Ward, *The Simple Cobler of Aggawam in America* (1645), ed. P. M. Zall (Lincoln: University of Nebraska Press, 1969), 14 ("It is said, That Men ought to have Liberty of their Conscience, and that it is persecution to debarre them of it: I can rather stand amazed then reply to this: it is an astonishment to think that the braines of men should be parboyl'd in such impious ignorance").

28. The exchange began with Roger Williams, "The Bloudy Tenent, of Persecution, for Cause of Conscience" (1644), reprinted in Caldwell, *Complete Writings*; the response was John Cotton, *The Bloudy Tenent, Washed, and Made White in the Bloud of the Lambe* (London: Hannah Allen, 1647); Williams replied once more with "The Bloody Tenant Yet More Bloody" (1652), in *Complete Writings*. All the texts were originally published in London.

29. John Locke, *A Letter Concerning Toleration* (1690), in John Horton and Susan Mendus, eds., *John Locke: A Letter Concerning Toleration in Focus* (London: Routledge, 1991), 12, 17–18; John Locke, *Two Treatises of Government* (1690), ed. Peter Laslett (Cambridge: Cambridge University Press, 1988), 382.

30. Locke, *Letter Concerning Toleration*, 32.

31. Ibid., 33.

32. "Those are not at all to be tolerated who deny the being of God . . . Oaths, which are the bonds of human society, can have no hold upon an atheist" (ibid., 47).

33. See, e.g., The Fundamental Constitutions of Carolina, §§ 95–109 (March 1, 1669), drafted by John Locke (subsequently edited and amended by others), available at www.yale.edu/lawweb/avalon/states/nc05.htm#b3. The provisions embody religious toleration for theists. Article 96, which provides for the Church of England to be the established and publicly funded church, is said (on what authority is uncertain) to have been added by authors other than Locke.

34. For a recent description of the prevalence of the liberty of conscience, see John Witte Jr., *Religion and the American Constitutional Experiment*, 2d ed. (Boulder, CO: Westview Press, 2005), 41–45.

35. See Curry, *First Freedoms*, 134.

36. William G. McLoughlin, "Isaac Backus and the Separation of Church and State in America," *American Historical Review* 73 (1968): 1392; *Isaac Backus on Church, State, and Calvinism*.

37. William G. McLoughlin, *New England Dissent, 1630–1833: The Baptists and the Separation of Church and State*, 2 vols. (Cambridge, MA: Harvard University Press, 1971), 1:512–30; William E. Nelson; *Americanization of*

the Common Law: The Impact of Legal Change on Massachusetts Society, 1760–1830 (Cambridge, MA: Harvard University Press, 1975), 105–8.

38. Isaac Backus, *A History of New England, with particular reference to the Baptists* (1871) (New York: Arno Press, 1969), 2:201–2.

39. Reproduced in John T. Noonan Jr. and Edward Gaffney, eds., *Religious Freedom: History, Cases, and Other Materials on the Interaction of Religion and Government* (New York: Foundation Press, 2001), 163; for Madison's amendments, see *The Papers of James Madison* (Chicago: University of Chicago Press, 1962–91), 1:174–75.

40. For the text of the law, see Robert S. Alley, ed., *James Madison on Religious Liberty* (Buffalo: Prometheus Books, 1985), 52.

41. Nelson Rollin Burr, *The Story of the Diocese of Connecticut: A New Branch of the Vine* (Hartford: Church Missions Publishing Co., 1962), 148–51.

42. Jefferson claimed the number as two-thirds as of the Revolution. "Notes on the State of Virginia," in Philip S. Foner, ed., *Basic Writings of Thomas Jefferson* (Garden City, NY: Halcyon House, 1950), 157.

43. Lunenberg petition of 1783, see Stokes, *Church and State*, 388.

44. Madison complained that the Presbyterian clergy were "as ready to set up an establishment which is to take them in as they were to pull down one which shut them out." Letter of April 12, 1785, to James Monroe, *Papers of James Madison*, 8:261.

45. James Buchan, *Crowded with Genius: The Scottish Enlightenment: Edinburgh's Moment of the Mind* (New York: Harper, 2003), 93–95.

46. See Madison's youthful letters to William Bradford of 1774–75, *Papers of James Madison*, 1:96, 105–6, 112, 161.

47. James Madison, *Memorial and Remonstrance against Religious Assessments* (1785), ibid., 8:295–306.

48. Ibid., 302.

49. "A Bill Establishing a Provision for Teachers of the Christian Religion" (1784), Noonan and Gaffney, *Religious Freedom*, 171–72. Madison pointed out that it was unfair and unequal to grant this exemption to these denominations alone, since there might be others that similarly did not want to pay compelled taxes to support religion (*Memorial and Remonstrance*, 300). In particular, Madison seems to have had in mind Baptists and some Presbyterians in Virginia, who did not want their taxes to go to support the mainstream Anglican church from which they dissented.

50. George Washington to George Mason (October 3, 1785), in John C. Fitzpatrick, ed., *The Writings of George Washington, 1784–1786* (Washington, D.C.: Government Printing Office, 1938), 285.

51. Thomas Jefferson, "A Bill for Establishing Religious Freedom" (1779), *The Papers of Thomas Jefferson*, ed. Julian P. Boyd (Princeton: Princeton University Press, 1950–), 2:545.

52. Thomas Jefferson, "Notes on Locke and Shaftesbury" (ca. 1776), *Papers of Thomas Jefferson*, 1:544–50.

53. See, e.g., Eric S. Lander and Joseph J. Ellis, "DNA Analysis: Founding Father," *Nature*, November 5, 1998, 13; Eugene A. Foster et al., "Jefferson Fathered Slave's Last Child," *Nature*, November 5, 1998, 27; Annette Gordon-Reed, *Thomas Jefferson and Sally Hemings: An American Controversy* (Charlottesville: University Press of Virginia, 1997).

54. Hamburger, *Separation of Church and State*, 113–17.

55. A letter to John Adams in 1817 praises the end of the state support of religion in Massachusetts; in it, Jefferson calls the New England Way "a protestant popedom." Thomas Jefferson to John Adams, in Ferguson, *American Enlightenment*, 73.

56. See Dreisbach, *Thomas Jefferson and the Wall of Separation*, 53.

57. In private, liberal New Englanders were not above admitting that their inherited, entrenched ways might be an establishment. Thus Isaac Backus reported that John Adams had told him that "we might as well expect a change in the solar system, to expect they would give up their establishment." Backus, *History of New England*, 2:202.

58. Cf. Curry, *First Freedoms*, 210.

59. Some scholars claim that, framed as a jurisdictional compromise to keep religious matters in the hands of the states rather than the federal government, the constitutional design of 1791 lacked internal logic. This argument has been used, most effectively by Steven Smith, to suggest that it is pointless to try to come up with a theory that would explain and justify how we as a society should structure the relationship between religion and government; religious diversity was too great to reach any national church-state consensus, Smith argues, and so federal nonintervention became the default. Steven D. Smith, "Separation and the 'Secular': Reconstructing the Disestablishment Decision," *Texas Law Review* 67 (1989): 955; the article became part of Steven D. Smith, *Foreordained Failure: The Quest for a Constitutional Principle of Religious Freedom* (New York: Oxford University Press, 1995). See also Steven D. Smith, "The Pluralist Predicament: Contemporary Theorizing in the Law of Religious Freedom," *Legal Theory* 10 (2004): 51. Smith broke new ground in emphasizing religious diversity as a key factor in producing the religion clauses of the First Amendment. It happens, however, that this diversity propelled the framers to converge on a logical, self-contained theory that justified the constitutional church-state arrangements they designed.

60. Proceedings and Debates of the Pennsylvania Convention, in *Documentary History of the Constitution*, 2:326, 592.

61. Petition Against Confirmation of the Ratification of the Constitution, January 1788, ibid., 710, 711.

62. Letter from Joseph Spencer to James Madison (February 28, 1788), ibid., 252 (spelling modernized).

63. Elliot, *Debates*, 3:659.

64. Elliot, *Debates*, 4:244 (North Carolina), 1:334 (Rhode Island), 1:328 (New York); *Documentary History of the Constitution*, 4:328, 334.

65. Elliot, *Debates*, 3:317–18.

66. *Papers of Thomas Jefferson*, 12:440.

67. Ibid.

68. *Papers of James Madison*, 11:298.

69. Ibid.

70. Ibid.

71. *The Federalist Papers*, ed. Clinton Rossiter (New York: Penguin, 1961), Federalist 10, 82–84.

72. Ibid., Federalist 51, 324 ("In a free government the security for civil rights must be the same as that for religious rights. It consists in the one case in the multiplicity of interests, and in the other in the multiplicity of sects. The degree of security in both cases will depend on the number of interests and sects; and this may be presumed to depend on the extent of country and number of people comprehended under the same government"). In both points, Madison owed something to David Hume, who had also struggled with the question of religious faction. The nature of the debt is the subject of a famous debate between Douglass Adair, who first drew attention to the parallel ("That Politics May Be Reduced to a Science: David Hume, James Madison, and the Tenth Federalist," *Huntington Library Quarterly* 20 [1957]: 343), and later writers, most prominently Edmund Morgan ("Safety in Numbers: Madison, Hume, and the Tenth Federalist," *Huntington Library Quarterly* 49 [1986]: 95). Several recent articles revisiting the debate have focused on the question of religion in Hume and Madison. Marc M. Arkin, " 'The Intractable Principle': David Hume, James Madison, and the Tenth Federalist," *American Journal of Legal History* 39 (1995): 148; Mark G. Spencer, "Hume and Madison on Faction," *William and Mary Quarterly* 59 (2002): 869. The best formulation is probably that Hume saw the question of faction in religious terms, leading Madison to do the same and then to expand outward to the problem of faction more generally.

73. Joseph Gales, ed., *Annals of Congress* (1789), 451.

74. Ibid., 796. This change was proposed by Fisher Ames of Massachusetts. For one view of Ames's ideology on the question and place in the debate, see Marc M. Arkin, "Regionalism and the Religion Clauses: The Contribution of Fisher Ames," *Buffalo Law Review* 47 (1999): 763, 786–90.

75. *Annals of Congress*, 757.

76. Ibid., 758.

77. Ibid., 759 (emphasis added).

78. One significant problem was left unaddressed by this dual formulation. Did the guarantee of the free exercise of religion entitle the citizen to an exception from a duly enacted law if he objected for reasons of conscience? The framers were not unaware of this issue, which had arisen wherever there were Quakers who sought exemptions from military service. Had the framers included a clause in the Constitution guaranteeing "the rights of conscience," that language might have been understood to guarantee a right of conscientious objection. By instead promising the free exercise of religion, the Constitution limited itself to protecting actions taken in furtherance of religious worship. It thus avoided promising that no one could be compelled to act against conscience in other contexts, such as wartime. It also left open the question of what would count as "religious exercise." Prayer and worship surely would qualify, but what about activities that, to the ordinary observer, would not seem religious in and of themselves but would be considered religious by those who wanted to perform them? To this problem the text of the Constitution provided no answer, and consequently, the issue remains incompletely resolved by the courts today. In general, though, it is left to Congress to provide for conscientious objectors the opportunity to avoid military service, and the constitutional right to free exercise has been limited to activities that are self-consciously religious. Since the 1980s, the Supreme Court has held that religious motivation provides no excuse for failing to obey a neutral, generally applicable law. See *Employment Div. v. Smith*, 494 U.S. 872 (1990) ("[D]ecisions have consistently held that the right of free exercise does not relieve an individual of the obligation to comply with a valid and neutral law of general applicability on the ground that the law proscribes [or prescribes] conduct that his religion prescribes [or proscribes]").

79. Locke, *Letter Concerning Toleration*, 40 (emphasis added).

80. James D. Richardson, ed., 10 vols., *A Compilation of the Messages and Papers of the Presidents, 1789–1897* (Washington, D.C.: Government Printing Office, 1896–99), 1:64, 268–70. Such declarations had been a regular feature of colonial life and had continued in the states, especially in Congregationalist New England. But even in Virginia, Jefferson and Madison had helped draft legislation authorizing the governor to issue them. The preconstitutional U.S. Congress, convened pursuant to the Articles of Confederation, had declared national days of thanksgiving several times between 1777 and 1783.

81. Dreisbach, *Thomas Jefferson and the Wall of Separation*, 35–37 (citing text of draft and reproducing image of draft). See also *Marsh v. Chambers*, 463 U.S. 783, 808, n. 19 (Brennan, J., dissenting).

82. See Dreisbach, *Thomas Jefferson and the Wall of Separation*, 25–54.

83. See Madison's detached memoranda, in Alley, *James Madison on Religious Liberty*, 93–94.

84. For an account of the Sunday mails controversy, see Richard R. John, *Spreading the News: The American Postal System from Franklin to Morse* (Cambridge, MA: Harvard University Press, 1995), 169–205.

85. See 20th Cong., 2d sess., January 19, 1829, Report no. 74, Sunday Mails, Report of Mr. Johnson of Kentucky, 211–12; 21st Cong., 1st sess., March 4–5, 1830, Report no. 87, Sunday Mails, Report of Mr. Johnson of Kentucky. Colonel Johnson, as he was widely known, was a Jacksonian Democrat who eventually served a term as vice president under Martin Van Buren.

86. In 1912, Congress passed H.R. 21279, which provided, "That hereafter post offices shall not be opened on Sundays for the purpose of delivering mail to the public." The argument that the individual religious conscience of postmasters who wanted to stay closed on Sunday ought to be accommodated played only a small role in the debate; Johnson replied that no one was obligated to take on the job of postmaster. In the states, where Sunday closing laws were prevalent, only California's Supreme Court went so far as to hold that Sunday laws violated the state constitutional ban on preferring one religious sect to others; it did so by overturning the conviction of a Jew who did business on a Sunday. See *Ex parte Newman*, 9 Cal. 502 (1858).

87. See 20th Cong., 2d sess., February 3, 1829, Report no. 75, Sunday Mails, Report of Mr. McKean from the Committee on the Post Office, 212–13.

CHAPTER 2. SCHOOLS AND MORALS

1. National Center for Education Statistics, U.S. Department of Education, Projection of Education Statistics to 2012 (2002), 13.

2. An Act to Provide for the Government of the Territory Northwest of the River Ohio, chap. 8, 1 Stat. 50 (1789).

3. Diane Ravitch, *The Great School Wars: A History of the New York City Public Schools* (Baltimore: Johns Hopkins University Press, 2000), 8–12.

4. The story of the rise of the common school has been told and retold. One thoughtful treatment of the subject is Charles Leslie Glenn Jr., *The Myth of the Common School* (Amherst: University of Massachusetts Press, 1988). An influential book in the field is Lawrence A. Cremin, *American Education: The National Experience, 1783–1876* (New York: Harper, 1980). For a still-valuable introduction to the earlier history of education, especially on the difficulty of comparing what came before the common schools movement and after, see Bernard Bailyn, *Education in the Forming of American Society: Needs and Opportunities for Study* (New York: Norton, 1960), especially 9–15. An excellent theoretical treatment of the schools ques-

tion—and of Catholic objections—is Macedo, *Diversity and Distrust*, 44–87.

5. Benjamin Franklin, *Idea of the English School* (Philadelphia: B. Franklin, 1751) ("Thus instructed, Youth will come out of this School fitted for learning any Business, Calling or Profession"), available at www.history carper.com/resources/twobf2/school.htm; cf. Bailyn, *Education*, 35.

6. For a detailed account of this process, see McLoughlin, *New England Dissent*; see also Sydney E. Ahlstrom and Jonathan S. Carey, *An American Reformation: A Documentary History of Unitarian Christianity* (Middletown, CT: Wesleyan University Press, 1985), 164.

7. Mark A. Noll, *America's God: From Jonathan Edwards to Abraham Lincoln* (New York: Oxford University Press, 2002), 166.

8. Alexis de Tocqueville, *Democracy in America*, eds. and trans. Harvey C. Mansfield and Delba Winthrop (Chicago: University of Chicago Press, 2000), 278. I first discussed many of the texts in this section in Noah Feldman, "Non-sectarianism Reconsidered," *The Journal of Law and Politics* 18 (2002): 65–117, and I draw on that analysis here.

9. Horace Mann, "Twelfth Annual Report to the Massachusetts Board of Education" (1848), in *Life and Works of Horace Mann*, 5 vols. (Boston: Lee and Shepard, 1891), 4:222, 311–13.

10. See, e.g., *Updegraph v. Commonwealth*, 11 Serg. and Rawle 394 (Pa. 1824). In this decision upholding a blasphemy conviction, the Pennsylvania Supreme Court declared that the Christianity that constituted a part of the common law was "not Christianity founded on particular religious tenets . . . but Christianity with liberty of conscience for all" (400). It went on to assert that "no free government now exists in the world, unless where Christianity is acknowledged, and is the religion of the country" (406–7).

11. Elwood P. Cubberley, ed., *Readings in Public Education in the United States: A Collection of Sources and Readings to Illustrate the History of Educational Practice and Progress in the United States* (1934) (Westport, CT: Greenwood, 1970), 207.

12. See George W. Potter, *To the Golden Door: The Story of the Irish in Ireland and America* (Boston: Little, Brown, 1960), 133–34 (calling the year 1846 "the vanguard" of an "emigration phenomenon not paralleled until the population uprootings of the two world wars of the twentieth century," and citing Irish immigration to the United States as 341,000 from 1831 to 1840; 1,321,725 from 1847 to 1854); see also Arnold Schrier, *Ireland and the American Emigration 1850–1900* (Minneapolis: University of Minnesota Press, 1958), 157 (noting that Irish immigration to the United States surpassed 100,000 annually only during the years 1846–54); Noel Ignatiev, *How the Irish Became White* (New York: Routledge, 1995), 38 (calculating Irish immigration to the United States as 800,000–1,000,000

between 1815 and 1845, but 1,800,000 in the decade 1845–55); Thomas T. McAvoy, *A History of the Catholic Church in the United States* (South Bend, IN: University of Notre Dame Press, 1969), 137–38 (places Irish immigration into the United States at 207,381 from 1830 to 1840, 780,719 from 1841 to 1850, and 914,119 from 1851 to 1860).

13. Ravitch, *Great School Wars*, 45 (quoting Power in *The Freeman's Journal*, July 11, 1840). Notice that in Power's formulation, the very word "sect" is associated with Protestantism.

14. Epistle and Dedicatorie, King James Version (1611, spelling modernized); for the text, see Alfred W. Pollard, ed., *Records of the English Bible: The Documents Relating to the Translation and Publication of the Bible in English, 1525–1611* (New York: Oxford University Press, 1911), 340–77.

15. Ravitch, *Great School Wars*, 34.

16. See E. R. Dille, *Rome's Assault on Our Public Schools* (Oakland, CA: Carruth and Carruth, 1889), 10 (quoting one Father Gleeson, who said, "We Catholics call for a reformation of the public school system of education, because it is dangerous to the well-being of the community, because it is the parent of infidelity, an abridgement of our Constitutional rights and destructive of parental authority." Dille retorted that "there is an irreconcilable and irrepressible conflict between the Roman Catholic and American theories of education, and it is for the American people to say which of them shall go to the wall, for it is war to the death between them"); see also Ray Allen Billington, *The Protestant Crusade: 1800–1860* (New York: Macmillan, 1938).

17. Cubberley, *Readings*, 212.

18. See John T. McGreevy, *Catholicism and American Freedom* (New York: Norton, 2003), 19–42.

19. *Quanta Cura*, encyclical of Pope Pius IX, promulgated December 8, 1864, ¶3 (the modern translation differs only in trivial detail). See Anne Fremantle, ed., *The Papal Encyclicals in Their Historical Context* (New York: Putnam, 1956), 137.

20. Horace Bushnell, *Common Schools: A Discourse on the Modifications Demanded by the Roman Catholics Delivered in the North Church, Hartford, on the Day of Late Fast, March 25, 1853* (Hartford, CT: Tiffany and Co., 1853), 6, 7, 24.

21. Catholic and Protestant versions of the Ten Commandments differ; McGreevy, *Catholicism*, begins with an account of a ten-year-old Catholic student refusing to recite the Protestant version of the commandments in Massachusetts in 1859 (8). See also Richard W. Garnett, "American Conversations Within Catholicism," *Michigan Law Review* 102 (2004): 1191, 1198, and n. 34. McGreevy emphasizes the intentional anti–public school activism of ultramontane priests, but in picking a fight on the ground of

the Bible, these recent immigrant priests were getting much more than they bargained for.

22. *Donahoe v. Richards*, 38 Me. 379, 398, 400, 413 (1854).

23. *A Full and Complete Account of the Late Awful Riots in Philadelphia* (Philadelphia: J. B. Perry, 1844).

24. "The Bible in the Schools—The Bible War in Long Island," *New York Times*, June 12, 1872, 5.

25. *Bd. of Educ. v. Minor*, 23 Ohio St. 211 (1872). Quoting Madison: "Religion is not within the purview of human government . . . Religion is essentially distinct from human government, and exempt from its cognizance. A connection between them is injurious to both. There are causes in the human breast which insure the perpetuity of religion without the aid of law" (254). And quoting Buddha: "Let a man overcome anger by love, evil by good, the greedy by liberality, and the slanderer by a true and upright life" (252). For the Cincinnati school controversy, see Robert Michaelsen, *Piety in the Public School: Trends and Issues in the Relationship Between Religion and the Public School in the United States* (New York: Macmillan, 1970), 89–98.

26. *Bd. of Educ. v. Minor*, 250–51.

27. Sister Marie Carolyn Klinkhamer, "The Blaine Amendment of 1875: Private Motives for Political Action," *Catholic Historical Review* 42 (1957): 15, 21 (quoting letter from Hayes to Blaine, June 16, 1875).

28. "A Coming Struggle," *New York Herald Tribune*, July 8, 1875, 4.

29. For the broader implications of this legal structure, see Gerald E. Frug, *City Making: Building Communities Without Building Walls* (Princeton, NJ: Princeton University Press, 1999).

30. "Army of the Tennessee—A Speech by Gen. Grant," *New York Daily Tribune*, October 1, 1875, 1. See also Steven K. Green, "The Blaine Amendment Reconsidered," *American Journal of Legal History* 36 (1992): 38, 47–48. Green's article broke new ground on the history of the Blaine amendment.

31. "Army of the Tennessee," 1.

32. "Non-sectarian Schools—Letter from Ex-speaker Blaine—Constitutional Provisions," *New York Times*, November 29, 1875, 2.

33. "The President's Message—Reforms for the Centennial Year," *New York Tribune*, December 8, 1875, 1.

34. Ibid.

35. A. D. Mayo, "What Does the Bible Represent in the American Common School?" *Universalist Quarterly and General Review*, 12 (1874): 261, 272.

36. *Congressional Record*, 44th Cong., 2d. sess., 1876, 5191.

37. Ibid., 5562.

38. Ibid.

39. It is possible to hear this states' rights argument echoed in contemporary Democrats' opposition to the anti-same-sex marriage amendment.

40. *Congressional Record,* 44th Cong., 2d. sess., 1876, 5583 (statement of Senator Whyte).

41. Ibid., 5589 (statement of Senator Bogy).

42. Ibid., 5591.

43. Ibid., 5587 (statement of Senator Edmunds).

44. Ibid., 5585 (statement of Senator Morton).

45. Ibid., 5594 (statement of Senator Saulsbury).

46. Ibid., 5586 (statement of Senator Kernan).

47. Ibid., 5590 (statement of Senator Bogy).

48. "Recent Publications on the School Question," editorial, *Princeton Review,* April 1870, 316.

49. See Green, "The Blaine Amendment Reconsidered," 38, 43.

50. See Joseph P. Viteritti, "Choosing Equality: Religious Freedom and Educational Opportunity Under Constitutional Federalism," *Yale Law and Policy Review* 15 (1996): 113, 146.

51. See Robert Larson, *New Mexico's Quest for Statehood 1846–1912* (Albuquerque: University of New Mexico Press, 1968).

52. Thomas M. Cooley, *A Treatise on the Constitutional Limitations which Rest upon the Legislative Power of the States of the American Union* (Boston: Little, Brown, 1868), 469.

53. See, e.g., Thomas M. Cooley, *A Treatise on the Constitutional Limitations which Rest upon the Legislative Power of the States of the American Union* (Boston: Little, Brown, 1927), 2:967.

54. See Christopher G. Tiedeman, *A Treatise on State and Federal Control of Persons and Property* (St. Louis: F. H. Thomas, 1900), 1:194–95.

55. For that phrase, see Catherine L. Albanese, *America: Religions and Religion* (Belmont, CA: Wadsworth, 1981), 249. For a controversial evaluation of the eventual fallout of Catholic responses to Protestantizing American liberalism, see Macedo, *Diversity and Distrust,* 132–38.

56. Thomas C. Hunt, Thomas Oldenski, Theodore J. Wallace, and Elaine Schuster, eds., *Catholic School Leadership: An Invitation to Lead* (New York: Falmer Press, 2000). In 1884, just 2,532 out of 6,613 parishes in the United States had their own Catholic schools; three years later, in 1887, the numbers were 2,697 out of 6,910. Thus, around 40 percent of Catholic parishes had their own schools—but not all the children in these parishes attended the schools. By 1900, there were 3,811 Catholic schools. Also see James Hennesey, *American Catholics: A History of the Roman Catholic Community in the United States* (New York: Oxford University Press, 1981), 187.

57. R. D. Cross, *The Emergence of Liberal Catholicism in America* (Cambridge, MA: Harvard University Press, 1958), 135.

58. On the debate, see ibid., 130–45; Robert T. Handy, *Undermined Establishment: Church-State Relations in America 1880–1920* (Princeton, NJ: Princeton University Press, 1991), 63–67; John Webb Pratt, *Religion, Politics, and Diversity: The Church-State Theme in New York History* (Ithaca, NY: Cornell University Press, 1967), 232–37; McGreevy, *Catholicism*, 105–26.

59. On Vatican I and papal infallibility, see Robert McClory, *Power and the Papacy: The People and Politics Behind the Doctrine of Infallibility* (Liguori, MO: Triumph, 1997); Hans Küng, *Infallible? An Unresolved Enquiry* (New York: Continuum, 1994).

60. See Cross, *Emergence of Liberal Catholicism*, 139, 144; see also Jay P. Dolan, *The American Catholic Experience* (New York: Doubleday, 1985), chap. 10.

61. See Aaron I. Abell, *American Catholicism and Social Action: A Search for Social Justice, 1865–1950* (South Bend, IN: University of Notre Dame Press, 1963), 25–26. See also Aaron I. Abell, *The Urban Impact on American Protestantism 1865–1900* (Hamden, CT: Archon, 1962). Hecker's mission generally sought to integrate Catholic faith with American political identity: "What a Catholic believes as a member of the Catholic Church, he believes as a citizen of the republic. His religion consecrates his political convictions and this consecration imparts a twofold strength to this patriotism. What a Catholic believes as a citizen of the republic, he believes as a member of the Catholic Church" (www.paulist.org/about/hecker.html).

62. See Cross, *Emergence of Liberal Catholicism*, 131.

63. Ibid., 140 (describing parallel efforts in Pittsburgh and Faribault, Minnesota).

64. Ibid., 144–45.

65. Martin E. Marty, Stuart E. Rosenberg, and Andrew M. Greeley, *What Do We Believe? The Stance of Religion in America* (New York: Meredith Press, 1968), 135.

66. National Center for Education Statistics, *Digest of Education Statistics 2002*, chap. 2, tables 37 and 62.

67. See McGreevy, *Catholicism*, 123–25, on the ebb of "establishment anti-Catholicism."

68. See Pratt, *Religion, Politics, and Diversity*, 207–8.

69. *Congressional Record*, 44th Cong., 2d. sess., 1876, 5581.

70. See Sidney Mead, *The Lively Experiment: The Shaping of Christianity in America* (New York: Harper, 1963), 157; A. M. Schlesinger, "A Critical Period in American Protestantism, 1875–1900," *Massachusetts Historical Society Proceedings* 64 (1932): 532–48.

71. See Abell, *American Catholicism*, 29.

72. Ibid., 35.

73. Ibid., 37, 38.

74. Ibid., 35–36.
75. Charles E. Rosenberg, *The Care of Strangers: The Rise of America's Hospital System* (Baltimore: Johns Hopkins University Press, 1995), 238–39.
76. Pratt, *Religion, Politics, and Diversity*, 216.
77. Quoted ibid., 216–17.
78. Ibid., 239.
79. See ibid., 246–51.
80. *State of Nevada ex rel. Nevada Orphan Asylum v. Hallock*, 16 Nev. 373 (1882).
81. *Synod of Dakota v. State*, 2 S.D. 366 (1891).
82. *County of Cook v. Chicago Industrial School for Girls*, 125 Ill. 540 (1888).
83. *Dunn v. Chicago Industrial School*, 280 Ill. 613 (1917).
84. *Bradfield v. Roberts*, 175 U.S. 291 (1899).
85. See Christopher J. Kauffman, *Ministry and Meaning: A Religious History of Catholic Health Care in the United States* (New York: Crossroad, 1995), 71.
86. See Sarah Barringer Gordon, *The Mormon Question: Polygamy and Constitutional Conflict in Nineteenth-Century America* (Chapel Hill: University of North Carolina Press, 2002).
87. Ibid., 112.
88. Ibid., 111–13.
89. Ibid., 196.
90. Ibid., 113–14.
91. *Reynolds v. United States*, 98 U.S. 145, 152–53, 161 (1878) (argument for the petitioner).
92. Gordon, *Mormon Question*, 133.
93. *Reynolds v. United States*, 165.
94. Ibid.
95. George Elliot Howard, *A History of Matrimonial Institutions* (Chicago: University of Chicago Press, 1904), 1:404–73.
96. See, e.g., ibid. 2:125–28; Lawrence Stone, *Uncertain Unions and Broken Lives: Marriage and Divorce in England, 1660–1857* (New York: Oxford University Press, 1995).
97. Howard, *Matrimonial Institutions*, 2:133.
98. See, generally, Perry Miller, *Errand into the Wilderness* (Cambridge, MA: Harvard University Press, 1956).
99. *Milford v. Worcester*, 7 Mass. 48, 54 (1810).
100. Ibid., 57.
101. See *Reynolds v. United States*, 166; Gordon, *Mormon Question*, 140–41; James Kent, *Commentaries on American Law* (Boston: Little, Brown, 1873), 2:81–82. On Lieber, see Frank Burt Freidel, *Francis Lieber, Nineteenth-Century Liberal* (Baton Rouge: Louisiana State University Press, 1948). Lieber's most important accomplishment was drafting a code of conduct

for Union forces during the Civil War that became a crucial piece of the international law of war.

102. *Reynolds v. United States*, 166.
103. Ibid., 167.
104. *Murphy v. Ramsey*, 114 U.S. 15 (1885).
105. *Davis v. Beason*, 133 U.S. 333 (1890).
106. See Noonan and Gaffney, *Religious Freedom*, 306.
107. Cf. Harold Bloom, *The American Religion: The Emergence of the Post-Christian Nation* (New York: Simon & Schuster, 1993).
108. See, e.g., Amy Fagan, "Marriage Bill Backed by Romney," *Washington Times*, June 23, 2004 (describing Massachusetts governor and identified Mormon Mitt Romney's testimony in favor of the federal constitutional amendment banning same-sex marriage).

CHAPTER 3. THE BIRTH OF AMERICAN SECULARISM

1. Ronald Numbers, *Darwinism Comes to America* (Cambridge, MA: Harvard University Press, 1998).
2. Cf. Martin F. Marty, *The Modern Schism: Three Paths to the Secular* (New York: Harper, 1969); Gary Scott Smith, *The Seeds of Secularization: Calvinism, Culture, and Pluralism in America, 1870–1915* (Grand Rapids, MI: Christian University Press, 1985), 157–79.
3. See G.E.E., "Christianity and Secularism," *Christian Examiner and Religious Miscellany* 55 (September 1853): 272–73. On Holyoake's life, see Joseph McCabe, *George Jacob Holyoake* (London: Watts & Co., 1920).
4. See, for example, George Jacob Holyoake, *The Principles of Secularism Illustrated*, 3d ed. (London: Austin & Co., 1870).
5. Ibid., 11.
6. Ibid., 19, 27, 33–34.
7. Cf. Hugh McLeod, *Secularisation in Western Europe, 1848–1914* (London: Macmillan, 2000), 164–66.
8. See Holyoake, *Principles of Secularism*, 8 (quoting a letter from Harriet Martineau that appeared in the *Boston Liberator*, November 1853); George Jacob Holyoake, *Sixty Years of an Agitator's Life* (1892) (New York: Garland, 1984); Lee E. Grugel, *George Jacob Holyoake: A Study in the Evolution of a Victorian Radical* (Philadelphia: Porcupine Press, 1976). Holyoake was read in America in the later nineteenth century. See Nelson R. Burr, *A Critical Bibliography of Religion in America*, 4 vols. (Princeton, NJ: Princeton University Press, 1961), 4:143. In contrast to Holyoake's immediate grassroots success in England, his closest American counterpart, the lapsed Universalist minister Abner Kneeland, spoke to occasional large au-

diences but was not the father of a movement. Kneeland declared himself a pantheist rather than an atheist, believing God and Nature to be synonymous. He faced five trials for blasphemy in Massachusetts and served sixty days in jail in 1838. He was the last person convicted and imprisoned for blasphemy in the United States. See Leonard W. Levy, ed., *Blasphemy in Massachusetts: Freedom of Conscience and the Abner Kneeland Case: A Documentary Record* (New York: Da Capo Press, 1973); and the classic treatment in Perry Miller, *The Life of the Mind in America: From the Revolution to the Civil War* (New York: Harcourt, 1965), 104–6.

9. George Jacob Holyoake, *Among the Americans, and A Stranger in America,* (1881) (Westport, CT: Greenwood Press, 1970).

10. Grugel, *George Jacob Holyoake.*

11. See James Turner, *Without God, Without Creed: The Origins of Unbelief in America* (Baltimore: Johns Hopkins University Press, 1985); Susan Jacoby, *Freethinkers: A History of American Secularism* (New York: Metropolitan, 2004). Jacoby does not identify secularism with Darwinian influence; indeed, she does not even mention Holyoake. Her approach—anachronistic, in my view—is to identify what I have called secularism as an outgrowth of earlier American religious skepticism, thus projecting secularism backward onto Thomas Paine, Jefferson, and others of the framing generation. Nonetheless, her focus is on elites, even if she does not emphasize the fact.

12. Francis Ellingwood Abbot, "The Nine Demands of Liberalism," *The Index,* January 1873.

13. Ibid.

14. Andrew Dickson White, *The Warfare of Science* (New York: D. Appleton and Co., 1876). The lecture was first published in the *New York Tribune,* under the auspices of Horace Greeley, the day after it was given at Cooper. John William Draper, *The History of the Conflict Between Religion and Science* (New York: D. Appleton and Co., 1876).

15. On White's life, see Andrew Dickson White, *The Autobiography of Andrew Dickson White* (New York: The Century Co., 1905). On Cornell's nonsectarianism and its relation to White's work, see George M. Marsden, *The Soul of the American University* (New York: Oxford University Press, 1994), 115–21.

16. White, *Warfare of Science,* viii.

17. Andrew Dickson White, *A History of the Warfare of Science with Theology in Christendom* (New York: D. Appleton and Co., 1896).

18. White, *Warfare of Science,* preface.

19. Marsden, *Soul of the American University,* 103–10, 114.

20. Ibid., 186–93.

21. Draper, *History of the Conflict,* v.

22. Ibid., vii.

23. Ibid., 102–18, 182–200.

24. Ibid., 201–27.

25. Ibid., 327–67.

26. For the reaction to White, see Glenn C. Altschuler, *Andrew Dickson White: Educator, Historian, Diplomat* (Ithaca, NY: Cornell University Press, 1979). For Draper, see McGreevy, *Catholicism*, 112.

27. White, *Autobiography*, 1:194.

28. On Draper's anti-Catholicism, see McGreevy, *Catholicism*, 185–86.

29. For a review of the extensive literature on this complex subject, see Burr, *Critical Bibliography*, 4:1049–72.

30. Robert G. Ingersoll, *The Works of Robert G. Ingersoll*, 12 vols. (New York: C. P. Farrell, 1900).

31. Ludwig Feuerbach, *The Essence of Christianity* (1841).

32. Robert G. Ingersoll, "The Gods," at www.infidels.org/library/historical/robert_ingersoll/gods.html.

33. Ibid.

34. Ibid.

35. Ibid.

36. Ibid.

37. Robert G. Ingersoll, "Human Rights," at www.skeptical-christian.net/lectures/human_rights.html.

38. Robert G. Ingersoll, "Free Schools," at www.sacred-texts.com/aor/ing/vol02/i0103.htm.

39. Proceedings of the Republican National Convention, Held at Cincinnati, Ohio (Concord, NH: Republic Press Association, 1876), 74; see also Hamburger, *Separation of Church and State*, 324.

40. The fascinating Abbot was a contemporary of Charles Sanders Peirce. Ralph Waldo Emerson supported Abbot's unsuccessful candidacy for a philosophy professorship at the newly founded Cornell. See Bruce Kuklick, *The Rise of American Philosophy: Cambridge, Massachusetts 1860–1930* (New Haven, CT: Yale University Press, 1977), 92–103. Abbot's intellectual and spiritual odyssey owed much to the early influence of Darwin; see Hamburger, *Separation of Church and State*, 289 and n. 6. Shortly after publicly abjuring even his liberal Unitarian faith, Abbot was also a protagonist in a famous court case over ownership of the property of the Dover, New Hampshire, church of which he had been minister. Under his influence, a group disbanded, then reorganized the church on principles they called Unitarian but that their opponents characterized as nonreligious. The state Supreme Court found that Abbot was no longer a Christian, denied the group's claim, and left title with the rump congregation. *Hale v. Everett*, 53 N.H. 106 (1868). Eventually Abbot returned to philosophy, publishing one book (devastatingly reviewed by Josiah Royce) in his lifetime. Another was published after Abbot's death by suicide at his wife's

grave on the anniversary of her death. See *American National Biography* (New York: Oxford University Press, 1999), 1:10–11.

41. Robert G. Ingersoll, "Convention of the National Liberal League," www.infidels.org/library/historical/robert_ingersoll/national_liberal_league. html.

42. Hamburger, *Separation of Church and State*, 298, says the league "regretted" the Blaine amendment because it did not go far enough, but this formulation obscures the basic fact that the league was prepared to support the amendment even though its members believed it incomplete; obviously, the Blaine amendment had a chance to pass, whereas the league's amendment was more purely symbolic. Ingersoll's close political relationship with Blaine underscores the alliance. Hamburger writes (324) that Ingersoll broke with the league to nominate Blaine, but there is no reason to think this was the case; it was perfectly consistent to support Blaine and his amendment while thinking the latter did not go far enough.

43. On the league, see ibid., 276–334. See Hal D. Sears, *The Sex Radicals: Free Love in High Victorian America* (Lawrence: Regents Press of Kansas, 1977), 39. A proposed constitutional amendment that Abbot printed weekly in *The Index* would have made the Free Exercise Clause and the Establishment Clause applicable to the states, not just the federal government.

44. Compare what Martin Marty calls "utter (maximal) secularity" and "mere secularity." Marty, *Modern Schism*, 10.

45. Robert G. Ingersoll, "Why Am I Agnostic?" at www.infidels.org/ library/historical/robert_ingersoll/why_am_i_agnostic.html.

46. Clarence Darrow, *Why I Am an Agnostic and Other Essays* (Amherst, NY: Prometheus Books, 1995), available at www.infidels.org/library/historical/ clarence_darrow/why_i_am_an_agnostic.html.

47. William Reed Huntington, *The Church Idea: An Essay Towards Unity* (New York: Hurd and Houghton, 1872), 134.

48. On Brann, see J. W. Shaw, *The Writings of Brann the Iconoclast* (New York: Blue Ribbon Books, 1938), 5–8; Charles Carver, *Brann and the Iconoclast* (Austin: University of Texas Press, 1957); Hamburger, *Separation of Church and State*, 365–69.

49. See David McAllister, *The National Reform Movement: Its History and Principles* (Allegheny, PA: Christian Statesman, 1898), 33–34. On the National Reform Association, see Steven Keith Green, "The Rhetoric and Reality of the 'Christian Nation' Maxim in American Law" (Ph.D. diss., University of North Carolina, 1997), 332–95; Hamburger, *Separation of Church and State*, 290–93.

50. McAllister, *National Reform Movement*, 105–40.

51. Ibid., 3–13.

52. Ibid., 161 (quoting Ingersoll).

53. Ibid., 205.

CHAPTER 4. THE FUNDAMENTALS, THE FUNDAMENTALISTS, AND THE
MONKEY TRIAL

1. See the preface to *The Fundamentals: A Testimony to the Truth*, eds. R. A.
Torrey, A. C. Dixon, and others (Grand Rapids, MI: Baker Books, 2003)
(reprint of original four-volume edition of 1917).

2. John R. Thelin, *A History of American Higher Education* (Baltimore: Johns
Hopkins University Press, 2004), 118–22, 128.

3. Gerald Priest, "A. C. Dixon, Chicago Liberals, and *The Fundamentals*,"
Detroit Baptist Seminary Journal, 1 (1996): 113–34.

4. Ibid.

5. "The teaching of Darwinism, as an approved science, to the children and
youth of the schools of the world is the most deplorable feature of the
whole wretched propaganda." Henry H. Beach, "The Decadence of Darwinism," *The Fundamentals*, vol. 4.

6. "Evolutionism in the Pulpit" by an Occupant of the Pew, *The Fundamentals*, vol. 4.

7. George Frederick White, "The Passing of Evolution," *The Fundamentals*,
vol. 4.

8. On the fundamentalist-modernist controversy, see Hutchison, *Religious
Pluralism*, 148–50.

9. Edward J. Larson, *Summer for the Gods* (New York: Harper, 1997), 40–41.

10. For the centrality of biblicism to American religion at the time, see Handy,
Undermined Establishment, 131–32.

11. Many mainstream liberal religious denominations embraced eugenics during this period. See Christine Rosen, *Preaching Eugenics: Religious Leaders
and the American Eugenics Movement* (New York: Oxford University Press,
2004).

12. Larson, *Summer for the Gods*, 18–20.

13. Key works establishing the modern synthesis are R. A. Fisher, *The Geneti-
cal Theory of Natural Selection* (Oxford: Clarendon Press, 1930); J.B.S.
Haldane, *The Causes of Evolution* (London: Longmans, Green, 1932). For
a discussion of the history, see Timothy Shanahan, *The Evolution of Darwinism: Selection, Adaptation, and Progress in Evolutionary Biology* (New
York: Cambridge University Press, 2004).

14. Larson, *Summer for the Gods*, 55.

15. Samuel Walker, *In Defense of American Liberties: A History of the ACLU*
(Carbondale: Southern Illinois University Press, 1999); Larson, *Summer
for the Gods*, 60–68.

16. Larson, *Summer for the Gods*, 60–73.

17. Ibid., 100–4.

18. Ibid.

19. See, e.g., Mary Sheila McMahon, "King Tut and the Scopes Trial," in M. L.

Bradley and James B. Gilbert, eds., *Transforming Faith*, (New York: Greenwood Press, 1989) 90, 94–99; cf. Larson, *Summer for the Gods*, 201–7.

20. Gaines M. Foster, *Moral Reconstruction: Christian Lobbyists and the Federal Legislation of Morality, 1865–1920* (Chapel Hill: University of North Carolina Press, 2002).

21. On journalists in the period, see George H. Douglas, *The Golden Age of the Newspaper* (Westport, CT: Greenwood Press, 1999), 157–70.

22. Larson, *Summer for the Gods*, 228–29.

23. Ibid., 201.

24. Will Herberg, *Protestant—Catholic—Jew: An Essay in American Religious Sociology* (Garden City, NY: Doubleday, 1955), 47.

25. Ibid., 52.

26. On Freud in America, see Nathan G. Hale, *The Rise and Crisis of Psychoanalysis in America, 1917–1985* (New York: Oxford University Press, 1995).

CHAPTER 5. THE COURTS AND THE RISE OF LEGAL SECULARISM

1. Robert Wuthnow, *The Restructuring of American Religion* (Princeton, NJ: Princeton University Press, 1988), 20–21. Although Wuthnow sets the date of the founding at 1897, the year is overwhelmingly cited as 1872. See, e.g., Peter H. Irons, *The Courage of Their Convictions* (New York: Free Press, 1988).

2. See, e.g., Shawn Francis Peters, *Judging Jehovah's Witnesses: Religious Persecution and the Dawn of the Rights Revolution* (Lawrence: University Press of Kansas, 2000). For a thoughtful review, see Neil M. Richards, "The 'Good War,' the Jehovah's Witnesses, and the First Amendment," *Virginia Law Review* 87 (2001): 781.

3. See, e.g., Irons, *Courage of Their Convictions*, 15–35; Peters, *Judging Jehovah's Witnesses*, 72–73.

4. *Minersville School District v. Gobitis*, 310 U.S. 586, 588 (1940).

5. *Cantwell v. Connecticut*, 310 U.S. 296 (1940).

6. *Minersville School District v. Gobitis*, 586, 596.

7. Ibid., 601.

8. Ibid., 603.

9. Ibid., 607.

10. *United States v. Carolene Prods. Co.*, 304 U.S. 144, 152 n. 4 (1938). Important legal discussions of the famous note include Bruce A. Ackerman, "Beyond Carolene Products," *Harvard Law Review* 98 (1985): 713; J. M. Balkin, "The Footnote," *Northwestern University Law Review* 83 (1989): 275; Robert M. Cover, "The Origins of Judicial Activism in the Protection of Minorities," *Yale Law Journal* 91 (1982): 1287; John Hart Ely, *Democ-*

racy and Distrust: A Theory of Judicial Review (Cambridge, MA: Harvard University Press, 1980), 75–77; Geoffrey P. Miller, "The True Story of Carolene Products," *Supreme Court Review* 1987 (1988): 397; Laurence Tribe, "The Puzzling Persistence of Process-Based Constitutional Theories," *Yale Law Journal* 89 (1980): 1063.

11. Peters, *Judging Jehovah's Witnesses*, 73–95, 99–100 (detailing several egregious incidents during the spring and summer of 1940, including one where a Witness was kidnapped from his Nebraska home and castrated, and another where a West Virginia sheriff's deputy detained several Witnesses, called in friends, bound the hands of the captives, placed guns and a rope upon the table, forced them to ingest castor oil, and marched them out of town); David R. Manwaring, *Render Unto Caesar: The Flag-Salute Controversy* (Chicago: University of Chicago Press, 1962), 165 (maintaining that in Wyoming, one Witness was tarred and feathered).

12. *W. Va. State Bd. of Educ. v. Barnette*, 319 U.S. 624, 626 n. 2 (1943).

13. Ibid., 627, 628.

14. The Senate confirmed Frank Murphy on January 15, 1940; James Byrnes on June 12, 1941 (the same day he was nominated); and Robert Jackson on July 7, 1941.

15. *W. Va. State Bd. of Educ. v. Barnette*, 637.

16. Ibid., 641.

17. Ibid., 642.

18. Ibid., 646–47 (Frankfurter, J., dissenting).

19. See Robert A. Burt, *Two Jewish Justices: Outcasts in the Promised Land* (Berkeley: University of California Press, 1988), 44.

20. Ibid.

21. Ibid.

22. I owe this parallel to Seth Zirkle of the Yale Divinity School.

23. *W. Va. State Bd. of Educ. v. Barnette*, 654 (Frankfurter, J., dissenting).

24. Ibid., 653.

25. Ibid., 658.

26. Until the end of his years on the bench, Frankfurter would stick to the view that the courts should exercise their power to overturn legislation sparingly, regretfully, and only as a last resort. Yet he lived to see this doctrine of judicial restraint, which reached its classic formulation in the hands of Progressives, become associated with conservatism and even reaction.

27. *W. Va. State Bd. of Educ. v. Barnette*, 670–71 (Frankfurter, J., dissenting).

28. Wuthnow, *Restructuring of American Religion*, 82.

29. *Zorach v. Clauson*. This monotheistic sentiment is a retrenchment from the Court's famous declaration that "this is a Christian nation" sixty years before in *Church of the Holy Trinity v. United States*, 143 U.S. 457, 471 (1892).

30. 36 U.S.C. § 302 (1998) (original version at ch. 795, § 302, 70 Stat. 732 [1956]).

31. On the emergence of the term "Judeo-Christian," the best source for the intellectual history is Mark Silk, *Spiritual Politics: Religion and America Since World War I* (New York: Simon & Schuster, 1988), 40–53. Silk points to academic uses of variants on the term already in 1940, in the context of grounding antifascism in religious terms, but he also says that "after the revelations of the Nazi death camps," the notion of Christian civilization "began to seem ominously exclusive" (44).

32. Interestingly, Mark Silk identifies Herberg in particular as an advocate of the "neo-orthodox [Christian] Hebraism" that Silk associates with the notion of the "Judeo-Christian" (*Spiritual Politics*, 49–50, citing Will Herberg, *Judaism and Modern Man: An Interpretation of Jewish Religion* [Philadelphia: Jewish Publication Society of America, 1951]).

33. Herberg, *Protestant—Catholic—Jew*, 10–23.

34. Ibid., 32–33.

35. Ibid., 87.

36. Ibid., 211.

37. Ibid., 218–19, 223.

38. C. Stanley Lowell, *Embattled Wall: Americans United* (Washington, D.C.: Protestants and Other Americans United for Separation of Church and State, 1966), 27–29.

39. *Everson v. Board of Education of Ewing Township*, 330 U.S. 1 (1947).

40. See Samuel C. Kincheloe, "Research Memorandum on Religion in the Depression" (New York: Social Science Research Council, 1937).

41. See Pratt, *Religion, Politics, and Diversity*, 235.

42. Ibid., 276–77.

43. *Everson v. Board of Education of Ewing Township*, 3.

44. *Cantwell v. Connecticut*.

45. *Reynolds v. United States*.

46. Hamburger argues that Black's youthful Klan membership was just the right preparation for a decision that, by separating church and state, amounted to anti-Catholicism. *Separation of Church and State*, 422–34. Similarly, McGreevy, *Catholicism*, emphasizes Black's interest in the writings of best-selling author Paul Blanshard as proof of anti-Catholicism. But Black's pervasive liberalism over hundreds of Supreme Court decisions undercuts these arguments, as does the fact that the legal secularism Black advocated effectively ended Protestant nonsectarianism even as it occasionally limited funding for Catholic institutions.

47. *Everson v. Board of Education of Ewing Township*, 9.

48. Ibid., 9–10.

49. Ibid., 11.

50. Ibid., 15–16.

51. Ibid., 18. This delicate dance, in which the prohibition on the state supporting religion had to match its steps to the corresponding requirement that the state not limit free exercise, was to become in later years a feature of subtle constitutional debate. Even as Black was announcing a major new restriction on what government could do in support of religion, he was simultaneously introducing the seeds of its downfall.

52. *McCollum v. Bd. of Educ.*, 333 U.S. 203 (1948).

53. Vashti McCollum, named after the wife of King Ahasuerus from the Old Testament Book of Esther, though known to the press and the vagaries of history as an atheist, called herself a humanist, declaring that "the term atheist . . . is too militant a term . . . and also implies a more profound student of theology than I am." Vashti Cromwell McCollum, *One Woman's Fight* (Garden City, NY: Doubleday, 1951), 10. Although much of the press during the trial discussed her father's rationalism, McCollum was actually raised Lutheran and attended both Presbyterian and Episcopalian services in her youth (her father did not become interested in rationalism until McCollum was already away at college) (10–16).

54. *McCollum v. Bd. of Educ.*, 238–56 (Reed, J., dissenting).

55. *Zorach v. Clauson*, 306, 314.

56. *McCollum v. Bd. of Educ.*, 213–32 (Frankfurter, J., concurring).

57. Ibid., 218.

58. Ibid., 231.

59. Ibid., 227–28.

60. Ibid., 228.

61. Ibid., 233 (Jackson, J., concurring).

62. *Engel v. Vitale*, 370 U.S. 431 (1962).

63. Ibid., 430.

64. *School District of Abington Township, Pennsylvania v. Schempp*, 374 U.S. 209 (1963).

65. *Brown v. Board of Education*, 347 U.S. 483, 494 n. 11 (1954). Footnote 11 rivals footnote 4 of *Carolene Products* for the title of history's most famous note. It has thus been the subject of extensive discussion. See, e.g., Edmond Cahn, "Jurisprudence," *NYU Law Review* 30 (1955): 150; Kenneth B. Clark, "The Desegregation Cases: Criticism of the Social Scientist's Role," *Villanova Law Review* 5 (1959): 224; Ronald Dworkin, "Social Sciences and Constitutional Rights—The Consequences of Uncertainty," *Journal of Law and Education* 6 (1977): 3; Richard Kluger, *Simple Justice: The History of* Brown v. Board of Education *and Black America's Struggle for Equality* (New York: Knopf, 1975); Mark G. Yudof, "School Desegregation: Legal Realism, Reasoned Elaboration, and Social Science Research in the Supreme Court," *Law & Contemporary Problems* 42 (1978): 57.

66. *School District of Abington Township, Pennsylvania v. Schempp*, 222, 224.

67. *Lemon v. Kurtzman*, 403 U.S. 602 (1971).

68. *School District of Abington Township, Pennsylvania v. Schempp*, 226.

69. *Wallace v. Jaffree*; *Lee v. Weisman*, 505 U.S. 577 (1992); *Agostini v. Felton*, 521 U.S. 203 (1997).

CHAPTER 6. THE VALUES EVANGELICALS

1. *Epperson v. Arkansas*, 393 U.S. 97 (1968).

2. See Wilber G. Katz and Harold P. Southerland, "Religious Pluralism and the Supreme Court," in William G. McLoughlin and Robert N. Bellah, eds., *Religion in America* (Boston: Beacon Press, 1968) 274–75.

3. Robert N. Bellah, "Civil Religion in America," *Daedalus* 96 (1967): 1. The beliefs were that God had led the American people from the bondage of Europe to the promised land of America; that he had, as Lincoln had suggested in his second inaugural, purged us of the sins of slavery through the blood of the Civil War; and that he continued to demand sacrifice from Americans in exchange for his special supervision of the people's manifest destiny. The state rituals in which these ideas found symbolic expression were things like the school prayers that the Supreme Court was in the process of dismantling. Bellah did not present his argument specifically as a response to legal secularism. But he pointed out that civil religion depended on public acknowledgment of God and wondered how the crisis of religious faith of the late 1960s would affect the American civil religion going forward. In retrospect, the context of Bellah's article suggests that he gave the name "civil religion" to a complex of theistic American beliefs in large part because the public manifestation of religion in American civic life was being challenged in decisions coming from the courts. Although Bellah initially presented his argument primarily as descriptive, it soon became clear that he believed American civil religion to be a valuable good, worth nurturing, defending, and steering in the right direction for the future.

4. An excellent standard work on evangelicalism is George M. Marsden, *Understanding Fundamentalism and Evangelicalism* (Grand Rapids, MI: W. B. Eerdmans, 1991). For a useful brief introduction to the issues, see Justin Watson, *The Christian Coalition: Dreams of Restoration, Demands for Recognition* (New York: St. Martin's Press, 1997), 9–27.

5. On these schools, see John C. Jeffries Jr. and James E. Ryan, "A Political History of the Establishment Clause," *Michigan Law Review* 100 (2001): 279, 282–83, 328–38.

6. Cf. Watson, *Christian Coalition*, 31–32.

7. See Roger Bruns, *Billy Graham: A Biography* (Westport, CT: Greenwood Press, 2004).

8. On the role of television and the history of the *700 Club*, see Alec Foege,

The Empire God Built: Inside Pat Robertson's Media Machine (New York: John Wiley, 1996); Jeffrey K. Hadden and Anson Shupe, *Televangelism, Power, and Politics on God's Frontier* (New York: Henry Holt, 1988); Razelle Frankl, *Televangelism: The Marketing of Popular Religion* (Carbondale: Southern Illinois University Press, 1987).

9. The name was suggested by New Right impresario Paul Weyrich. See William Martin, *With God on Our Side: The Rise of the Religious Right in America* (New York: Broadway Books, 1996), 200. See also Ruth Murray Brown, *For a "Christian America": A History of the Religious Right* (Amherst, NY: Prometheus Books, 2002), 155–65. On Falwell's theology, see Warren L. Vinz, *Pulpit Politics: Faces of American Protestant Nationalism in the Twentieth Century* (Albany: State University of New York Press, 1997), 169–89.

10. Nonetheless, circulation of the *Moral Majority Report* was just 482,000. See Brown, *For a "Christian America,"* 158 (questioning membership numbers). On Reagan's faith, see Paul Kengor, *God and Ronald Reagan: A Spiritual Life* (New York: ReganBooks, 2004).

11. See Frank S. Ravitch, *School Prayer and Discrimination: The Civil Rights of Religious Minorities and Dissenters* (Boston: Northeastern University Press, 1999).

12. *Roe v. Wade*, 410 U.S. 113 (1973).

13. For Catholic attention to abortion pre-*Roe*, see McGreevy, *Catholicism*, 250–81.

14. Even Planned Parenthood did not focus on abortion on demand at the time. See ibid., 257.

15. Both women represented the plaintiffs before the United States District Court for the Northern District of Texas, *Roe v. Wade*, 314 F. Supp. 1217 (1970). Weddington alone, however, argued before the Supreme Court, joined by Roy Lucas, Fred Bruner, Roy L. Merrill Jr., and Norman Dorsen on the briefs.

16. A crucial voice in the process of making abortion a central issue for evangelical activism was that of Francis A. Schaeffer, *A Christian Manifesto* (Westchester: Crossway Books, 1981). On his influence, see Watson, *Christian Coalition*, 22 and nn. 78–79.

17. Kerry N. Jacoby, *Souls, Bodies, Spirits: The Drive to Abolish Abortion Since 1973* (Westport, CT: Praeger, 1998).

18. Ronald Reagan, "Abortion and the Conscience of the Nation," *The Human Life Review*, Spring 1983, available at www.humanlifereview.com/reagan. See also Kengor, *God and Ronald Reagan*, 177–78. On Reagan's earlier reticence, see Jacoby, *Souls, Bodies, Spirits*, 176.

19. Jacoby, *Souls, Bodies, Spirits*, 189.

20. See Bob Jones III, "The Moral Majority," *Faith for the Family*, September 1980, at www.bju.edu/resources/faith/1980/issue7/majority.html.

21. Cf. Jeffries and Ryan, "Political History of the Establishment Clause," 349.

22. Ibid., 358–65.

23. Richard John Neuhaus, *The Naked Public Square: Religion and Democracy in America* (Grand Rapids, MI: W. B. Eerdmans, 1984).

24. Ibid., 172–76.

25. Ibid., 78.

26. Foster, *Moral Reconstruction.*

27. Neuhaus, *Naked Public Square,* 147–55.

28. Ibid., 264.

29. On Neuhaus's conversion, and on his efforts toward ecumenism, see "No Good Reason to Stand Apart: An Interview with Richard John Neuhaus," *Catholic Dossier* 7, no. 5 (September/October 2001), www.catholic. net/rcc/Periodicals/Dossier/2001-10/interview.html.

30. William J. Bennett, *Virtues of Leadership* (Nashville: W Publishing Group, 2001); *The Moral Compass: Stories for a Life's Journey,* ed. with commentary William J. Bennett (New York: Simon & Schuster, 1995); *The Book of Virtues: A Treasury of Great Moral Stories,* ed. with commentary William J. Bennett (New York: Simon & Schuster, 1993).

31. See, e.g., *Planned Parenthood of Southeastern Pa. v. Casey,* 505 U.S. 833 (1992). But see also *Stenberg v. Carhart,* 530 U.S. 914, 956 (2000) (Kennedy, J., dissenting) (finding that Casey "was premised on the States having an important constitutional role in defining their interests in the abortion debate" and chastising the majority for finding unconstitutional a Nebraska law banning partial-birth abortions because "[States] may take sides in the abortion debate and come down on the side of [life] in the unborn").

32. Annual statistics may be viewed at www.scotusblog.com.

33. *Lynch v. Donnelly,* 668.

34. Ibid., 634.

35. Ibid., 683.

36. Ibid., 689–91 (O'Connor, J., concurring).

37. Ibid., 688.

38. *County of Allegheny v. ACLU Greater Pittsburgh Chapter,* 492 U.S. 573 (1989).

39. Ibid., 598–600.

40. *Rosenberger v. Rectors of the University of Virginia,* 515 U.S. 819 (1995).

41. Ibid., 825.

42. Ibid., 827–28, 837. Although the university offered this rationale to each court, considerable wavering throughout the litigation casts some doubt upon its origin. The university argued before the trial court that resource limitations necessitated that it be able to decide which activities furthered its educational mission. *Rosenberger v. Rectors,* 795 F. Supp. 175, 181 (1992). Before the Supreme Court, the university argued that "it would

defeat the ability of public education at all levels to control the use of public funds." *Rosenberger v. Rectors*, 515 U.S., 838. It is thus unclear whether the university's Establishment Clause rationale was an actual motivation or a concoction for litigation.

43. See, e.g., *R.A.V. v. St. Paul*, 505 U.S. 377 (1992); *Police Dept. of Chicago v. Mosley*, 408 U.S. 92 (1972); *Members of City Council of Los Angeles v. Taxpayers for Vincent*, 466 U.S. 789 (1984); *Turner Broadcasting System, Inc. v. FCC*, 512 U.S. 622 (1994).

44. *Rosenberger v. Rectors*, 515 U.S., 841–42.

45. E.g., *Good News Club v. Milford Central School*, 533 U.S. 98 (2001); *Capital Square Review and Advisory Bd. v. Pinette*, 515 U.S. 753 (1995). See also *Lamb's Chapel v. Center Moriches Union Free School Dist.*, 508 U.S. 384 (1993) (preceding *Rosenberger v. Rectors*).

46. See, e.g., Michael McConnell, "Originalism and the Desegregation Decisions," *Virginia Law Review* 81 (1995): 947.

47. *Zelman v. Simmons-Harris*, 536 U.S. 639 (2002).

48. Michael McConnell Support Letter, available at www.usdoj.gov/olp/ michaelmcconnellsupportletter.htm.

49. *Employment Div., Dept. of Human Resources of Oregon v. Smith*, 494 U.S. 872 (1990).

50. *Locke v. Davey*, 540 U.S. 712, 124 S. Ct. 1307 (2004).

51. E.g., Brief of Amici Curiae the Becket Fund for Religious Liberty, the Catholic League for Religious and Civil Rights, and Historians and Legal Scholars in Support of Respondent, *Locke v. Davey*; Richard Garnett's amicus brief in *Locke v. Davey*.

52. *Romer v. Evans*, 517 U.S. 620 (1996).

53. *Lee v. Weisman*.

54. *Santa Fe Independent School District v. Doe*, 530 U.S. 290 (2000).

55. *Mueller v. Allen*, 463 U.S. 388 (1983); *Bowen v. Kendrick*, 487 U.S. 589 (1988); *Zobrest v. Catalina Foothills School Dist.*, 509 U.S. 1 (1993); *Rosenberger v. Rectors*; *Agostini v. Felton*; *Mitchell v. Helms*, 530 U.S. 793 (2000).

56. E.g., *County of Allegheny v. ACLU Greater Pittsburgh Chapter*.

57. *Engel v. Vitale*.

58. *Wallace v. Jaffree*.

59. *Lee v. Weisman*.

60. *Santa Fe Independent School District v. Doe*.

61. *Edwards v. Aguillard*, 482 U.S. 578 (1987).

62. See Deborah Caldwell, "Banning Halloween," at www.beliefnet.com/ story/48/story_4828_1.html. In fact, not only secularists but also some evangelicals have sought to ban Halloween celebrations, apparently on the theory that the customs surrounding it glorify the devil.

63. Some of Senator Lieberman's ideas are set out in Joseph I. Lieberman, *In Praise of Public Life* (New York: Simon & Schuster, 2000), 139–51 (argu-

ing importance of religion to American public life). The *New York Times* editorial page disapproved. "Mr. Lieberman's Religious Words," *New York Times*, August 31, 2000, A24.

64. *Lemon v. Kurtzman; Meek v. Pittenger*, 421 U.S. 349 (1975); *Wolman v. Walter*, 433 U.S. 229 (1977). In each of these cases, the Court upheld and distinguished *Board of Education v. Allen*, 392 U.S. 236 (1968), in which it had held that a state may lend books directly to both public and parochial school students.

65. *Zelman v. Simmons-Harris*.

66. After hours, classrooms made available for general civic activities must be made equally available for religious activities. See *Lamb's Chapel* and its progeny.

CHAPTER 7. OUT OF MANY, ONE

1. Christopher L. Eisgruber and Lawrence G. Sager, "The Vulnerability of Conscience: The Constitutional Basis for Protecting Religious Conduct," *University of Chicago Law Review* 61 (1994): 1245.

2. On the problem of pluralism, see Smith, "The Pluralist Predicament."

3. See, in particular, John Rawls, "The Idea of an Overlapping Consensus," *Oxford Journal of Legal Studies* 7 (1987): 1. The idea is already implicit in Rawls's *A Theory of Justice* (Cambridge, MA: Harvard University Press, 1971), in the heuristic of the veil of ignorance that blocks participants in the original position from knowing their comprehensive theories of the good. For other expressions, see, e.g., Kent Greenawalt, *Religious Convictions and Political Choice* (New York: Oxford University Press, 1988), 49–84; Bruce A. Ackerman, *Social Justice in the Liberal State* (New Haven, CT: Yale University Press, 1980), 103.

4. It is true that legal secularists will still insist on banning certain kinds of religious speech altogether: teachers will not be free to preach religion in public school classrooms, and in addition, secularists would like to prohibit prayers in public political contexts, such as legislative sessions or presidential inaugurations. Such limitations can be defended by saying that the government is just limiting what its employees can say or do in the exercise of their official capacities.

5. I intend this point both theoretically and empirically. For the sociology of the experience of exclusion by evangelicals, see Watson, *Christian Coalition*.

6. See Richard Rorty, "Religion as a Conversation Stopper," in Richard Rorty, *Philosophy and Social Hope* (New York: Penguin Books, 1999), 168–74; Stanley Fish, *The Trouble with Principle* (Cambridge, MA: Harvard Uni-

versity Press, 1999), 256 (arguing that in fact the conversation "will never get started").

7. For a particularly rich treatment of this subject, see Stout, *Democracy & Tradition*, 64–91.

8. On different numberings, see Noonan and Gaffney, *Religious Freedom*, 5–9.

9. In this context it may be useful to compare Stout's highly sophisticated account of how moralities that are "akin to each another" might proceed to decide difficult questions on a "piecemeal" basis even if a single "set of moral uniformities" were to prove elusive. Stout, *Democracy & Tradition*, 229–45. Stout strives to avoid a relativist conception of truth, which he denies holding, yet he does so by distinguishing truth (nonrelative) from relativist conceptions of adjudication and justification (239). This subtle position is unlikely to be appealing to those who, like most values evangelicals, believe that truth is accessible and justifiable, and that it has direct consequences for adjudicating concrete moral questions.

CHAPTER 8. RECONCILIATION AND THE AMERICAN EXPERIMENT

1. Stephen M. Feldman, *Please Don't Wish Me a Merry Christmas: A Critical History of the Separation of Church and State* (New York: New York University Press, 1997). This unrelated Feldman—who lived in Oklahoma while writing the book!—may someday get his wish. I, for one, have started to feel sorry for people who, having wished me a Merry Christmas, seem suddenly overcome with concern that perhaps it is not my holiday. "Not to worry," I want to say to them. "I'm not offended! I hope you have a Merry Christmas, too!"

2. George W. Bush, President's Remarks at National Day of Prayer and Remembrance at the National Cathedral (September 14, 2001), transcript available at www.law.ou.edu/hist/bush-addr-nation-prayer-and-remembrance.shtml.

3. See Watson, *Christian Coalition*, 123–74 (discussing evangelicals' experience of victimization and demands for multicultural-style recognition). On this phenomenon more broadly, see Stephen L. Carter, *The Culture of Disbelief: How American Law and Politics Trivialize Religious Devotion* (New York: Basic Books, 1993).

4. Cf. Bill O'Reilly in the *New York Post*, December 9, 2004, arguing that restrictions on Christmas celebration are designed to win a broader secular agenda, including same-sex marriage, abortion rights, and so forth. www.billoreilly.com/site/product?pid=18833.

5. *Pierce v. Society of Sisters*, 268 U.S. 510 (1925).

6. See Madison's detached memoranda, in Alley, *James Madison on Religious Liberty*, 93–94. Where officially mandated prayer in schools has the effect of making the classroom into a chapel and the teacher into a religious authority, the problem is the same. Yet a moment of silence that enables children to pray privately if they wish, and neither coerces nor institutionalizes worship, would not violate the principles I have sketched here and might represent a reasonable compromise on this still-contentious issue.

7. Cf. Jeffries and Ryan, "Political History of the Establishment Clause" (arguing that the desire to fund Christian academies drove evangelical support for school vouchers).

ACKNOWLEDGMENTS

This book is the product of six years of research, and during that time I had the benefit of advice and instruction from wonderful colleagues at the Society of Fellows at Harvard, the New York University School of Law, the New America Foundation, and, for a term each, the Yale and Harvard law schools. I would not have had the confidence to continue the project had I not been encouraged by the incomparable Bernard Bailyn in some preliminary work on the origins of the Establishment Clause. (I hasten to add that he bears no blame for the final product.) Bill Nelson, Steven Smith, and Nelson Tebbe generously commented on the manuscript. I had extraordinary research assistance from Gail Abbey-Lange, Zach Intrater, Robert Sarvis, and Katherine Worden. Elizabeth Evans of the NYU Law Library was tireless in tracking down unlikely sources. Paul Elie drew on his deep knowledge of religious history in helping me shape my argument, and Heather Schroder focused me on keeping the message clear. Heidi Lubov organized my professional time and so enabled me to think more clearly. Most important, my wife, Jeannie Suk, makes it all worthwhile. Her constant challenges to every aspect of my thinking inevitably transform my views, much as she has transformed my life.

INDEX